VALUE IN SOCIAL THEORY

VALUE IN
SOCIAL THEORY

A SELECTION OF ESSAYS
ON METHODOLOGY
BY
GUNNAR MYRDAL

Edited by Paul Streeten

HARPER & BROTHERS
PUBLISHERS * NEW YORK

CONTENTS

v

Contents

Contents

INTRODUCTION

by PAUL STREETEN

IF a man has been successively university professor, government adviser, member of parliament, director of a study of the Negro in American life, cabinet minister, bank director, chairman of a planning commission and international civil servant; if, a citizen of a small country, he has occupied these positions in the last thirty years in different countries, has travelled widely both east and west, and has remained all the time a curious observer, we should not be surprised if he came to ask himself certain fundamental questions: Can one be at the same time objective, practical and idealistic? What is the relation between wanting to understand and wanting to change society? How can we free ourselves from thinking in terms possibly appropriate to an earlier age, but no longer appropriate to ours, though still powerful in our intellectual tradition? What are the new presuppositions of social thought which can do justice to the changes in social organization?

Yet, Gunnar Myrdal asked himself these and similar questions as a young man in Stockholm, before embarking on the voyage described above. His subsequent career looks almost like a series of attempts to extort from concrete problems time and time again the replies to these and similar fundamental questions. His biography might be an exercise in practical methodology.

So at least it may appear from the point of view of this book. The following collection of essays is intended to illustrate his repeated attempts to explore the logical, political and moral foundations of social thought and action, as he pursued diverse academic and political activities.

The volume is a companion to Myrdal's youthful and iconoclastic *Political Element in the Development of Economic Theory.*[1] From his young days as a rebel against the firmly

[1] 1930; English edition, London, Routledge & Kegan Paul, Cambridge Harvard University Press, 1953.

established authority of laissez-faire, to his current writings on under-developed countries, the clarification of the status of the social scientist has been Myrdal's constant and meticulous concern. His views, although a series of variations on the same theme, have undergone a gradual change.

One justification for collecting these scattered reflections is that the reader interested in the relation between values and analysis of facts in social theory might not look for its treatment in the sources on which this volume draws. The whole of Part II consists of excerpts and summaries from *An American Dilemma*.[1] In Part III I have included an early article on Ends and Means, written in German, which has not hitherto been available in English.

The book is neither a complete collection of Myrdal's writings on value, nor is it confined to this topic, nor does it avoid overlapping. To give a complete collection would be impossible, for all Myrdal's writings are pervaded by methodological reflections and provide illustrations of their application. Few workers in the statistical and empirical field and even fewer men of action can have been more conscious of and scrupulous about the theoretical foundations of their activities. To include all relevant material would have meant to reprint virtually everything Myrdal has written. The most important omission is his most recent *Economic Theory and Under-developed Regions*[2] which treats almost entirely of the same questions as this book. Thus the *Political Element*, on the one hand, and *Under-developed Regions* on the other, form, as it were, the youthful and the mature companions to this volume that spans the eventful quarter century between the last glimpse of a golden European age and the challenge of rising Asia and Africa, which Myrdal calls the great awakening.

Discussions not directly relevant to the central problem were included in order to illustrate how Myrdal's method

---

[1] *An American Dilemma*, The Negro Problem and Modern Democracy, by Gunnar Myrdal, with the assistance of Richard Sterner and Arnold Rose (Harper, New York and London, 1944). Harper & Brothers and Mr. Ordway Tead, editor, social and economic books, most generously gave their permission to reprint and to use material from *An American Dilemma*.

[2] Duckworth, London, 1957. Only the last chapter is reprinted here in chapter XI.

works in practice.[1] If, then, the selection is neither complete nor solely concerned with the central theme, it is also, inevitably, repetitive. But the repeated assaults are never identical, and may themselves serve to illustrate what Myrdal calls the logical crux of science :[2] the continual encounter—sometimes constructive, sometimes destructive—between the *a priori* and the *a posteriori*, between vision and experience, in which each, in the process of shaping the other, is itself shaped by it.

In the following sections I shall attempt to select some of the issues raised by Myrdal and to contrast his approach with the more conventional type of welfare economics which is still vitiated by many of the 'Victorian' presuppositions criticized by Myrdal.

I. Is and Ought[3]

One of the peculiarities of political economy is the clash between the words and deeds of its protagonists. For over a century, economists have repeatedly declared that economic science is concerned only with observing, describing, analysing, and predicting events, and never with recommending, giving advice, or prescribing. Senior, John Stuart Mill, Cairnes, Bagehot, Sidgwick, John Neville Keynes,[4] J. B. Clark, and in our times Professors Pigou and Robbins, as well as almost any textbook on economics, have affirmed that economics is about what *is* and *could* or *might* be, never about what *ought* to be.

[1] See e.g. chapters iv, vi and viii in this volume. For further examples, see particularly *An American Dilemma*, the whole Introduction and chapters 1 and 3; the discussion of Caste and Class in a Negro Community; chapter 33 on Individual Leadership and Mass Passivity and appendix 9 on Negro Leadership; also some early Swedish writings, such as the appendix to the Report of the Swedish Population Commission, a book on monetary policy in the Depression, an appendix to the Swedish Bill of 1932 on Deficit Finance, and other writings on fiscal and agricultural policies, in the Thirties, referred to in the Postscript to this Volume, and chapter IX of *Monetary Equilibrium* (1931, English edition, William Hodge, 1939).

[2] See chapter xi.

[3] The remainder of this Introduction is a revised and expanded version of an article that appeared in the *Quarterly Journal of Economics*, Vol. LXVIII (August, 1954), which is used with the kind permission of its editor and the Harvard University Press.

[4] For references see Gunnar Myrdal, *Political Element*, pp. 3f.

Yet, in spite of these declarations of the scientific, neutral character of economics, virtually all economists have in fact advised, recommended, exhorted, warned, etc.,—and all this with the aid of arguments derived directly from the 'science' of economics.

It is possible to argue that for the economists in the great utilitarian tradition the distinction between *is* and *ought* is not fundamental. Like other rationalist systems of philosophy, utilitarianism holds that *ought* can be deduced from *is* and *could be*. There is, indeed, evidence that the distinction between science and politics (or ethics) was thought to be merely classificatory. Economics as a *science* (in the narrow sense) is about facts, economics as an *art* is about values and policies. If this interpretation is adopted, the declarations as to the scientific character of economics amount to no more than a convenient classification into 'pure' or 'theoretical,' and 'applied' or 'practical,' economics.[1]

The difficulty that stands in the way of accepting this interpretation is the extreme importance which authors attach to the value-free character of economics, and the fervour with which they denounce in their methodological introductions any attempts to derive recommendations from the analysis of facts. I think they mean what they say, yet they never practise it.

The sharp division between *is* and *ought*, between positive and normative pursuits, is so widely accepted to-day that the inconsistency of the writers in the classical tradition might strike one as either gross carelessness or dishonesty. But one must remember that the habits of rationalistic philosophies, particularly those of the philosophy of natural law and of utilitarianism, according to which values and rules are either identical with, or can be derived from, facts, have deep and tough roots. Neither Adam Smith nor James Mill believed that there is anything improper in formulating a *science* of values and rules, and some of the confusion to-day may be merely

[1] See, e.g., J. N. Keynes, *Scope and Method of Political Economy.*, p.39. 'The problem whether political economy is to be regarded as a positive science, or as a normative science, or as an art, or as a combination of these, is to a certain extent a question merely of nomenclature and classification.' See also *Political Element*, pp. 8 and 219.

the reflection of an ideological lag between words and deeds.

On the other hand, to-day we accept perhaps too easily the belief that the distinction between *is* and *ought* is always obvious, clear-cut, and easy to draw.[1]

Myrdal's views on this issue have undergone a gradual change. There are passages in the *Political Element*, which imply that an honest effort and hard work can always sort out the values from the facts. The smuggling in of the value premises is done, on this view, at a rather superficial level But there is a gradual shift from this *psychological* view (which, as Myrdal says in his 1953 Preface, implies a naive empiricism) to a more complicated analysis of the entry of value judgments. In the *Crux of All Science* the values enter, not as wishes distorting thought, but as essential principles, forming the structure of theoretical thought, giving it meaning and direction. But if values enter inevitably into the way in which we attempt to analyse reality, good will and honesty have nothing to contribute to the clarification at this deeper level. The whole conception of scientific analysis is changed. Values are not something to be discarded, nor even something to be made explicit in order to be separated from empirical matter, but are ever-present and permeate empirical analysis through and through.

2. PROGRAMME AND PROGNOSIS

In Appendix 2 of *An American Dilemma*, entitled 'Note on Facts and Valuations,'[2] Myrdal draws a distinction between ' programmes ' and 'prognoses.' These two key concepts open

[1] Hume's complaint was that 'in every system of morality which I have hitherto met with, I have always remarked, that the author proceeds for some time in the ordinary way of reasoning, and establishes the being of a God, or makes some observations concerning human affairs; when of a sudden I am surprised to find that instead of the usual copulations of propositions, *is*, and *is not*, I meet with no proposition that is not connected with an *ought*, or an *ought not*. This change is imperceptible; but is, however, of the last consequence. For as this *ought*, or *ought not*, expresses some new relation or affirmation, it is necessary that it should be observed and explained; and at the same time, that a reason should be given, for what seems altogether inconceivable, how this new relation can be a deduction from others, which are entirely different from it.' *A Treatise of Human Nature*, Book III, Part I, end of Section II.

[2] Chapter vii in this volume.

the door to his approach to the whole problem of value and I shall attempt to use them in this Introduction for this purpose.

'Programme' should be understood as a plan of intended action, e.g., a party programme, the objectives of trade unions, farmers' or traders' associations, etc. A programme is the formulation of a policy. It consists of certain objectives or ends, and rules about the manner in which these objectives are to be pursued.

By 'prognosis' is meant a forecast of the probable or possible course of events. A prognosis is based on observation and analysis, and consists of the application to particular instances of generalizations about the actual and hypothetical connections between facts and events.

This distinction is related to the more familiar one between *analysis* and *policy*. 'Prognosis' stresses the predictive character of analysis; 'programme' is a concrete formulation of policy. The distinction is also related to the familiar *means-ends* dichotomy, but it is not the same. The means-ends model was constructed in order to salvage something of what appeared to be a normative science, in an age when the rationalistic faith in discoverable values had declined, and scepticism and relativism had grown stronger.[1] If the dichotomy is tenable, a teleological argument can be conducted on objective lines, as long as the hypothetical clause about ends is inserted. All valuations are bundled together under the rubric 'ends,' and the appropriateness of means can then be discussed 'scientifically.'

But people attach value not merely to 'ends', in the sense of the desired ultimate results of a course of events, but also to the means by which ends are achieved. This complex of desired ends, means and procedures, and effects other than ends which may be inevitable outcomes, all of which is conditioned by valuations, one may call 'programme'.

In terms of the distinction between programme and prognosis much of social analysis looks like the attempt to derive programmes directly from analysis and prognosis. Critics have repeatedly pointed out that such attempts stem from a confusion, and that clear thinking requires that ends (which

[1] See Chapter x

are a part of programmes) be separated from means (analysis and prediction). The most recent formulation of this view can be found in the theory of the *social welfare function*.[1] The social welfare function is a hold-all for all valuations, set out in a definite order, a device which is supposed to purify economic investigation of all vestiges of unscientific matter. But the interdependence of programme and prognosis is in the nature of social theory, and the obstacle to their separation is not just muddle-headedness.

The purists claim that it is possible and desirable to separate sharply (*a*) the prognosis based on an objective analysis of a situation in which programmes are taken as data, from (*b*) the programme based on this analysis. In fact, there is mutual interaction, and each is partly determined and modified by the other.

The criticism of the view that independent prognosis is possible is similar, as far as I can see, to the criticism of modern physicists of the assumption that observer and observed do not affect each other. It has been found that it is inherently impossible to observe exactly both the position and the velocity of a particle, even if all experimental errors are eliminated.

This discovery did not lead to the abandonment of observation, but to a reformulation of the model used. Similarly, the fact that programme and prognosis affect each other forces us to abandon such models as 'economics is the science of the allocation of scarce means with alternative uses between competing ends' and to replace them by more appropriate models, which take account of this interaction.

3. PROGRAMME DETERMINED BY PROGNOSIS

Pigou prefaced his *Wealth and Welfare* with a quotation from Charles Booth: 'discontent, to be effective, must be shot through with the colours of hope.' He was convinced that in his analysis hope could be found. A programme, to be effective, must take

[1] A. Bergson (Burk), 'A Reformulation of Certain Aspects of Welfare Economics', *Quarterly Journal of Economics*, LII (Feb. 1938), 310-34; P. A. Samuelson, *Foundations of Economic Analysis*, Chap. VIII; K. J. Arrow, *Social Choice and Individual Values*; A. Bergson, 'On the Concept of Social Welfare', *Quarterly Journal of Economics*, May, 1954.

account of the probable and possible future course of events, in other words, it must be based on analysis and prognosis. Programmes are altered in the light of new knowledge about the facts. Programmes without prognoses are idle wish-dreams or empty protests.

More particularly, analysis and prognosis can point out the implications of alternative choices, and the consistency or inconsistency of objectives contained in a programme. They may indicate the proper policies for achieving given objectives, in so far as values are not attached to the policies as such, and the probable consequences of given policies. They may show to what extent the short-term interests manifested in a programme are compatible with the long-term interests of a group, to what extent the objectives expressed in a programme diverge from the actual conduct of the group in question (pointing out rationalizations and hypocrisy), and to what extent this conduct is consistent.

It appears therefore that the ends are never given, in the sense required by those who believe in the possibility of a neutral welfare theory. Ends are modified:

1. In the light of fuller knowledge of the facts.

2. In the light of what is believed can, and what cannot, be altered. But amongst these 'data' are the ends of other people; therefore ends are altered in the light of the programmes, and the power behind the programmes, of others. Many conservative recommendations rest on the conviction that 'you can't change human nature', whereas socialists derive hope from the belief that institutions can sometimes do so. Disputes between revolutionaries and reformists are often about whether certain institutions can be changed. Opinions as to the factual problem of what are the constants will condition men's moral and political convictions.[1]

3. In the light of other ends which develop as one set of ends is explored, and in the light of undesirable, previously unforeseen, results which clash either with the 'given', or with the newly discovered, ends.

To put the same thing another way: Analysis and prognosis modify programmes in the following ways:

[1] But the convictions may also colour their view of the 'facts'. See below,

xvi

1. Programmes may become more consistent through being better informed, and thus more effective.

2. Value standards, previously only implicit, or altogether absent, may be activated as a result of the facts turned up by analysis. (See Section 5).

3. Confusions not only about the relations of facts, but also about one's own desires may be cleared up. Rationalizations and pseudo-interests may give place to knowledge of real interests.

4. Divergencies between words and deeds, action and belief, may become apparent.

For any of these reasons, programmes may be altered as a result of the clarification of certain facts. This relationship, however, is complicated because there is no *logical* connection between false beliefs about the world and valuations based on them, on the one hand, and correct beliefs and valuations based on them, on the other hand. If it were not for this complication, it might still be possible to maintain the dichotomy between ends and means. If we were given programmes based on erroneous factual beliefs, we might be able to deduce logically what programmes would be pursued if the errors were corrected. This is the view expressed by Max Weber in his discussion of the objectivity of social science.[1] In fact, this is impossible. The question, how do individuals and groups react to changing insight into reality, can be answered only by psychology and sociology, not by logic.

4. PROGNOSIS DETERMINED BY PROGRAMME

It is obvious that a programme is based on, and modified in the light of, analysis and prognosis, though not always logically. A programme without prognosis is an impotent utopian dream. On the other hand, a prognosis without programmes is necessarily incomplete. Prognosis depends upon programmes in two distinct ways. First and obviously, the programmes of *others* are data for the social observer and theorist. What physical facts and events are to the natural scientist, that valuations,

[1] Max Weber, *Gesammelte Aufsätze zur Soziologie und Sozialpolitik*, p. 416; *Political Element*, pp. 202-3.

beliefs and programmes, however wrong-headed or ill-conceived, are to the social scientist. Second, and perhaps less obviously, the observer and theorist himself has something like a programme which determines his analysis and prognosis.

(a) *Programmes as Social Data.* Social analysis treats the intentions and plans of individuals and groups as the most important part of its data. We can forecast what is likely to happen under specified conditions only if we know what certain people will want to do in those conditions and how successfully they will act. Not value systems in the abstract, not given sets of ends, but programmes, in so far as they are backed by power, are an essential element in analysis and prognosis.

Prognostic disputes have raged over the question of whether the removal of food subsidies, or a rise in rents, or devaluation, would have inflationary or deflationary effects. Yet, the answer hinges almost entirely on the programme and power of trade unions. If workers attempt to fix real wages, money wages will rise as a result of the above policies, and the effect will be inflationary. If they fix wages in money terms (either because they suffer from a 'money illusion', or because they are relatively weak) the effect may be deflationary.

(b) *Selection and Relevance.* The selection of empirical data relevant to any question under examination is subject to a judgment as to what *ought* to be admitted as good evidence. Factual propositions imply injunctions about what kind of events we *should* expect if we accept certain views about the real world, and valuations about the credit-*worthiness* of beliefs. Clearly these judgments are not moral or political value judgments (although they may be connected with these). This is not the place for a discussion of the nature of these judgments and rules, but they appear to be in some respects like moral value judgments and imperatives. They, too, require a decision, imply a choice, and cannot be subsumed under clearly definable general canons. Above all, they cannot be derived from the facts, because there are no facts without them.

Moreover, the element in these judgments which resembles value judgments is particularly prevalent in social studies.

Here evidence cannot always be provided at will, situations are complex and often unique, and scientific experiment almost impossible. Hence the scope for appraisal and judgment is much wider than in many of the natural sciences.[1]

The importance of valuations in the formation of empirical hypotheses is brought out even more clearly when we consider probability prognoses in the form of statistical propositions. First, the decision as to what deviations in any given set of observations from a probability hypothesis should be considered as refuting this hypothesis, is quite independent of the observations, and determined entirely by the use to which we put the hypothesis. The purpose of our investigation thus determines the decision to accept or reject an empirical theory.

Second, when we are faced with a choice between alternative statistical prognoses, we require a programme to select the best one. One such programme is that formulated by Wald, which is equivalent to a Neumann-Morgenstern theorem in the theory of games, according to which we choose that hypothetical prognosis on which we are likely to lose least if it turns out to be false. *Safety first* bids us minimize the maximum of possible losses. By looking upon uncertain future natural events as if they were a partner in a game, we can apply the Neumann-Morgenstern strategy to the selection of empirical prognoses. Thus an evaluation of gains and losses is an essential prerequisite for prediction, where alternative probability hypotheses are available. In the words of R. B. Braithwaite, '. . . we cannot be good, or at least deliberately good, without being wise. The modern principles of statistical inference show that, *vice versa*, judgments of value are, in the last analysis, inextricably involved in choosing the best way to scientific knowledge: we cannot be wise without making judgements of good and evil.'[2]

(c) *Models and Concepts: the Index Number Problem.* All concepts

---

[1] These differences are, however, sometimes exaggerated. In astronomy, experiments are not possible; metereology deals with complicated forces; and the objections to controlled human experiments are partly moral, and not in the nature of society.

[2] R. B. Braithwaite, 'Moral Principles and Inductive Policies', *Proceedings of the British Academy*, XXXVI (1950), 65f.

are abstractions. They are normative, not only in the sense much discussed recently, that they may have emotive connotations and may be used to persuade or to commend, as well as to describe, but also in the more fundamental sense that a rule or judgment is required to determine what particular objects or experiences should be lumped together under any given concept. What is known in economics and statistics as the index number problem is a problem common to all thinking. But the difficulties become particularly glaring in the social sciences. Trouble arises when we mistake for concrete things what in fact are theories or models, and thus forget that there is usually a *choice* of alternative theories or models to explain a given set of experiences.

Examples of the muddles caused by this mistake are such models as 'Man v. Nature,' 'Real Social Income,' 'Consumption,' 'the Economy', etc. A particularly apt example is the means-ends model itself. By arranging and presenting the facts in a certain way, policy questions are already implied, which would not have arisen if a different model had been chosen. (See section (d).)

The same is true of all important concepts in economics. To say anything, not merely about prices, real wages, national income, etc., but, e.g., about the economic consequences of the war, about the economic prospects of a country, almost anything about capital—ideas with normally little emotive content—implies nevertheless *choosing*, hence *valuing*, although this fact is often concealed by our mistaking models for concrete objects.

The literature is replete with declarations that comparisons between the utilities of different men cannot be made by positive economists because such comparisons are value judgments. Yet, by using appropriately question-begging pseudo-positive terms, i.e., models with implicit valuations disguised as descriptive concepts, the valuations reappear. Thus shortly after Jevons says solemnly: 'there is never, in any single instance, an attempt made to compare the amount of feeling in one mind with that in another,' (*Theory of Political Economy*, p. 14) he speaks ingenuously of aggregate and average psychological functions, belonging to groups of people, nations, or trading bodies, as if the impossible were possible after all. Similarly, modern welfare economists speak of increases in social income and welfare after having declared firmly that interpersonal comparisons of real income and welfare are impossible.

In some instances it is, of course, possible to lay down a definite rule to eliminate ambiguity. But even then the decision will be guided by the *purpose* of our investigation, by the *question* we are asking. We shall be prepared to modify the rule according to what our *interest* requires. The point is that the concepts and propositions of even the most purely empirical investigation derive their meaning and significance from a purpose, an interest, and involve choice and, therefore, valuation.

'National income' has no meaning, unless we specify whether we are interested in an underdeveloped or a developed society, in one with little or much state activity, in a nation's productive capacity, its standard of living, or its equality, etc. 'Capital' has no meaning unless we know whether the inquirer is an accountant, a businessman, or a pure theorist who postulates equilibrium. Yet, many speak of 'national income', 'capital', etc., as if they were speaking of gallons of water.

All this may sound too obvious to be worth saying. Yet the belief is widespread that we can confine ourselves to the discovery of facts and thus avoid choice and valuation.

(d) *Inadequacy of the Means-Ends Scheme.* In social analysis valuations enter not only at the ultimate (or initial) stage in decisions about sets of given ends, but at every stage. People do not attach value only to ultimate ends (whatever this may mean); and they are not indifferent between the means which promote these ends, even where the means are technically and otherwise exactly equivalent.

It is important to avoid a terminological confusion here. It is, of course, possible to *define* anything to which value is attached as an "end". But such a trick would not meet the purpose for which the means-ends dichotomy was constructed. As we have seen, it was meant to circumscribe a neutral sphere in which objective statements can be made, and into which no valuations enter. But if values are attached to means, the

Introduction

qualifications required by the acceptance of the ends become necessary at every stage. If end E can be brought about by courses a, b, and c, and if no direct values are attached to a, b, and c, a scientific discussion of these course, which abstracts entirely from valuations, is possible: how long they take, how effectively they promote E, what other results E_1, E_2, etc., besides E they are likely to have, etc. It is then possible to arrive at the conclusion, say, that a is the most effective course, *if E* is desired and if E_1, E_2, etc. are insufficient deterrents (or welcome by-products). This is the model commonly envisaged by practitioners of economics.

But this procedure is no longer open if direct values are attached to a, b, and c themselves. For then we can only say, tautologically, choose a *if* you want a, choose b, *if* you want b, etc.: whereas before we could say, choose a, but not b or c, if you want E. Since the hypothetical clause referring to valuation has to be introduced at every stage, empirical analysis disappears altogether.

The following quite unwarranted assumptions would be required if we were to discuss objectively means in relation to "given" ends:

1. People attach to means no direct value, but only instrumental value.

2. People attach to ends direct value only, and never consider them as means to other ends.

3. No other effects of means than the "given" ends have direct value.

Very rarely can one reach exactly the same end by alternative, politically entirely indifferent, means. The means affect the 'end' in the wider sense. Whereas the means-end model, to be useful, must assume that the same place can be reached by alternative paths (see section e), in fact different paths usually lead to different places in this field. This fact greatly restricts the sphere in which prognosis can progress without assuming or committing itself to specific valuations almost all the time. It narrows the realm of 'neutrality' and 'objectivity,' as defined by the means-ends protagonists.

To illustrate: If consumption were the only end, and if production and exchange were only means to its achievement certain rules about the optimum conditions of production and exchange could be laid down. The formulation of these rules has been the aim of an important branch of traditional welfare economics. But the disturbing fact is that neither the conditions in which production is carried on, nor the relationships generated by exchange are purely instrumental. They are *human* conditions and *human* relations, which are valued as much as, and in some cases more strongly than, the end of consumption. Nor, of course, is consumption *simply* a given end. Not only are there good and bad ways of earning money, but there are also good and bad ways of spending it.

The foregoing was an attempt to criticize the means-ends model in its own terminology. A different approach, pointing to the same conclusion, may bring out the argument more clearly.[1] Somebody may at this stage of the argument reply: 'Granted that problems of policy as a whole cannot be reduced to a means-ends model. Nevertheless, means-ends problems are ubiquitous, though always involving abstractions from the total situation, and they are the only ones which an economist as such is competent to deal with. Furthermore, surely not all the deliverances of an economist will be policy deliverances. If so, how are the purely descriptive parts of his analysis related to the policy part?'

Those who find the means-ends model helpful look upon problems of economic policy as if they were, in principle, like puzzles. There is the obvious difference that puzzles are constructed by some people in order to be solved by others, whereas problems of policy usually are not. But in both cases, granted consistent premises, there is always a 'correct' solution. There is always an unambiguous 'scientific' test of whether we have solved the puzzle. Thus if the end is, say, the avoidance of more than 2 per cent. unemployment for five years, statisticians can tell us whether we have succeeded or not. No doubt, many problems of economic policy are of this type.

If all policy problems were of this kind, not much more could be said in principle. Some people, perhaps the technocrats, believe that they are. It is certainly tempting to assimilate

[1] See T. D. Weldon, *The Vocabulary of Politics* (Penguin, 1953), esp. Chap. 3, section 7 and Chap. 5.

all problems to this type, and to say that a problem has been solved when certain ideal rules are obeyed. But the question, e.g., whether the avoidance of unemployment should be a primary objective of policy is altogether different. We might indeed say that absence of unemployment diminishes the chances of social rebellion and is to be commended solely on this ground. Thus considered as a mere means, statisticians could presumably again tell us whether this is correct or not. Many ends are, at least partly, intermediate ends in this sense. And some theories maintain that all problems could be subsumed under one single ultimate end. But this is not a plausible view.

If we believe that unemployment spells misery and loss of human dignity, and that it violates our belief in the brotherhood of men, but that some of it may at times be necessary to prevent greater evil, no simple criterion could be formulated, which would show whether, by avoiding unemployment, we have done the right thing. However, although we cannot apply simple and definite tests and present a 'scientific' solution, the answer is not arbitrary. Through observation, conversation, and experience we can learn to *judge* and *appraise* these matters.

Although value judgments enter into our judgment of the situation, they are not of the type of 'ends' as in the puzzle-solving model. A good deal of political and economic discourse is neither purely descriptive, nor just rhetorical emotive persuasion, nor a combination of the two. It is more like the exercise of a skill, or an art, like playing the piano, or giving a lecture, or writing a poem. The strictly scientific aspect of political discussion, as defined by the means-ends dichotomists, is comparable to the theory of the skill: it lays down precise rules, clear tests. But the best theory can produce neither a skilful performance nor good judgment of a performance. A skilful performance can neither be tested by hard and fast standards, nor is it merely an arbitrary or subjective decision whether we judge it good or bad.

An economist, like a novelist, is good not because (a) he knows the facts, and (b) has the right value judgments (political or literary). The answer to the question, 'How do we know that he is a good economist or novelist?', whatever it may be (and it is not an easy one), will certainly not be, 'Because his work follows certain definite canons.'

Analysis and prognosis and their appraisal are skills, which cannot always be subjected to the rules of the means-ends game. Although they inevitably involve judgments which have some of the characteristics of valuations, they are not for that reason 'subjective', arbitrary, or mere matters of taste.

(e) *Implications for Welfare Economics.* There are, roughly speaking, two modern versions of welfare economics, the Paretian and the Bergsonian. Both versions depend, to some extent, on the validity of the means-ends model. The Paretian optimum conditions of production and exchange are claimed to be—in the more modest formulations—necessary, though not sufficient, conditions for an economic optimum, on certain additional assumptions which it is not necessary to enumerate.

If the puzzle-solving model is rejected, according to which recommendations of means become a merely *technical* matter, and if the more empirical approach suggested in the previous section is adopted, it becomes pointless to speak of a social or of an economic *optimum* which is achieved if certain specifiable conditions are fulfilled; and yet it is meaningful and important to speak of *improvements*.

But only if we are prepared to speak of an 'optimum' are the Paretian conditions *necessary* conditions (on certain assumptions). If we reject the applicability of an 'optimum', it is perfectly possible, even granted the stringent assumptions about values and facts of this theory, to envisage all kinds of improvements which do not meet the Paretian criteria. All desirable redistributions of wealth which would not allow compensation of the losers would be such improvements. The Pareto criteria would turn out to be not only insufficient, but also unnecessary.

Similarly, the social welfare function is a device which makes an ordering of all possible states necessary. Given a social welfare function, the solution of the optimum · is like the solution of a puzzle though it may require great technical virtuosity. But no social welfare function is ever given, at any rate in a· democratic society. We never order all possible total situations according to a system of values, but have rather muddled preferences for aspects and features of a limited number of actual and possible situations. These preferences change as a result of the discussion and adoption of policies intended to minister to them.

If the economist is to give advice in concrete situations, it is more helpful for him to think in terms of *improvements* than in terms of ideals or *optima*. Nobody really knows what an optimum economic system is like, but many can make wise proposals for betterment. The fallacy of the means-end pattern of thinking lies in the belief that 'improvement' always logically implies an 'optimum' or 'ideal'. It may, if we judge the change with reference to a given ideal, such as the number of correct answers in a quiz where the only alternatives are 'Yes' or 'No'. But 'improvement' need not imply 'optimum', as may be illustrated in the example of writing a good article. An article is never completed; there is *always* scope for improvement. Nobody can lay down criteria and say: 'This is what the end-product ought to be like'. Yet, it would be foolish to deny that there are ways of knowing when it has been improved. The mistake of fitting the 'good article' into the quiz schema is analogous to the mistake of fitting all economic policies into the means-ends pattern.

(f) *Bias.* So far we have discussed some of the ways in which analysis and prognosis depend upon and presuppose judgments, valuations, and programmes, without, however, necessarily being distorted by them. But there are numerous interpretations of facts in social theory whose function it is not to clear up muddles or to show up inconsistencies, but, on the contrary, to justify inconsistent beliefs, to bridge over contradictions. Many well-known types of social prognosis are biased in a more or less conscious way, so as to justify valuations and the behaviour that springs from them.

When contradictions within a programme, or between the programme and certain facts, are pointed out, two reactions are possible: either the programme is altered in accordance with fuller, more rational understanding, or the belief about the facts is adjusted to fit the programme. Prognoses that are used to justify programmes in this manner may be manifestations of 'blind spots', prejudices, biases, or, more grandiosely, ideologies. The distortion may range from blatant lies to the very categories of thought, which, if the sociologists of knowledge are right, are conditioned by our interests and valuations.

At this stage, the philosophies of natural law and of utilitarianism are turned upside down. According to these two philosophies, values and rules can be derived from a contemplation of the facts, the natural order according to the former, happiness or welfare according to the latter. But to-day we are more inclined to believe that it is possible, and perhaps inevitable, that our values and rules determine the manner in which we approach, see, arrange, and interpret, the facts. It is not so much that values follow from 'the nature of the case', as that what we believe to be the nature of the case follows from our values.

Although in some cases a rational examination of political ideas may make them more effective by grounding them on a better knowledge of the facts, in other cases rational or rather pseudo-rational examination makes them into sterile ideologies. But their power over the irrational nature of men may be thereby increased. One of the most important facts of social life is that people are often highly irrational.

The critics of abstract, rationalistic systems in economics have, for over a hundred years, pointed out the historical and political value premises which underlie this type of theorizing, without, however, clarifying where they seek the Archimedean point from which to lift their own theory—the institutional or historical criticism—beyond ideology. It appears that the way towards a bias-free study of economics lies in the awareness of one's historical, political, institutional and moral valuations, and thus in an open recognition of the limitations of any theory, including one's own. Paradoxically, by abandoning the claim to absolutism, universality, and 'pure' science, a way is opened to a more limited but also more rational, to a more modest but also more objective, approach to the study of society. Some of the problems raised by ideologies are more fully discussed in section 7.

5. INTERDEPENDENCE BETWEEN PROGRAMME AND PROGNOSIS

It appears therefore that programmes are modified in the light of prognoses, but prognoses also depend upon, and are altered with, changing programmes. Valuations depend on what changes we believe to be feasible. But the 'constants' which determine what is feasible may in turn be altered by people's valuations. Faith can move mountains.

It is therefore impossible to take either the ends, in so far as they enter into programmes, as 'given' independently of the analysis of means, or to postulate a 'pure' analysis of means, a science of social engineering. Programmes depend on prognoses, which in turn depend on programmes, etc. It has been said that public knowledge of Keynesian analysis removes the world which Keynes analysed, and that successful practice of Marxism removes the conditions to which Marxian analysis applies.

In the following I shall try to give a few illustrations of the way in which prognosis alters programmes, the transformation of which in turn modifies prognosis.

(*a*) *Prophecies: Cure through Prognosis.* Prognosis may serve the programme of changing the way of life (the programmes) of others. The oldest illustrations of this are the reform endeavours of the prophets of the Old Testament. Jonah's prognosis was the destruction of Nineveh in forty days. God's programme for Jonah was not to make him into a successful forecaster, but to mend the ways of the people of Nineveh. As a result of Jonah's prognosis, this programme was achieved. Incidentally, Jonah's prognosis was falsified, which may have contributed to his anger.

In the same tradition of cure through prognosis stand the interpretations of history of Hegel, Marx, Spengler, and perhaps Toynbee. In some cases the cure lies in the fulfilment of the prognosis (Hegel, Marx), in others it lies in its falsification (Spengler, Toynbee). These interpretations contain analysis and prognosis, which are both determined by, and, in turn, determine social programmes.

The prognosis need not be guided primarily by the intention of improvement, but may have that effect nevertheless. The studies of Booth and Rowntree stated certain facts about poverty in England. As a result of this knowledge, consciences were stirred into action. But the methods which were taken to alleviate poverty, together with the general rise in the standard of living, led to a new interpretation of poverty. The poverty line, i.e., the standard condemned by public opinion, rose with rising living standards. Or, to put the matter another way, analysis and action to relieve poverty brought out a new aspect of poverty: it was considered to lie not merely in destitution, i.e., inability to afford the physically essential minimum, but also in inequality. Poverty, it has become clear, is partly relative, though not entirely, for it is possible for all to be *equally* poor. The idea of what constitutes poverty has changed as a result of inquiring into poverty and of attempting to reduce it.

Other examples of the same process are Myrdal's study of the conditions of Negroes in the United States, Ferguson's and Cunnison's study of juvenile delinquency in Glasgow,[1] and reports on living conditions in poor countries.

(b) *Dangerous Thought: Destruction through Prognosis.* In other instances prognosis has the effect of destroying some of the values, and hence some of the social relations, upon which it is based. This is often neither foreseen nor desired by the prognosticators. Indeed, proposals based on prognosis often fail to produce the intended results, just because the prognosis alters the data on which it is based.

A simple illustration would be those theories that assume the 'money illusion' on the part of wage earners. Workers are supposed to object to a reduction in money wages while prices are constant, but not to a rise in prices with wages constant. Such a theory in itself may make workers more real-wage conscious.

There is an element of erosion in almost all growth of knowledge on social relations. A good deal of our behaviour is habitual, semi-instinctive, subject to taboos and conventions. Analysis, which is based on the assumption that people behave in this way, brings taboos and conventions into the open,

1. T. Ferguson and J. Cunnison, *The Young Wage-Earner: A Study of Glasgow Boys* (Oxford University Press, 1951).

increases people's awareness of them, and leads to the desire for conscious manipulation. But the manipulation destroys the fabric on which, according to the initial prognosis, it is supposed to work. The price for eating of the tree of knowledge is the loss of Paradise.

Some objections to too much knowledge of the working of one's psyche have been raised on those grounds. In economics, the knowledge of the irrational, quasi-conventional character of competition led to monopolistic agreements; knowledge of the outwardly imposed rules of the gold standard game led to a desire of every nation to be master of its own fate; and generally, greater awareness of the network of economic relations led to a desire to manipulate it, and thus to its disintegration. Increased organization by individuals and groups led to increased disorganization at large.

The social effects of birth control, of divorce, of control of property, markets, prices, currencies, and the use of propaganda, all result from growing knowledge and sophistication. The automatic adjustments of liberal society presupposed acceptance of traditional behaviour, and absence of the desire to question, experiment, and control rationally. Successful prognosis seemed to make it unnecessary to adjust ourselves to the world, and created the desire to adjust the world to our desires. But the cumulative effect was to produce an altogether new social situation, adjustment to which is more problematic than ever.[1]

We have seen above that Marxist theory, like prophecy, is a prognosis intended to create action. The theory and practice of modern state planning, on the other hand, is an attempt to meet the disintegrating pulls of a growing number of increasingly self-conscious, rational planning units. (Some of these pulls are themselves state interventions).

It is possible to draw different conclusions from this tendency. Some might argue that 'too much knowledge is a bad thing.' There are various versions of the Japanese concept of 'dangerous thought', and almost every society attempts to protect itself to some extent by restricting open discussion of its most sacred

[1] See Myrdal: 'The Trend towards Economic Planning", *Manchester School* (January, 1951).

institutions. Others might argue that the trend is both inevitable and desirable. What is required is more knowledge,
i.e., knowledge that takes these socially disintegrating effects
of partial knowledge into account.[1] But these questions are not
my concern here.

(c) *Harmony through Prognosis.* In many theories a fuller
understanding of the facts is believed to lead to greater social
harmony. This is obviously so in all theories which consider evil
as a form of ignorance. But although many believe implicitly
in such a theory, few do so now when it is stated explicitly.

Yet, it is clear that knowledge *may* contribute to social
harmony, and often does. It can remove opposition based on
false views about reality, and a good deal of opposition does in
fact have this origin. It can bring out more clearly the implications of commonly accepted standards;[2], and it can help
to contribute to the formulation of common standards (respect
for honest research, tolerance, etc.) In many situations, even
where short-term interests clash, it can be shown that it is in
everybody's interest to co-operate, because large potential
gains could thereby be realized, out of which all members to
the agreement could benefit.[3] A whole theory of welfare
economics has been constructed on this argument.

On the other hand, fuller knowledge may also sharpen
conflicts. Harmony may rest on muddled thinking, and
conflicts may be brought to light by clarification. In particular,
the reluctance to make sacrifices to achieve accepted objectives

[1] Socially sophisticated countries like England, where people know that institutions can be eroded, often refuse to allow rational considerations to erode them.

[2] For a recent expression of this view see Milton Friedman, in *A Survey of
Contemporary Economics*, II, 456: 'I venture the judgment that currently in the
Western world, and especially in the United States, differences about economic
policy among disinterested citizens derive predominantly from different predictions
about the consequences of taking action, differences that can in principle be
eliminated by the progress of positive economics—rather than from fundamental
differences in basic values, differences about which men can ultimately only fight.'

[3] This, of course, is the classical argument for the greatest happiness principle,
for free trade, etc. In commenting on his terms of trade argument for the im-
position of a tariff, Edgeworth quoted with approval a remark by J. S. Nicholson
that some demonstrations are 'part of the casuistry of economics, like the discussions of moral philosophers concerning the occasional justification of mendacity.
Free trade, like honesty, is still the best policy'. R. W. Stevens, 'New Ideas in
International Trade Theory', *American Economic Review*, June 1951, p. 375 note.

may be increased. Everybody wants peace, full employment happiness and prosperity for all. But not everybody is prepared to do what is required to achieve these goals.

Moreover, knowledge of appropriate means gives power. Given divergent values, a clearer view on policies may therefore sharpen conflicts. Programmes backed by knowledge will be more powerful and, for those who do not share them, more dangerous.

Public opinion polls are a simple illustration of how a certain kind of knowledge (viz., of other people's opinions) may either increase or reduce agreement. Knowledge as to how votes are distributed may make some people switch their votes to the majority, and may induce others to back a minority.

To say more about the relation between social knowledge and social harmony would require specific sociological assumptions. Here it must suffice to note that totalitarian philosophies postulate a single rigid programme which must not be subject to modifications. Prognosis will tend to take the form of ideology: it will not show up, but rather will plaster over cracks in the analysis in order to justify the programme.

But this view is not confined to totalitarian philosophies. Programmes that cannot be modified by prognosis are to be found in any utopian system of political theory. The means-ends pattern fits best into these views. According to the liberal doctrine of the ultimate harmony of interests, either in its natural law version or as utilitarianism, conflicts result from ignorance, knowledge must promote harmony.

But closer inspection shows that the harmony aspect of these theories is in fact ideology. They are usually the formulation of the aspirations of a *particular* group (exporters, manufacturers, e.g., advocating free trade) put forward as in the *general* interest. Ideological concepts such as utilities, pleasures, social income, etc., are used in order to postulate a harmony where in fact there is conflict.

In times of crisis or war, even in a political democracy, the situation of a single, generally agreed, programme is approximated, and the means-ends dichotomy becomes a plausible assumption. But in a democratic society, in times of peace and at least moderate prosperity, programmes and the power

behind them are conflicting and dispersed; and prognoses and programmes become intricately inter-connected in a way which cannot be fitted into the means-end pattern. In a society that values independent research and programmes based on this research, and in which knowledge is widely disseminated, prevailing programmes will be modified in the direction of greater efficiency and consistency, though not necessarily greater harmony. As a result, probably future social trends are altered and prognoses will have to be modified. In the light of this revised knowledge, programmes will again be altered, some tensions will be resolved, others created.

All groups will be aware of the possibility that their programmes may have to be altered by new situations, and that they must be limited by the aspirations of others. Dictatorial programmes may be justly reflected in a means-end pattern. But democratic programmes are piecemeal, empirical, and elastic. The means-end pattern does not fit them.

(d) *Speculation and Oligopoly.* The strictly economic activities which illustrate this interdependence most clearly are speculation and oligopoly. The programme here is to make profits. The prognosis is the intentions and the behaviour of others (rival speculators, or rival sellers). Every sound speculator and oligopolist takes into account the manner in which the expectations of others (their prognoses) are affected by the intentions of others (their programmes), including his own. A's prognosis, hence A's programme, is a function of B's, C's, D's, etc., prognoses and programmes, B's prognosis and programme are a function of A's, C's, D's, etc., and so on. Any prognosis affects programmes, and any programme affects prognoses. Policies are sensible if certain facts are true ; but whether they are true depends on whether people pursue certain policies.[1]

[1] The common sense view that people's reactions to prognoses (that are made public) may, but do not necessarily, falsify all such prognoses, and that social scientists therefore may hope to predict, at least sometimes, and perhaps normally, both in public and correctly (although these predictions may be different from private ones because they have to take their own effects on people's actions into account) has been proved rigorously and elegantly by Emile Grunberg and Franco Modigliani in 'Predictability of Social Events', *Journal of Political Economy* (December, 1954).

Introduction

6. The Task of the Social Sciences

What follows from all this with respect to the task of the social scientist? It does not follow that social science is impossible, or that it must plunge at once into valuations and ideologies. On the contrary. To be useful and truthful, the social scientist, and in particular the economist, should start with actual political attitudes of people, or groups of people, not with their rationalizations and pseudo-theoretical ideologies. He should abandon speculation about 'general welfare', 'maximum satisfactions', etc., for at least two reasons: first, because these concepts have no clear implications and lend themselves easily to implicit interpretations and persuasive definitions; second, because, even if they had clear implications, actual concrete valuations are not concerned with them at all.

Concrete valuations in concrete historical situations, or in possible situations that might arise, and the attitudes which reflect them, should form the starting point of analysis. Political programmes are not good enough. They too contain empty rationalizations such as 'general welfare'; and they are conditioned by the desire to reach 'agreed formulae' and gloss over disagreement. Neither the party programmes in the United States, nor those of the parties in Britain would provide a sufficiently concrete basis for analysis.

On the other hand, the social scientist must not 'go behaviourist' either. The observed behaviour of groups in actual situations is not a sufficient guide to the formulation of concrete political attitudes. It is certainly a partial way of discovering attitudes, but it does not tell the whole story. The relevant attitudes to be discovered must also refer to readiness to act in certain ways in the future, and under different conditions. And since these potential reactions cannot be deduced *logically* from present reactions, an altogether different method suggests itself. It is the task of social or group psychology to attempt to unify group reactions under something which is analogous to character or personality in individual psychology. No anthropomorphism is involved here if it is possible to discover and predict regularities and unity in the reactions of groups to different actual and potential situations. The political

attitudes thus mapped out can then yield value premises which are sufficiently concrete to be used for analysis and prognosis.

To map out this unity is obviously not a matter of looking for 'given' welfare functions, sets of ends, etc. It is more like the exercise of artistic imagination and sympathetic understanding than like solving puzzles, though puzzle-solving will have a part to play. The conclusions of Section 4 (d) are thus confirmed: problems of economic policy have a good deal in common with problems of artistic workmanship, as well as with problems of engineering.

Some of the difficulties discussed in the preceding sections would still remain, in particular:

1. Values are attached to means, and to incidental consequences, as well as to ends.

2. It may be difficult to separate professed valuations from actual ones.

3. The transition must be made from valuations derived from false beliefs about reality to valuations derived from correct beliefs.

Thus ideology may creep into the theory of the personality, or the character of groups. Since the unity of group personality is neither one of deductive logic nor one of complete observation, but partly at least one of intuitive understanding, the scope for bias and controversy is enlarged. Yet an inadequate theory based on a correct view of social attitudes seems preferable to a logically perfect theory based on an altogether false view, i.e., the means-end dichotomy.

The growing complexity of social life, and the increasing importance of controlling groups, such as monopolies, public corporations, trade unions, planning bodies of various types, etc., whose activities are replacing the more conventional and automatic adjustments of the past, make it more important to study the valuations that underlie the actions of these bodies. In this analysis account should be taken of the probable reception of new theories and their social repercussions.

Once we have mapped out the valuations of different groups in society, two types of interconnected study can be pursued. First, one might pose the question: what policies are appropriate to these concrete valuations? And second: what social factors determine the formation and the strength of these valuations? It will be necessary to revise continually the results of the inquiry into one of these two questions in the light of the results of the other.

The main thread in Myrdal's thought that links the *Political Element* with *Under-developed Regions* is the idea that the fundamental presuppositions in which we attempt to understand society must be transformed if, as a result of the changes and new techniques of control, we are to make possible a new epoch of development. He showed in the *Political Element* that our thinking about society is invalidated by relics of old systems of thought (harmony, analysis of stable equilibrium, utility welfare); he criticized the separation of means from ends as a doctrinal bias of the same origin in the 1933 article; he gradually evolved and used presuppositions and models (in *Monetary Equilibrium, An American Dilemma, An International Economy*) more appropriate to an 'age in which the policies of integrated nation states have reduced some inequalities but given rise to new internal and international tensions, in which the basic work of industrialisation has benefited only a few, countries, in which the state and large private institutions have assumed power, and public and quasi-public relations have replaced private relations, in which science has been institutionalised, in which rational questioning of accepted ways has been extended, and in which Western ideals have spread throughout the world; and he is now using these new presuppositions of social thought (cumulative causation, integration of economic and non-economic forces, value premises from concrete aspirations of important groups) to understand the problems and to further the aspirations of our age.

7. IDEOLOGIES

In a previous section [4, (f)] I have indicated that analysis and prognosis may be distorted by valuations and programmes. A somewhat fuller treatment of this problem may be forgiven, both because it is central in Myrdal's essays and also because discussion in general in this field is obscured by a reluctance of many writers who insist that valuations somehow seep into social analysis to state clearly (a) where precisely this seepage occurs, and (b) how the Archimedean point[1] can be found from which their own theory is lifted into objectivity.

Without entering into a discussion of these problems themselves, it may be useful to compile, in note form, a short list of some of the ways in which valuations may be thought to affect analysis and to consider the change in Myrdal's thought in the light of this classification. There appear to be roughly four possiblities:

1. Valuations determine the *content*, and thus the *validity*, of the analysis *psychologically*. (Views of this kind were held by Bacon, Nietzsche, Sorel and Pareto).

(a) The analysis is consciously false; the propositions are lies.

(b) The distortion is semi-conscious: wishful thinking; special pleading.

(c) The distortion is unconscious; the conclusions are rationalizations.

It may, of course, be that one group of men implant what they know to be false notions into the minds of others by manipulative efforts. If the victims are not aware of being manipulated, their beliefs would fall under (1c), whilst the activity of the manipulators (propaganda, conditioning) falls under (1a), at least as long as they have not fallen victims to their own devices.

Freudian rationalization is a method of resolving conflicts peculiar to the individual, whereas rationalization here considered serves to resolve social conflicts. Ideology is for society what guilt and self-justification are for an individual. But tensions in the structure of society will tend to manifest themselves in the psychological problems of individuals and the two spheres are not strictly separable.[2]

[1] The expression is E. Grünwald's. Cf. *Das Problem der Soziologie des Wissens*, Wien-Leipzig, 1934, p. 206.

[2] Thus guilt can be a symptom of personal conflicts which, however, may reflect social forces. The connection between Protestantism and the rise of capitalism has been discussed by Weber and Tawney. Guilt over enjoyment may be connected with capital accumulation by men who valued thrift, hard work, and self-denial. The secularized guilt feelings of many modern Americans at not getting the most out of life may be similarly connected with a later stage of capitalism at which the problems of excess capacity and surplus production have replaced that of capital accumulation.

In all cases, (a), (b) and (c) only *false* statements are contaminated. Ideology is defined as 'false consciousness'. Valuations may provide a motive for finding a *logical* (as well as an illogical) basis for a desired conclusion, but the analysis is not then distorted. There is a sphere of objective thought.

The Archimedean point is given by exposing the motives. (There is, however, a danger that this effort itself is contaminated by unexpressed valuations).

2. Valuations determine the *content* and thus the *validity* of analysis by affecting the structure (categories, presuppositions, premises, etc.) of thought. (Hegel's and Marx's theories are not psychological but epistemological in this sense). Contamination is not a matter of individual or even social psychology, but everyone in a given situation who thinks at all has to think in a certain value-determined way. Probing of motives cannot eliminate implicit valuations, for they are an essential condition of all thought.

Nowadays, a similar point is made by stressing the manner in which language influences the way we see, select, and analyse events, and thus opens the door to bias. First, it enters not only —as is generally recognized—into the selection and criticism of evidence, but also into our classifications and frames of reference. Particularly in social studies do we take our vacabulary from the field of study itself.[1] Thus the valuations of the market place and of the political arena are carried unobtrusively into scientific analysis.

Secondly, language introduces a bias by adopting identical terms for situations that are similar in some respects, dissimilar in others. To use the same concept, or model, or metaphor to refer to different situations is a source of both danger and opportunity. Danger, because the reference may distort or misrepresent the facts; opportunity, because it may enlarge our vision by drawing attention to hitherto unnoticed features.

Thirdly, there is the danger of seeing real essences behind terms of mere classification.[2]

---

[1] Cf. the perceptive reflections of Marc Bloch, *The Historian's Craft* (Manchester University Press, 1954).

[2] In so far as only the *emotive* use of words is stressed, the linguistic analysis should be classified under 1. Valuations enter at the pyschological level and could be eliminated by a purged language.

In whatever manner we analyse the seepage of valuations into analysis, it follows that not only false, but all statements under this second heading are 'ideological' and hence logically suspect, unless areas are cleared which are claimed to be exempt from bias. Thus some writers say that

(a) only at certain historical *periods* (e.g. in a class society), others that

(b) only certain *fields of study* (e.g. social studies), others that

(c) only certain *classes* (e.g. the bourgeoisie) are subject to contamination, have 'false consciousness.'[1] But the corollary that only certain periods, fields of study, classes, or men are free from bias, can, of course, itself be a fruitful source of ideology. Combining (a), (b) and (c), we arrive at the Marxist view that there is a proletarian social science in the late stages of capitalism to which truth is guaranteed. Particularly Georg Lukács has argued that only proletarian class-conscious thought represents reality 'adequately'. Mannheim (in his earlier work) believed that only the 'socially unattached' (i.e. radical) intellectuals can seek the required 'dynamic synthesis', a 'total perspective', that overcomes the inadequate, partial and biased conceptions of other groups. Hegel thought that reason revealed itself to philosophers (particularly Hegelian philosophers) at a certain stage of history. Nearer home, Marshall, Pigou and others in the tradition of Benthamism imply that in the midst of interest classes only the State is an agency that can see and promote disinterestedly the public good.

On the other hand, some authors argue that it is not only valuations, but other extraneous spheres that determine thought, e.g., social or economic *conditions* (as contrasted with *interests, aspirations, valuations*), natural environment, nationality, race, generation. This determination may be conceived as either causal, or as an expression of some kind of unity.

The Archimedean point cannot be reached empirically, nor logically, but only metaphysically. The 'intellectuals', 'the

[1] The expression occurs in one of Engels' letters to Mehring. Cf. Franz Mehring, *Geschichte der deutschen Sozialdemokratie* (1921) vol. i, p. 386.

working class', or 'action', 'commitment', 'a synthesis' or 'an absolute sphere of values', guarantee objectivity. Or, using the linguistic approach, only a 'perfect language' that exactly fits the facts, could enable us to pull ourselves up by our own shoestrings. The attempt to save the theory from self-contradiction succeeds only through an arbitrary step into metaphysics. The choice lies between dogmatism and absurdity.

3. Valuations have merely *selective* significance. They do not affect the content or validity of thought, but its direction.

(a) They may be *positively selective:* valuations determine *that* a proposition is made then and there. The questions asked are value-determined, but not the answers. The relation between values and theories is not causal, but like the kind of determination by which a question 'determines' an answer.

(b) They may be *negatively selective*, preventing certain propositions from being made in certain situations. (Max Scheler suggested this, although his views are not consistent).

Thus the Ricardian theory of distribution, the Malthusian theory of population, the Marxist theory of the increasing misery of the masses, the Keynesian theory of employment, and the various theories of secular stagnation, secular inflation, and secular dollar shortage, may all be projections on to a vast historical screen of the snapshots of a few years or decades and the magnified protests to which these short-run experiences gave rise.

An Archimedean point is not here required, for validity is independent of valuations. The distinction, however, between type 3 and type 2 ideology is blurred when we remember that an inadequate, partial conception of reality may lead to bias not by commission but by omission. The Archimedean point would consist in scaling down the claims of the theory to less generality; but it then often loses all interest.

4. Valuations determine whether certain propositions are understood, recognized, publicly accepted.[1] Again, no Archimedean point is required.

---

[1] E.g., it could be argued that the appeal of Keynes' theory to the public resulted from protests against the depression.

Introduction

According to which of these views is held, the role of criticism is (1) to show up the more or less sinister motives in the false explanations of the opponents, or to psycho-analyse their theories, (2) to analyse the structure of their thought, (3) to fill in gaps in the selection, or (4) to relate ideas to their social setting. It is also obvious that these four views have radically different implications for the question as to what extent unexpressed value premises invalidate social theories. Yet, eminent exponents of these theories of ideology have shifted uneasily between self-destructive and fairly obvious positions. To say that the tests of logic change with one's values is open to the old objection to scepticism: if the theory is untrue, no more is to be said; if true, its own objectivity must be denied. On the other hand, to say that we meet with obstacles in our attempts to be impartial in thinking about political matters serves as a useful reminder that scientists, too, are human. But the ambiguity between these two views lends apparent force to many theories.

Unlike many methodologists who are quite naive about their own theory, Myrdal gradually develops a kind of methodology of methodology—a critical theory that criticizes itself. Myrdal started with a largely psychological approach. In the *Political Element* there is the suggestion (recanted in the 1953 Preface) that if economic theory were stripped of its implicit valuations, a corpus of hard facts and relations would remain that could then be successfully harnessed to any set of valuations explicitly introduced from sociological and psychological research.

In his later writings the epistemological approach gains ground, until, in the *Crux of All Science* the structural interdependence of valuations and facts is presented as a necessary condition of *all*—sound and unsound—theory and research, of both logical and illogical conclusions. His view seems to shift towards the selective role of value judgments (category 3a) and resembles Schumpeter's. According to Schumpeter, scientific procedure 'starts from the perception of a set of related phenomena which we wish to analyse and ends up— for the time being—with a scientific model in which these phenomena are conceptualised and the relations between them explicitly formulated, either as assumptions or as propositions (theorems) . . . that perception of a set of related phenomena is a pre-scientific act. It must be performed in order to give to our minds something to do scientific work on —to indicate an object of research—but it is not scientific in itself. But though prescientific, it is not preanalytic. It does not simply consist in perceiving facts by one or two of our senses. These facts must be recognised as having some meaning or relevance that justifies our interest in them and they must be recognised as related —so that we might separate them from others—which involves some analytic work by our fancy or common sense. This mixture of perceptions and prescientific analysis we shall call the research worker's Vision or Intuition.'[1] Like Myrdal, Schumpeter stressed the 'endless give and take' between theory and facts. 'This work [of model-building] consists in picking out certain facts rather than others, in pinning them down by labelling them, in accumulating further facts in order not only to supplement but in part also to replace those originally fastened upon, in formulating and improving the relations perceived—briefly in 'factual' and 'theoretical' research that go on in an endless chain of give and take, the facts suggesting new analytic instruments (theories) and these in turn carrying us towards the recognition of new facts.'[2] On Schumpeter's view, as on Myrdal's, the source of ideological bias is the initial vision of the phenomena we propose to treat scientifically.

But for Schumpeter the vision is, on the one hand, either corrected or ignored by sound analysis (as in Adam Smith), or, on the other, it dominates and sterilises analysis (as in Marx). For Myrdal the vision plays a more constructive part. It is not merely the starter (as for Schumpeter) but the driving power of the analytical engine.

Myrdal never identifies valuations simply with the interests, ambitions or aspirations of a group. He is too subtle a psychologist for that. The valuations that he claims should form the bases of social theories are more like the complex of attitudes that unify a personality or a

[1] 'Science and Ideology', *The American Economic Review*, March 1949, p. 350.
[2] *Ibid*.

style. The beliefs, moral principles sympathies, preferences, ideals and actions that characterize a group cannot be deduced logically from a set of abstract premises, nor are they the mechanical product of certain interests. And they are never 'given' once and for all, but change under the strains and stresses to which their relations to each other and to experience give rise. Although many prognoses are formulated to justify programmes, the relation between them is not static but one of cumulative interaction.

An attempt to explore the values underlying Myrdal's own persistent demands for the discussion of the role of values would show an increasing emancipation from liberal presuppositions in his own criticism of liberalism.

The strict separation of *ought* from *is*, which dominates modern liberal economic theory (and, in different versions, modern philosophy) is not, as it claims to be, morally neutral, nor simply a discovery of philosophical analysis. For no observation or logical analysis can *discover* that we *ought to* separate values from facts, or ends from means. No amount of description or deduction can show that we can fully analyse actual political and moral choices without introducing values into our analysis. Since most people act upon the belief that only where objective criteria for choice hold is choice worthy of serious attention, the denial of any objective basis, if accepted widely, will radically influence people's choices.

The philosophy which denies the logical connection between facts and values and deduces from this denial its own moral neutrality (suppressing a series of necessary unwarranted premises) suits admirably a liberal philosophy of tolerance, in which different political views have an equal right to exist, though it is not explicit whence it derives this claim. (The liberalism may have radical connotations as in utilitarianism and logical positivism, or a conservative slant as in the philosophy of linguistic analysis).

In his article on Ends and Means Myrdal abandons the belief in the possibility or desirability of a strict separation of ends from means, which still underlay the criticism in the

Political Element. Myrdal shows not merely the impossibility of this separation but also its ideological function.[1]

Once the dichotomy between values and facts is rejected, all kinds of questions about Myrdal's own method arise. (1) Since the choice of value premises in social analysis is itself a moral and political decision, why are we told to confine ourselves to those of actual and powerful groups as psychology and sociology formulate them? To admit *any* premises as equally valid would be to fall victim to relativist liberalism—itself a political theory. But to admit those only that are 'practicable', 'significant', 'relevant', 'real', etc., may lead into another trap. True, having shown the fallacies in the claims for a strict separation of facts from values, Myrdal has opened the door to a new connexion between them. But has the criticism of the 'naturalistic fallacy' in utilitarianism only led to its substitution by pragmatism? The reasons that Myrdal gives for his selection of value premises—'the rule of economy', 'relevance', 'significance'—may not convince those who choose their premises on different principles.

(2) Is it necessary that the analysis of stable equilibria must lead to laissez-faire conclusions, whilst the analysis of cumulative causation leads to policies that are both anti-laissez-faire and against 'one-factor-theories'? 'Equilibrium is just equilibrium', and to remove *bad* stable equilibrium overwhelming government action may be thought desirable. On the other hand, the spiral, if virtuous, may make government action unnecessary; and if government action is directed at one strategic factor, the inter-action of others may make one-cause-remedies suitable.

(3) Whence the characteristic blend of optimism and pessimism that pervades Myrdal's writings and that once led him to describe himself as a cheerful pessimist ?

[1] In the *Political Element* Myrdal showed how the philosophy of natural law harboured a contradiction and a compromise between a radical and a conservative strand. In a different connection, Ernst Troeltsch suggested that the Christian idea of natural law fulfilled a similar function for the thought of the Church, enabling it to come to terms with non-Christian social facts and ideals. (Cf. *Aufsätze zur Geistesgeschichte und Religionsuoziologie*, Tubingen, 1925, vol. iv, pp. 156-180). Similarly, the 'naturalistic' relic in the modern, post-Humean, juxtaposition of ends and means serves to reconcile the rigorous demands of scientific neutrality with the ethics of liberalism. Can political thought ever be purged of all 'naturalism'?

Starting with a vision of a world of free and equal men, he warns us against confusing hopes and prospects. He is pessimistic with respect to the latter and untiringly cheerful in attempting to make true the former. Is his pessimism educational, a caution against disappointments and despair, and a call for courage in the face of failure ? Is his optimism a reminder that the unexpected may happen, that cheerful programmes may alter the gloomiest prognoses, a conclusion from the doctrine of the vicious circle turned virtuous, or a moral protest against fatalistic determinism?

Myrdal combines the ideals that were common to nineteenth century liberalism and socialism with an opposition to their doctrine of 'inevitable progress' as much as to the more modern doctrine of 'inevitable decline'. He unites emphasis on the need for the scientific analysis of society and on the presence and positive function of value clashes that is reminiscent of Marx, with a faith in a better society whose shape the imagination of free men can design, that recalls the Utopian Socialists.

8. SUMMARY

Analysis and prognosis cannot be neutral, in the sense that they belong to a sphere of actual and possible causal relations which can be permanently separated from valuations and the programmes which they inspire.

1. Analysis and prognosis presuppose programmes in the sense of interests which determine selection and appraisal of evidence. To ignore this side of the picture is analogous to adhering to naive empiricism in the theory of knowledge.

2. The relation between analysis and policy, and that between prognosis and programme, cannot always be adequately analysed in terms of means and ends. The application of analysis to policy is a matter of skill, not one of subsumption under given canons.

3. Modern welfare economics, in both its Paretian and Bergsonian versions, misapplies the means-ends model to social situations. It thus mistakenly holds that 'optima' must be sought where 'improvements' are appropriate and logically

sufficient, and that valuations must be 'given' from outside, although in fact they may result from empirical appraisals.

4. Analysis and prognosis may harbour ideologies. They may be formulated in a manner which does not bring out the facts, but which rather attempts to reconcile conflicts in beliefs and valuations. Awareness of his own valuations, and of the limitations of his conclusions, are among the theorist's safeguards against falling into the ideological trap.

5. Although analysis and prognosis must take the actual or possible beliefs and valuations of people as data, by analysing them and bringing them into the open, they tend to change them. A fuller analysis and prognosis will take cognizance of these changes, but the interconnection is a continuous process. Prognosis must therefore be subject to continuous revision.

6. Social scientists should attempt to base their prognoses on concrete actual or potential valuations of groups in concrete situations. An understanding of the unity of complex attitudes is the task of social psychology or sociology.

7. As a result of social change, the presuppositions in terms of which we attempt to understand it, must be transformed if, by the achievement of new techniques of control, we are to make possible a new epoch of development. For the new programmes of our times, new theoretical prognoses are needed.

PART I

CHAPTER ONE

INTERNATIONAL INTEGRATION[1]

1 THE PLACE OF VALUE PREMISES IN SCIENTIFIC ANALYSIS

'ECONOMIC INTEGRATION' is a value-loaded term.
It carries the implication that the attainment of economic integration—in some sense—is desirable.

That a term is value-loaded is, even when used in scientific
inquiry, not of itself a ground for objection. It has been a mis-
guided endeavour in social science for a little more than a
century to seek to make 'objective' our main value-loaded
concepts by giving them a 'purely scientific' definition, supposedly free from any association with political valuations.
To isolate them from such association, new and innocent-
looking synonyms were often invented and substituted. On
logical grounds, these attempts were doomed to failure. The
load of valuations was not there without a purpose and a
function, and they soon pierced through the strained 'purely
scientific' definitions and even crept back into the specially
fabricated synonyms.

There is no way of studying social reality other than from the
viewpoint of human ideals. A 'disinterested social science' has
never existed and, for logical reasons, cannot exist. The value
connotation of our main concepts represents our interest in a
matter, gives direction to our thoughts and significance to our
inferences. It poses the questions without which there are no
answers.

The recognition that our very concepts are value-loaded
implies that they cannot be defined except in terms of political

[1] Appendix from *An International Economy, Problems and Prospects*, pp. 336–340,
Routledge and Kegan Paul, 1956.

valuations. It is, indeed, on account of scientific stringency that these valuations should be made explicit. They represent value premises for scientific analysis; contrary to widely held opinions, not only the practical conclusions from a scientific analysis, but this analysis itself depends necessarily on value premises.

A value premise should not be chosen arbitrarily: it must be relevant and significant in relation to the society in which we live. It can, therefore, only be ascertained by an examination of what people actually desire. People's desires are to some extent regularly founded on erroneous beliefs about facts and causal relations. To that extent a corrected value premise—corresponding to what people would desire if their knowledge about the world around them were more perfect—can be construed and has relevance.

By no econometric trick, however, can a value premise be generated by pure reasoning or inferred from facts other than people's actual valuations. Therefore, no discussion of closer international economic integration has any meaning, except within the framework of a set of political valuations which should be made explicit. If a meaning is attached to the concept 'integration,' without any value premise being stated, there is nonetheless an implied one, usually corresponding to the author's own political preferences or those of his national milieu. Since the premise is concealed, this is not only presumptuous, but actually amounts to a fraud, even though an unconscious one.

The proper method of proceeding, instead, would be to seek the foundation for the analysis in an empirical study of people's opinions on the matter under investigation. We should map the field of interests and ideals as they exist and should confront these volitional forces with each other and with all other facts of the political, social, and economic situation of the world. I believe that the future of practical social science lies in seeking this foundation of a very much modernized political science, making full use of empirical sociology and social psychology.

This was, of course, not possible for the present restricted study of the problem of international economic integration. We have had to be content with what is generally known about what people in fact desire, based to a large extent on impressions and conjectural inferences. Nevertheless, it is important that the true relations between valuations and research in social science be recognized and that the proper place be reserved in our reasoning for people's political valuations.

A corollary to this general philosophy of the correct method of social science is the open recognition of the fact that ordinarily the meaning of value-loaded concepts is indeterminate within a certain field. In fact, people have different and conflicting valuations and, therefore, mean different things when they talk about economic integration as being desirable. It is not a mark of clear thinking that the concept be determined by a definite— and arbitrary—definition; inherent vagueness must be recognized and accounted for.

The unity of a culture consists, however, in the fact that to a relatively large degree there exists a certain community of valuations, which implies that the field of vagueness is limited. This is particularly true of our most general valuations. In this book the concept 'economic integration' has been related to the old ideals in Western civilization of liberty and equality and, more specifically, equality of economic opportunity. The trend of development in our advanced countries has been continually towards greater emphasis—and greater national realization—of these ideals. The 'awakening' of the backward peoples consists very much in their, too, embracing these Western ideals.

2 THE CLASSICAL THEORY OF THE PERFECT MARKET

These ideals were, of course, also basic to the classical economic doctrine. To an economist it would, indeed, be most natural to associate the notion 'economic integration' with the theoretical model of the perfect market, governed by the market forces. Such a definition would not necessarily prevent the concept from implying the desirability of a dynamic process instead of a static balance.

Viewed from this angle, an economy would be fully integrated when the prices of identical goods and services everywhere tended to become the same and when, in addition, labour of a given kind commanded the same wage, when there was one market for capital with a single rate of interest at comparable levels of risk, and when the rent for the same kind of land had been equalized—in a less than completely atomistic economy with appropriate amplifications added for non-competing groups, location of land, etc.

The doctrine of the perfect market represented, as we know, more than a theoretical tool for economic analysis, namely a valuation of how society ought to operate. From this political angle the significant characteristics of the classical construction refer naturally more to the beneficial effects expected to accrue to the participants in an economy that adhered to the doctrine, and less to the specific policies, or rather absence of policies, by which these effects were supposed to be realized.

The free market economy would, as I have already pointed out, lead to an equalization of the remunerations of the factors of production. In human terms this would take us a long way towards the achievement of the ideal of equality of opportunity, as every kind of productive effort would, without discrimination, be awarded the same pay. And the freedom to move in society without artificial barriers, which for this purpose was assumed in the free market economy, represents by itself an important element of this ideal.

The beneficial effects of the free market economy were, furthermore, assumed—and considerable theoretical exertions went into 'proving' them scientifically—to include maximizing the total production. In a dynamic setting this would correspond to creating the conditions for rapid economic progress.

Another old Western ideal, closely related to, but not identical with, the demand for equality of opportunity—the equalization of incomes and wealth—was given its due a little more than a century ago by the explicit recognition that the free market economy ought to be perfected by redistributional reforms. The principle of noninterference should, according to the classical doctrine, be adhered to in the sphere of production and exchange, where natural forces worked themselves out to common advantage; but in the sphere of distribution corrections would have to be applied by means of taxation and other interferences with the working of the price mechanism.

It was held that otherwise the free market economy would not lead to a desirable social development. This was motivated by the hedonistic law of decreasing marginal utility, according to which a more even distribution would increase 'social welfare'.

The theory of the free market economy was, therefore, from John Stuart Mill on, always presented with a major reservation underlining the legitimacy of redistributional interferences, and it was believed that they would not change materially the operation of the free market economy in the sphere of production and exchange. This represents an extension of the ideal of ' equal opportunity' to incorporate in addition an extra degree of 'equalization of realized income and wealth'.

Of these three main valuations at the basis of the classical economic doctrine the first one—the demand for equalization of the remunerations of the factors of production—relates directly to the ideals of liberty and equality. During the last hundred years, if anything has changed, it has been towards giving increased emphasis to the demand for equality of opportunity. The two other valuations are partly instrumental to this one. Redistributional reforms are needed in order to give reality to the attempts to establish equality of opportunity. Similarly, a fair degree of economic progress in terms of a rapidly rising level of production is, as we have found, a precondition for all effective attempts to equalize opportunities.

'Economic integration' as an ideal quite clearly cannot be defined by relating the concept to the classical doctrine of a free market economy; the actual process towards integration within the advanced countries has taken them further and further away from this theoretical model. Nevertheless, the present study is in line, on a deeper level, with the traditions of political economy, since it is based on those more fundamental valuations, centred on equality of opportunity, upon which the classical doctrine also was founded.

3 THE CLASSICAL THEORY OF INTERNATIONAL TRADE

The classical theory of international trade was an adjunct to this doctrine of a free market economy. It assumed that all national economies were completely integrated domestically as perfect markets. This was, of course, an unrealistic assumption: only a few countries, and they only in the last two generations, have gradually reached a state that we can meaningfully say approaches national integration; and these higher integrated economies are not of the free market type.

Internationally, the factors of production were assumed to be immobile.[1] This was a strange assumption, as in the nineteenth century and until the First World War there actually occurred, in the partial world which was then actively participating in international intercourse, very substantial movements of labour and capital which considerably contributed to

[1] From the point of view of their basic valuations as those were sometimes expressed in general terms, it may perhaps be thought that in the back of their minds the classical authors had a theoretical model of a worldwide perfect market; the theory of international trade would then represent an approximation to greater realism. At the same time they were undoubtedly, however, good nationalists and citizens of a country conscious of the advantages of being ahead of the rest of the world. ". . . it must be realized that this consumption which was regarded as the end of economic activity was the consumption of a limited community, the members of the nation-state. To the extent to which they repudiated former maxims of economic warfare and assumed mutal advantage in international exchange, it is true that the outlook of the Classical Economists seems, and indeed is, more spacious and pacific than that of their antagonists. But there is little evidence that they often went beyond the test of national advantage as a criterion of policy, still less that they were prepared to contemplate the dissolution of national bonds. If you examine the ground on which they recommended free trade, you will find that it is always in terms of a more productive use of *national* resources. . . . I find no trace anywhere in their writings of the vague cosmopolitanism with which they are often credited by continental writers. I do not claim this as a virtue—or as a deficiency; the question of the extent to which, at the stage of history, it was incumbent on political thinkers to transcend the ideas and the criteria of the nation-state is a matter of great difficulty. All that I contend is that we get our picture wrong if we suppose that the English Classical Economists would have recommended, because it was good for the world at large, a measure which they thought would be harmful to their own community. It was the consumption of the national economy which they regarded as the end of economic activity." (Lionel Robbins, *The Theory of Economic Policy*, Macmillan, 1952, pp. 9 ff.)

Marshall was entirely in line with classical tradition when he wrote: ". . . the notion of national trade has been bound up with the notion of solidarity between the various members of a nation." He observes in this connection that "it is becoming clear that this (Great Britain) and every other Western country can now afford to make increased sacrifices of material wealth for the purpose of raising the quality of life throughout their whole population. A time may come when such matters will be treated as of cosmopolitan rather than national obligation; but that time is not in sight." (Alfred Marshall, *Industry and Trade*, Macmillan, 1919, pp. 4 ff.)

6

the maintenance of international balance. The assumption has become increasingly realistic, though, during the last decades.

Since factor movements were excluded by hypothesis, complete international equalization of factor prices was not attained even in theory. Such equalization of factor prices as was possible was supposed to come about through the international specialization and division of labour made possible by trade, which was to achieve this purpose by equalizing the prices of goods everywhere in the world, within the limits set by transport costs. The practical conclusion of the theory was therefore the desirability of free trade.

As a matter of fact, international trade is now less free than ever. The national economies are not free market economies and are becoming less so as national integration proceeds. The very effective aid to attaining international balance which, until the First World War—and against the assumption of the classical theory—large-scale factor movements actually gave to trade, has almost disappeared.

As between developed and undeveloped countries, international trade does not equalize factor prices but rather tends to set up a cumulative process away from equilibrium.[1] The political development has now brought to the forefront the very large, and growing, disparities between these two types of countries, and economic development of the undeveloped ones has become a recognized main goal of international economic integration.

International economic integration, like national integration, is ultimately a much broader problem than trade and even than economics. It involves problems of social cohesion and practical international solidarity, and the building up of machinery for accomplishing inter-governmental agreements and large-scale political settlements, as a half-way house to the common decisions on economic policy that may be out of reach for our age.

A definition of 'international integration' in terms of free

[1] I have developed this thought in *Development and Under-development. A Note on the Mechanism of National and International Economic Inequality;* lectures given in Cairo under the auspices of the National Bank of Egypt, and in *Economic Theory and Under-Developed Regions*, Duckworth, 1957, which is a completely revised version of the Cairo lectures.

international trade is, therefore, as false as one in terms of the perfect market. However, to the extent that the classical doctrine of international trade was founded upon the basic ideals, enumerated in our account of doctrine of the perfect market, the analysis in this book on an International Economy is again, on a deeper level, in line with the more fundamental intentions of the doctrine.

The rejection of the classical doctrines as appropriate terms for the definition of our value premise, 'international integration', does not imply, however, that important elements of theoretical analysis, contained in these doctrines and amplified by the work of generations of economists in the classical line, do not preserve their usefulness as tools in economic research.

CHAPTER TWO

THE RELATION BETWEEN SOCIAL THEORY AND SOCIAL POLICY[1]

1. SOME HISTORICAL HINTS

IT might be useful to recall at the start that the social sciences have all received their impetus much more from the urge to improve society than from simple curiosity about its working. Social policy has been primary, social theory secondary. This holds true, of course, for the long ages from Aristotle onwards when the social sciences were still merged into the general speculation which we have later come to call moral philosophy. It also holds true for the period of the Enlightenment, when the social sciences made the decisive leap towards their modern development into full-fledged and gradually separated empirical disciplines. Looking close, one sees that they still remained, and to a considerable extent remain to-day, merely branches of the two dominant philosophies of Enlightenment: natural law and utilitarianism. It is an under-statement to say that at this early stage no clear distinctions between theory and policy are observed. In fact the absence of such a methodological distinction is only a negative characterization of these philosophies: in the former philosophy there is a direct identification of what *is* with what *ought to be* in the concept 'natural'; in the latter philosophy an indirect identification is implied in the assumption that 'happiness' or 'utility' both *is* and *ought to be* the sole rational motive for human action. Social values existed as facts and could be objectively ascertained. Social theory explained reality but, as values were real, at the same time defined rational social policy.

[1] Opening Address at the Conference of the British Sociological Association, 1953. Reprinted from *The British Journal of Sociology*, September, 1953, pp. 210–242.

9

For their subsequent development up to the present day it was of importance that the social sciences were imbued with very radical policy premises. One such premise was that labour has moral superiority as title to property. In its modern form this idea stems from Locke, becomes the basis for Ricardo's theory of real value and is to-day reflected in, for example, lower rates of taxation on 'earned income'. Another radical premise is the idea that 'all men are born equal'. Primarily this was understood in the moral sense that all have the same basic duties and rights in society. But in addition there was a strong tendency to believe that all persons were also fairly equal in natural endowments: in capacity to do things and to enjoy happiness. An important corollary to this second premise —which incidentally also agrees, though only approximately, with the first one—is that the attainment of a more equal distribution of income and wealth will enhance 'general welfare' in that it hurts the rich less than it benefits the poor.

A further consequence of these ultra-radical tenets of the philosophies of the Enlightenment and thus of the social sciences as they were beginning to emerge in their modern form, is that they implied the environmental approach. Man could be improved and his lot made happier by changes in the institutions of society which condition him. In a sense, the deepest difference between a radical and a conservative attitude towards social policy springs from a difference in views as to the fundamental cause of the ills of society: whether they are due to 'human nature', in which case there is not much to be done about them, or whether they depend on the actual organization of society, which can be reformed. From the environmental point of view the task of social theory is to clarify, by a study of the social facts, how by social policy men and society can be improved.

To the environmental approach the social sciences have, on the whole, stuck tenaciously. Not that 'human nature' was ever totally expelled from social theory. Thus, Malthus's doctrine— that, if not checked, the human procreative urge tended to defeat all attempts by social policy to improve the lot of the masses— was in the early part of the last century a powerful conservative argument based on 'human nature' and served in the social sciences as an effective offset to their radical policy premises.

In one particular respect the secularist rationalism of the Enlightenment, by placing *homo sapiens* in the natural biological order as an animal, strengthened conservative inclinations. Thus, the biologists' assumption that black men were of inferior 'race'—a word, incidentally, not applied to human beings much earlier than about two hundred years ago—replaced the old argument of the theologians that they were pagans as the principal intellectual defence of slavery. Generally speaking, this new stress on 'human nature' was, however, canalized into the natural sciences dealing with man, while the social sciences directed their interests towards human behaviour and social institutions. The clash between the two thought elements which we carry with us from the Enlightenment is still often apparent when social scientists and natural scientists meet over an issue, be it the psychological characteristics of twins or the nature of homosexuality. As we know, the history of much basic controversy in psychiatry could very appropriately be written in terms of the question whether mental illnesses have a purely somatic causation or are also conditioned psychologically and, consequently, socially, and whether, therefore, a psychological and social therapy can be effective.

Taking the long view, the environmental approach—and the radical premises—have gradually won. The assumption of the Enlightenment philosophers that men are, when viewed as groups, equal even in natural endowments, has increasingly been proved to be scientifically correct. The more we have perfected our methods of measuring intelligence and other mental capacities and qualities, the less we have been able to ascertain any innate inferiorities in groups of people, whether we have distinguished men and women, rich and poor, whites and Negroes. Even physical differences between ethnic groups have, when measured more accurately, turned out to be smaller and less socially important than was previously believed. The political importance of this trend in social science is illuminated by the fact that it was violently broken and forced in the contrary direction under the impact of extreme reaction in Nazi Germany.

If the social sciences were thus from the outset endowed with a radical urge towards social policy, this momentum was continually fed by new impulses. Of sociology in particular, and most clearly in Britain, Scandinavia and America, it can, I believe, be said that its growth was time and time again stimulated by social reform movements. Important surveys of living conditions in Britain were prompted by the growing awareness of grave social problems. Many, perhaps most, social scientists even up to our own time were originally led to the social sciences by their interest in social reform.

When all this has been said, a number of qualifications are necessary in order to preserve a balanced picture. First, the radical premises were most explicitly spelled out in the period of the Enlightenment and in the first half of the nineteenth century when the social sciences in their modern form had their beginning. But at that time there was very little social reform. And the reforms propounded on the practical level of social policy by the social scientists of that period were not very radical, viewed in the light of what has later been accomplished and become accepted as standard. Then and later, the reformers did not usually draw the revolutionary conclusions with respect to the practical problems of the day which their philosophical premises warranted, but preserved these for their more abstract expositions.

True, there were radicals and revolutionaries during the whole development; but by insisting on social changes which were out of reach politically, they placed themselves as doctrinaires outside the main line of the social sciences. As scientists the conservatives profited during the whole period from their greater 'realism'. For their conservative inclinations directed their interests upon society as it actually was and kept them from constructing utopias.

Later, as time went on, the clear-cut radical premises to which I have referred were also apt to become less explicit in the minds of the gradually more specialized social scientists than they had been for the philosophers. Thus, as we know, the psychologists who some forty to fifty years ago first set out to measure intelligence actually assumed that there were considerable innate differences between social groups. And it was to their surprise that their research carried them to conclusions very different from their hypotheses, a development which I therefore consider to be one of the great triumphs of scientific endeavour.

The secular trend has, however, corresponded to the radical momentum originally given to social theory in the era Enlightenment. Social policy has expanded in scope and influence and, on the whole, with accelerating speed. And in our scientific work we have all the time and in all fields been entitled, while still remaining 'realistic', to count on more and bigger induced changes in social institutions. The chief explanation for this trend of social policy is without doubt the increase of productivity and economic resources which has allowed a greater social generosity. But the influence of social theory has, directly and indirectly, acted as a continuous force.

As this historical sketch shows, one of the main problems raised by a consideration of the relation between social theory and social policy is, of course, the general value problem. In the period of the Enlightenment and in the beginning of the nineteenth century there was little awareness even of its existence. For according to the philosophies which formed the seed-bed for the social sciences, there were objective values which, like other social facts, could be ascertained by reasoning or by observation and calculation. Rational policy conclusions could be drawn in terms of what was 'natural' or, later, of what led to the maximum 'general welfare'. However, over the last century or so it has become an ambition of social scientists to draw a sharp dividing line between science and politics and to lay stress on the view that, in principle, scientific research cannot arrive at policy inferences. In actual practice no such line was ever observed, nor is it observed to-day. Our whole terminology and all our thought-ways are still saturated with the old value metaphysics of natural law and utilitarianism.

To this fundamental methodological problem of social facts and social values and of how rationally to apply value premises to factual research, I shall return at the end of my lecture. The major part of this paper I want to devote to the sociological and institutional aspects of the relation between theory and

13

policy: the processes in society by which the social sciences have been, and are, influencing social policy, and the reactions upon the social sciences of changes in these processes.

We are all aware of the fact that in our generation the role of the social theory in the formation of social policy is beginning to change radically. The social sciences are increasingly called upon to develop a social technology, a set of tools for social engineering, as the natural sciences did long ago. This change in the practical importance of the social sciences in society is not of their own making. It is only a reflection, or a considerably lagging concomitant, of a much more fundamental change in society itself.

A main feature of this deeper change is that in recent decades the total volume of state interventions has been growing continuously. At the same time businesses have become bigger; in so doing they have developed interests which cannot be reduced to terms of the pecuniary interests of their individual members, and their managers have come to realize that their contacts with society must be wider than those merely of buying and selling. Larger and more abstract units of interest organizations—of industries, farmers, workers and consumers—have asserted themselves and taken over social functions. Private relations have increasingly become public or quasi-public relations; secondary contacts have replaced primary contacts. More and more things are settled for the individual by law, regulation, administration, or collective bargaining and agreement

In our part of the world this development has in the main *not* been the effect of conscious attempts towards planning. The causal order has in our countries, as a matter of plain historical fact, rather been the contrary. It was usually the growing mesh of unco-ordinated public interventions called forth by special interest groups or made necessary by situations of crisis and also the disorganizing effects of the activity of the larger and more powerful interest organizations that called for co-ordination and central planning. This secular trend is prompted by deep-rooted and constant social forces of which technical development is only one. The trend has more recently been pushed on by successive and cumulative waves of violent crises, a course of events which had its beginning with the First World

War, and the end of which is not yet in sight. On a deeper level of causation, the development is also related to changes in the attitudes of individuals to society.

I am not here attempting to analyse the involved dynamics of social relations making up this secular trend towards the more closely integrated state.[1] But I want to raise the question: how is the growing volume of public, quasi-public, and private intervention and planning, i.e., of social policy in its broadest sense, changing the role of the social sciences in our society?

2. THE TRADITIONAL ROLE

Let us start by attempting to characterize the traditional situation as it still was before the First World War. The easiest approach is perhaps to state what functions social scientists did not have. To begin with, they were neither the final authors nor the executors of social policy. They did not even train the civil servants. On the Continent, civil servants were usually recruited from among young persons with a university degree in law; in Britain, I understand, studies in mathematics or the dead languages were considered to be a more appropriate educational background for civil servants than studies in social science. In all civil services there were, in addition, engineers with a technical training to run the railways and other socialized branches of the national economy and, of course, doctors in the hospitals, officers in the army, teachers in the schools, and clergymen in the church. The people employed by the interest organizations were usually picked from their ordinary membership. Business had not come to think of seeking advice from social scientists about how to handle their practical problems. Some statisticians were everywhere needed. But neither the state and the municipalities, nor the interest organizations and private businesses felt much need for economists and, naturally, still less need for sociologists, psychologists, political scientists or anthropologists.

The teaching of the social sciences was almost wholly directed towards training the next generation of social scientists who, in

[1] Cf. "The Trend towards Economic Planning", the *Manchester School of Economic and Social Studies*, January 1951.

their turn, were supposed to hand down their methods and knowledge to a third generation, and so on. As the social sciences for various reasons had, and have, a very small place in the curricula of primary and secondary education, the social scientists did not even have the task incumbent upon most university disciplines of training teachers for the schools, a task which allows for the satisfaction of quantity, at least. The closed cycle of the social sciences revolved almost entirely, generation after generation, within the academic sphere, with a fringe of learned amateurs outside the universities who could afford it as a hobby. Social science studies were not very useful for anything but a university career.

Within this sheltered existence to which the social sciences were confined, they developed rapidly. They usually started from principles and broad theories; economics was, of course, the most successful in developing early an abstract model-explanation in terms of social causation. Facts, however, as they were increasingly observed and taken into account, worked changes in the theories, and so we gradually achieved a more systematic knowledge. None of the social sciences went far into therapy, as did medicine, or into technology, as did the natural sciences; and in the circumstances this is understandable. Social scientists were not called upon to perform practical tasks.

Nevertheless, the social sciences had a very great influence on social policy. My thesis is that, while there was little participation on the part of social scientists in the actual technical preparation of legislation and still less in administering induced social changes, their influence was nevertheless very considerable, and that this influence was due in the main to their exposition and propagation of certain general thoughts and theories.

Malthus's theory of population pressure was in its time one such powerful influence and moulded a whole generation's general attitude towards social policy; in our time very different general thoughts on the population issue have in a radical way determined social policy in Scandinavia and Britain. Ricardo's thoughts about prices and distribution and about currency, taxation and tariffs, Marx's thoughts about surplus value and the economic determination of history, Darwin's and Spencer's about social evolution and the survival of the fittest and, in our time, Keynes's about how the state by increasing total demand can prevent or mitigate depressions and mass-unemployment, are other such general theories which have strongly influenced the direction of social policy. It is also my considered opinion, reached after careful study, that the important changes in race relations now slowly taking place in America are to a considerable extent the result of the sociologists' exposure of the stereotyped superstitions present about the Negro in the popular mind; it is becoming more and more difficult for people to preserve their defensive rationalizations without appearing uneducated, which they are reluctant to do.

By stressing the policy importance of the general ideas emerging from the social sciences I do not, of course, want to deprecate penetrating theoretical thinking and the collection and analysis of facts. The progress of science is attained only by hard work. Even general ideas of the type which I have mentioned have often developed and have always been modified as a result of involved thinking and intensive research. But it is only natural that public interest should be focused rather on the general conclusions we reach as the result of our work.

As a matter of fact, the general ideas I referred to gained much of their social prestige from popular awareness of their cumbersome derivation. It is not as a facetious cynicism but as an observation of an important social phenomenon that I note that, in order to exert influence on society, we must as social scientists not only master the art of writing well and forcefully, and sometimes do so in terms so simple that we can be understood by the general public, but also, at other times, become so involved and intricate that we cannot possibly be followed by others than our peers. To sociologists it is, of course, a commonplace that orderly society is founded upon a lot of inherited magic, some of which is functional, i.e., useful for a purpose. In old times we kept ourselves socially distinguished from ordinary people by the academic dress which is now reserved for solemn occasions only. Our hallmark is learnedness; it is an essential instrument of our profession;

Value in Social Theory

to exert influence in society we must always merit its popular recognition.

In his first polemic pamphlet Malthus had developed a very simple idea which had been floating around in social discussion for a long time. It was the political circumstances of the epoch, Malthus's emphatic single-mindedness and also, to some extent, the literary qualities of his exposition which made it a hit. After the reverberations, Malthus felt that he needed heavier armour and went into painstaking empirical research. Also, when Ricardo spoke in the House of Commons, where he was an independent member, or elsewhere pronounced himself in general terms on policy issues, his prestige basis was partly some very involved reasoning which became patently demonstrated in his rather inaccessible *Principles*. The *Communist Manifesto* contained in simple terms all the dynamic ideas of Marxist scientific socialism, but it was only the bulky and unwieldy *Das Kapital* which could become a bible for the fateful political doctrine. Again, the policy idea of Keynes to which I referred was not new; it is simple and can very well be developed in a couple of pages: Keynes did this himself on several occasions. It was the mass-unemployment in the 'thirties which created a receptive climate for the idea; but it was his big volumes and the large outburst of learned literature following his own books which gave it weight. Still another example is provided by the long series of public inquiries and local surveys of conditions of life and work among the poor, which have been carried out in Britain since the first half of the last century and which have been the basis for the development here of empirical sociology: even if their main and very considerable policy importance was the simple one of compelling recognition of inequalities and wrongs in society, it was the amassing of data which gave credence and status.

The writings I have referred to have all been landmarks in the growth of the social sciences. Malthus's thoughts on population were destined to become the basis for the classical economic theory of distribution and economic development, mainly *via* their consequences for land rent and wage theories. Ricardo built this basis and his thoughts dominated economic thinking for half a century and have retained importance to this day. Marx's writings and the century-long discussion they inaugurated have had deep and lasting influence on all the social sciences and particularly on historians', sociologists' and economists' attitudes to social stratification, social development, and business fluctuations. Even if there had never been a political movement inspired by his ideas and, indeed, quite apart from it, he would have his distinguished place in the history of social sciences. In more recent time, the new approach to the economic processes which is associated with the name of Keynes has gradually reshaped our entire economic theory.

At the same time, these elements in the development of the social sciences have all had very important repercussions on public opinion and on social policy, and this is what concerns us here. In one sense of the word this influence of the social sciences on social policy can be called ideological. When addressing themselves to the public, the social scientists have always appealed to the people's rationality. The argument has been directed against social superstitions and narrowness in people's points of view. In doing this the social scientists have carried on the most glorious tradition of the Enlightenment.

And as there has never been unanimity among the social scientists, least of all in the realm of those general ideas, what the public has been confronted with has been a continuous discussion—a discussion above opportunist party lines, taking the longer and broader views, performed mostly by persons whose sheltered and, in our countries, distinguished, position as scholars has assured them liberty of thought and expression. This discussion of broad issues carried on by the independent social scientists has, I believe, a very essential function to fulfil in our type of democracy. To a considerable extent, it has continuously given a voice also to the unpopular ideas. And it has assured a disposition and a momentum for change in people's thinking about society, and prevented 'Gleichschaltung' which is such a deadly danger in every state.

This discussion by social scientists could keep its level and exert its wholesome influence on the broad trend of public opinion only to the extent that its performers could actually feel free to pursue the truth without anxiously seeking public acclaim or avoiding popular anathema. Some were men who had an elevated position in society or disposed of independent means which formed the basis for their freedom; in the past the princes or the church gave shelter to others; there were always a few who, having no secure institutional refuge, were prepared to pay the price of voluntary poverty, and even risk persecution, for their freedom to seek the truth and publicly proclaim the results of their intellectual endeavours. As time passed, a protective wall of tolerance was gradually built up around scientific pursuit, which became fortified to the extent that in a few of our most civilized countries the scholar's freedom became an unquestioned and almost unconscious part of our mores. It is a very remarkable thing that modern democracy, building upon an age-old heritage, succeeded so relatively well, notwithstanding local and temporary short-comings, in preserving, in protecting against its own transitory whimsies, and even in adding new lustre to a social institution, the University, among whose main functions is that of giving livelihood, status, and, consequently, independence to scholars and prestige to science.

We shall perceive more clearly the role of the social scientists in democratic society if we realize what a very different sort of institution the elected assembly is as a forum for discussion of social issues. Politicians have only a limited freedom and can, therefore, only to a limited extent be men of ideas. Their specific status is uncertain and temporary in nature. It is derived from the assent of the public, awarded for a limited time; in more recent times they have not been able, as Ricardo did, to buy a safe seat in Parliament, but have had to fight for it.

The primary aim of politicians must always and rightly be power; for if they do not win and retain power all their strivings come to naught. Seeking power demands yielding on ideas. Political action is, furthermore, collective, and for this reason also politicians must, to be successful, accept compromises. More often than not a political agreement is made possible only by leaving the motivation blurred. The member of a parliament and, even more, of a government must get accustomed to being praised and criticized for collective actions which he has tried, without success, to prevent, and for which he has then to stand, and perhaps to take primary responsibility.

Politicians must develop a relish for living intensively in the present moment and letting its accidental constellation of circumstances dominate their perspective. They have to watch carefully that they do not elevate themselves more than a tiny inch above the short and narrow view, the popular aggressions, the ingrained prejudices of the public which grants them power. In general, political leadership in a democracy implies keeping oneself at the head of the flock wherever it is drifting. Holding political power often means largely relinquishing any real influence on the course of events.

When we realize these institutional facts conditioning the politicians in a democracy, we should not wonder that so many of them render only a thoughtless reflex of the ripples on the surface of the wide sea of public opinion. Nor should it surprise us that some politicians even become demagogues, recklessly exploiting the aggressions and the prejudices of the multitude for their own personal benefit. The thing to be explained is rather that so many politicians do exert real leadership, that they succeed continuously in taking the longer view without losing power, and that they can strive, not only to give the electorate an articulate voice, but gradually to educate it. This happens more often in a country like Britain where the general level of political culture among the people is high, where the political life is organized by a stable system of parties, corresponding to real differences in long-range ideals and interests, and where in the parliament a tradition of statesmanship has developed over the centuries and become cherished. Ultimately it is based upon the presence of general ideals and a desire for rationality among the public at large. The honest and responsible politician, striving against all the odds of his profession, can contribute greatly to raising the intellectual level of the public upon whose support he depends, and this should not be denied. But the steady pedagogical urge to rationality in political questions must be provided largely by people who have their status independently of the general public and for this reason can afford not to sacrifice long-range influence for immediate power.

Another very important source of rationality in politics is the experts in the civil servants' ranks. Their specific function is to prevent attempts to realize the phantasmal and, in addition, to keep the details of the policies in order. Their realm is not the broad issues or the dynamics of ideas. Indeed, they would destroy their usefulness by failing to hide intellectual originality, should they possess it.

Within their sphere of immediately practical problems, the civil servants in all democratic countries actually exercise an influence on the course of politics very much greater than their formal position as obedient instruments in the political process would suggest and much greater than is commonly realized. They do so, however, mainly by influencing the politicians, not the general public. In theory they should keep mute, and in Britain the theory is observed in practice. In Sweden or America, where it is not observed, their influence on the public is somewhat greater.

But there it can also be seen that when the civil servants transgress the limit of their special competence and occasionally pronounce themselves on the broader issues of our time, they often disclose an astonishing lack of perspective and sometimes a general ideological confusion. Their field is the details and the routine, not the larger motives for policies, the general relations between social facts or the broad trends of social development which raise basic issues. But the intellectual insufficiencies demonstrated by the expert civil servants, when they enter, by mistake or design, the realm of ideas, are sometimes so extraordinarily large that it must be assumed that they are caused by a combination of, on the one hand, psychic inhibitions acquired in their role as instruments in the political process and, on the other hand, easily understandable inclinations, conscious or not, to put on a protective disguise. For in many cases they are obviously more intelligent than their pronouncements.

It can also be observed that a government expert who persistently expresses himself on the broader issues of our time, and does it with intellectual success, will easily make himself impossible in his proper role. If, for instance, George Kennan is now becoming uncomfortable to his government, it is not because of his mishap among the journalists in Berlin, which could have been forgotten, but because of his significant articles, his brilliant book and his outspoken lectures. It is because he has ideas, expresses them publicly, and does it effectively. He is welcome among the professors.

The journalists are, like the politicians, catering to their public. They are working for a market, employed in the public opinion industry. They cannot afford any large-scale deviations, i.e., not much independent expression. This is, incidentally, what every journalist will tell you if you sit down with him, though to express it publicly belongs to the taboos of the profession. The risk they run in thinking outside the pattern of popular opinion is that of losing not only their jobs and their livelihood, but, more fundamentally, their opportunity to reach the printed column from which springs their social usefulness and their status in society.

The limits on their freedom arise from the disposition of their publishers and public, the institutions under which they work, and these are under the influence of the temper of the time. Under the impact of the cold war, the limits in Western countries for the discussion of international questions—and, because of political association, also most internal questions— are thus becoming more and more narrow, even outside the Communist fold where they are also very narrow but differently drawn. The reason against straying beyond the limits is, as I said, not only, and for the larger part of the profession not even mainly, the fear of getting into difficulties, but the positive urge to retain an influence on day-to-day affairs.

It is interesting to follow over the years the writings of a high-class columnist such as Walter Lippmann and to watch how skilfully he balances, adjusting, as time passes, the deviations of his opinion so as not to transgress the bounds of the practical politics of the day in America. As under the impact of the cold war the temper of his compatriots' ire has been rising, the bounds have steadily contracted and his articles have at times become blunted; in fact, it is almost a public wonder and a testimony to his skill and integrity that they are not more blunted and that he preserves his audience. Lippmann would, like Kennan, be very welcome among the professors. If he stays on as a journalist and accepts the limitations of horizon and intellectual freedom which this deliberate choice implies, he does so in the attempt to exercise some power in the shorter run and within the narrow but certainly not unimportant bounds of actual day-to-day political decisions in his country.

Democracy is a most paradoxical form of government. Our devotion to democracy—to the point of being prepared to die in defending it—should not close our eyes to the fact that, by itself, it does not guarantee a reasonable degree of rationality in the collective decisions of the state. Its course has often been disastrous and may be so to-day. Nor does it guarantee free thinking or the basic civil rights which are its *raison d'être*. I have just pointed to the intellectual sacrifices demanded from its public servants: the politicians, the civil servants, the journalists. When a situation becomes tense, as for instance in inter-racial relations, the pressure of conscience upon the private citizen can also be frustrating, even crushing. And, by itself, democracy does not contain the certainty of its own growth or even survival.

In the institutional set-up of modern democracy which I have sketched, a function most important for its survival and growth falls on the social scientists: the long-range intellectual leadership thrusting society forward to overcome primitive impulses and prejudices and to move in the direction of rationality. Our independent status should not be merely a personal pleasantness and distinction; it should be used as a basis for exerting influence over the development of the thinking of the general public which fixes the limits to the freedom of the journalists, awards conditional power to the politicians and allows them to decide upon the policies which set the frame for the craftsmanship of the civil servants. We can speak to the journalists and the politicians; but we have also the opportunity to go over their heads and influence those who ultimately award all the power—the people. It is not only a few books but many books in all lands which have exerted a cumulative influence upon society much larger than any of the contemporary holders of political power. Our kind of power, which I have called influence, is most of the time only feebly related to the politics of the day; but if historical research lifted its eyes above the political constellations and machinations and sought the sources of the ideas out of which social change comes, it would be led to books and their authors.

Whatever new functions the social scientists may in time acquire as the engineers of social policy, it would, therefore, be a most serious loss if they became shy in dealing with the broader issues. The urgent need for continuing stimuli to rationality is revealed by every popular debate in the press, on the platforms or in the parliaments: on capital punishment, flogging, use of leisure time, teaching in schools and the orientation of youth, divorce—to choose, within the field of questions central to sociology, only a few revealing examples of the continued presence of public stupidity which come to one's mind when studying a week's newspapers in this not un-civilized country.

It is in international problems, however, that people's opinions are apt to be least affected by rational knowledge and calm reasoning.[1] Particularly in agitated times such as ours, we can therefore least of all in these questions rely upon the politicians and the journalists to keep their nerves and to talk and act with superior wisdom. Yet the globe is shrinking and our lives are increasingly dependent upon how these international problems are dealt with. The present trend is catastrophic. In these circumstances what is urgently needed is a free, full, frank, calm and penetrating discussion on the highest intellectual level of the diverse causes of international tension. In the last instance this need can only be met by the independent scholars who can afford the freedom of detachment, serenity and courage.

In my opinion, it is a most unfortunate and potentially enormously dangerous effect of the cold war on the Western societies—most apparent in America, least in Britain—that even academic discussion now tends to be hampered by anxious fore-thoughts and fixed in opportunist stereotypes. Loyalty to provoked popular prejudice or the transient policies of the government of a state was never the signum of science; only loyalty to truth. To this question I will come back.

[1] "Psychological Impediments to Effective International Cooperation", Kurt Lewin Memorial Lecture; Supplement No. 6 to the *Journal of Social Issues*, New York, 1952.

3. NEW FUNCTIONS

From the viewpoint of this lecture, a chief characteristic of the new society which is gradually emerging is the continuous growth in the volume of public, quasi-public and private interventions in social life. A further, and consequent, characteristic is that these interventions—i.e., social policy in its broadest sense—are no longer sporadic but take more and more the form of a continuing activity, steered to influence and to control a social process in a certain direction. Social policy is less and less effected simply by legislative *fiat;* it is more and more brought about through 'administration' stretching over time. These changes are making new demands on the social sciences. As I have already stated, they are now required to include annexes of therapy and technology, such as medicine and the natural sciences have long had.

On this point I might be permitted to refer first to economics in order to make my exposition more specific. For two hundred years economists had a very great influence upon economic policy, mainly by means of the general academic discussion whose role and paramount importance I have already commented upon. When the First World War broke out, one immediate effect was the need for a whole system of new direct economic controls. Economists were, however, usually not brought in to plan and to handle the controls, nor would they have been very suited to this type of responsibility, trained as they were in the pre-war liberal tradition. Quite apart from the fact that they lacked experience of the practical tasks of constructing and operating economic controls, few of them were interested or ideologically prepared for doing so. Instead, the controls were usually built and managed by civil servants of the traditional kind, rarely with economic training, and by practical men of all sorts drawn from the world of business, politics, or the legal profession. Nor, at that time, was it yet the vogue for the interest organizations and big business to possess economic research staffs.

It was the Great Depression in the 'thirties and the need for planning and operating anti-depression measures which began to draw large numbers of economists into government

26

offices and, with some lag, into the offices of big business and the interest organizations, which felt that for defensive or aggressive purposes they would have to equip themselves as well as the government had done.[1] A new generation of economists who, on the whole, were better equipped, ideologically and intellectually, for the task of planning and controlling also became available at about the same time.

This movement gathered momentum. When the Second World War broke out, bringing with it a considerable increase in the demand for economists to be used in all sorts of practical tasks, the economic officers were at hand and they drew on their colleagues and their assistants from the universities. Economists became accustomed not only to collaborating in drawing up plans for controls but increasingly also to participating in their execution. Meanwhile, in many of our countries, the administrations had gradually changed their principles of recruitment, taking in more young people with a social science background as regular civil servants.

When the war ended, the need for economic controls remained. The old international automatism has gone for ever, and governments find themselves in a situation where they have to carry on a managed economy. They need economists to follow carefully economic developments month after month, to warn of the need for action, to advise on its nature and sometimes to direct its course. These are tasks of economic engineering. Big business and the interest organizations have similar tasks for their economists.

Other social scientists have also been drawn upon for tasks of social technology. Already during the First World War the American army made good use of the psychologists' new testing techniques; and political scientists, historians and geographers were aiding in the political warfare of that period. After the war psychologists and sociologists were increasingly in demand in big business for planning and directing advertising, propaganda and public relations. In America industrial psychology developed into a specialized subject of great practical importance; so did public opinion and market re-

[1] This change went further before the war in Scandinavia and America than in Britain.

search. Many social scientists took employment in big business or with organizations; others set up as independent consultants, hiring themselves out for specific jobs. To a considerable extent university institutions, too, adjusted themselves to this commercialization of the social sciences by offering, for a fee, to provide governments, as well as business and private organizations, with specialized services.

When the Second World War broke out, there was thus a large body of social scientists trained to deal with problems of applied science and accustomed to co-operate with practical people on practical tasks. Many of them were during the war employed by the military and political authorities on all sorts of problems arising from the war effort or expected to follow in its wake, as indeed were many of those who had stayed on in academic work. This development proceeded farthest in America but was well on its way in other western countries too.

After the Second World War the political control of Japan and the induced social changes in Japanese society during the American occupation were from the beginning steered by the advice of social anthropologists; on a smaller scale, their British colleagues had even earlier begun to advise on colonial matters. In both Japan and Western Germany the opinion experts have continuously been taking the political pulse of the defeated nations. In both countries a host of economists, sociologists, psychologists, political scientists and educators has been engaged in advising on all the diversified practical problems which the occupation authorities had to tackle. Meanwhile, the demands at home from government agencies, organizations and business have continued to sustain a steadily expanding market for social scientists willing to devote themselves to practical problems.

I believe that we should be careful not to claim for ourselves too much success in these new functions. Even our economic technology is still a very crude art. No experienced economist would pretend that we are doing anything by fumbling in the dark and trying to learn as we proceed. The attempts to recondition the Japanese and the Germans have had very obvious flaws. But in both cases the cause of the partial failures is not the participation of social scientists in the planning and execution of policy, but rather the inherent difficulties of the tasks, the limitation of experience, the confusion in the policy goals set and the rapid sequence of changes in the goals. I believe that disappointment with the results reached so far in economic planning and control and in these other social experiments will not deprive the social sciences of their new tasks but rather will raise the demand for more, and more sustained, efforts to improve our technological methods.

The commercialized social research utilized in planning advertising, propaganda and public relations is quite evidently not always carried out with such circumspection and methodological care as to satisfy scientific standards. And when occasionally it is in this sense fully respectable, it often does not meet the practical demand for clear-cut answers and ready advice without much work and cost. I shall have some very critical remarks to make in a few minutes on the application of the methods of social science to psychological warfare. But even with respect to these most questionable technological extensions of the social sciences I retain the belief that we have seen only the beginning of a development which is bound to continue rapidly.

The common characteristic of the new practical functions I have touched upon so far is that the task is to observe and to analyse actual situations and short- and long-term developments and, on this basis, to plan rationally the immediate policy reactions to events of a government, an interest organization, or a business firm. Social development is throwing more long-term policy functions also upon the social scientist. Economists are engaged by government agencies as well as by local authorities and big business firms to make development plans based on intensive study of natural resources and other pre-conditions of development. Concrete economic planning of this type is bound up with long-term investment policy and trade policy. All governments in advanced countries are now committed to secure full employment and a rising standard of living and these goals are important in all development plans.

In our type of countries in Western Europe and gradually also in America housing has increasingly become subject to public planning and control. Competent planning in this field must be concerned with how many buildings to build and when, how to build them, where to build them, and sometimes also who should live in them and under what conditions. Housing policy, moreover, has to be fitted into the economic development plans. Houses are a very durable form of capital, and the policy perspective is therefore a long-term one.

Obviously, all the social sciences—from economics and demography to social psychology and psychiatry—become involved in different aspects of the problems raised by the increasing responsibility of government for housing. In housing policy important questions of standards are involved, and this is also true of nutrition policy and health policy as they are gradually taking shape, and thus medical science and the natural sciences are also being applied in social technology. We have not come very far yet. In fact, not many years ago in all our countries—and often to-day in countries where a rational housing policy has been lagging—national and local housing policies were framed without much consideration even of the prospective family curve and other simple demographic determinants of housing demand.

Even the full employment goal in economic policy does not raise problems for the economists and the statisticians alone. The level of employment is, for instance, tied to migration between localities and countries and mobility on the labour market: Britain's recent sad experiences in attempting to settle some Italians in the coal mines raises important questions which have to be studied by sociologists, social psychologists and psychiatrists. The same is true in considerations of 'employable' and 'unemployable' workers. As a warning to us of how easily we are swayed by convenient assumptions, we might recall the many learned studies in the 'thirties which tended to demonstrate that a considerable percentage of the unemployed were 'unemployable'. Most of the so-called unemployables were nevertheless rapidly absorbed into useful work when labour demand rose in the period of full and over-full employment during and after the war.

A third category of policy functions developing in our generation relates to international co-operation through the inter-governmental organizations which under great difficulties are seeking to survive and perform useful, even necessary work. It is easy for the thoughtless haughtily to deem them futile and, perhaps, to want them liquidated. This is a very large subject: here I will restrict myself to the *obiter dictum* that if we are not engulfed in a third world war, which is quite possible and which would reduce most of our present endeavours to futility, multi-lateral inter-state organizations of this type are bound increasingly to become the institutional framework for foreign policy and diplomacy; at the same time social policy is increasingly becoming an international concern and thus part of foreign policy and diplomacy. In a very real sense, these organizations represent the alternative to the chaos of inter-national anarchy. If a major war is avoided, they will, through all difficulties, come gradually to be the organs for an increasing volume of concerted policy actions on the international level. My main reason for this qualified optimism is the very trend of international disintegration. Anarchy is so costly that corres-pondingly great gains from agreement on concerted action are possible. It is the very irrationality of the present situation which, in time, will engender rational attempts to seek inter-national re-integration—if a general war does not break upon us.

But at present there are large realms of potential social engineering in the international field which, from a social science point of view, are lying fallow and being dealt with only by the limited means of traditional diplomatic methods. There was a resolution at the UNESCO General Conference of 1951 advising that teams of social scientists should be commissioned to investigate on the spot, at an early stage, situations of developing international tension; the machinery should be set in motion upon formal request by the Economic and Social Council. As yet this resolution has not been acted upon.

Meanwhile considerable international work is going on, particularly in the economic field; and it is not altogether restricted to studies. One of the most practical attempts is technical assistance to under-developed countries. This activity of international social engineering can be criticized from many points of view. The administration of technical assistance may

Value in Social Theory

often be ineffective and unreasonably wasteful and costly; as a whole, the programme may be badly co-ordinated; directly and indirectly the responsibility for these short-comings rests on the governments. And the approach is certainly not founded upon a thorough study of the social implications of applying modern industrial technology to primitive societies or to societies which for a long time had been stagnant at a low level of economic productivity and with frozen social institutions ill-adapted to development.

Probably these beginnings will be deemed dilettante in ten years' time. If so, this itself will, however, only be a reflection of the fact that the problem has been drawn into the realm of the applied social sciences and become the object of sustained and intensive study, with the result that superior advice and direction to this activity could be rendered. The new principle of multi-lateral technical assistance has such an importance that, in spite of everything, our beginnings, even if poor, have already demonstrated revolutionary potentialities.

It is an unfortunate indication of the sorry state of our world to-day that very much less public interest—and, in comparison, only infinitesimal funds—are devoted to the work for international integration and peace than to the cold war and the preparation for a possible third world war. Social scientists of all kinds are now being called upon to plan the strategy and tactics of psychological warfare. In the cold war and in the preparation for a possible hot war on a world scale there are, of course, many other practical tasks for social scientists besides advising on propaganda.

How the Russians are framing their foreign propaganda, and the extent to which they in a similar way attempt to plan total war by substituting refined scientific methods for old-fashioned common sense hardened into Marxian dialectics, is difficult to know. In America, however, it is a fact that, as the cold war has mounted and the possibility of a third world war seriously entered into calculations, the social scientists like the natural scientists have been increasingly drawn into war work: directly for the Government and its multifarious political and military agencies or indirectly on 'projects' of all sorts, farmed out to the universities and paid for by the Government. A very

32

large number of social scientists in America are now employed, wholly or partly, in this way, and perhaps soon the majority may be so engaged. In other western countries the same trend is noticeable, though it has not proceeded anything like as far as in America.

Of all these variegated activities linked to the cold war and the preparation for a possible third world war, the easiest to observe and form a judgment upon is naturally that of psychological warfare. In America the demand for an intensification of this type of foreign propaganda has for many years been raised from time to time. More recently, in connection with the change of Administration, this popular demand gathered great strength and for some time exaggerated ideas about the potentialities of psychological warfare were prevalent.

My own views on the application of social science methods to psychological warfare are sceptical, but mainly because I am utterly sceptical about the effectiveness of foreign propaganda as it is usually conceived and applied. From all I have observed of foreign propaganda during and after the war I retain the strong impression that in most cases the effects are less than zero, i.e., negative, whenever it transgresses the simple task of honestly spreading news and accurate information, including accurate information about the policy of the government sponsoring the propaganda. I believe this holds true even with respect to propaganda emanating from a totalitarian country. And very definitely, psychological warfare and democracy are uncomfortable bed-mates.

A democratic government, trying to influence foreign nations by a cleverly loaded propaganda, is bound to see its efforts defeated by the fact that a democracy is not single-minded. It will never be possible to co-ordinate all the people who act and speak. Not only ordinary people but persons in high position will continually be talking out of the backs of their heads—from the point of view of the directors of the propaganda—and what they say will have to be hurriedly broadcast around the world to prevent it from being even more effectively used by the counter-propaganda. The life of a democratic country cannot be directed to suit the strategy of propaganda; in fact, not even its foreign policy can be so adjusted.

And the propaganda itself will in a democracy be criticized by the press and in the parliament. In a time of national fear such as the present, the safest way for a propaganda agency to get by may then be to make itself agreeable to the more primitive and extreme attitudes in its own country. What then happens to international propaganda is about the following: it easily succeeds in influencing opinion at home which was not its aim, and to stampede it into ever more compact extreme views; this tends, however, to isolate the nation not only from its enemies but often also from its friends. This propaganda further ties the hands of the nation's own political leaders and deprives them of their opportunities for real leadership by reducing abnormally the number of political alternatives and narrowing irrationally the field of negotiation. On the other hand, meanwhile, the nations to which the propaganda is diverted tend rather to become confirmed in their previous views by the propaganda and the counter-propaganda which it engenders.

The startlingly bad psychology of psychological warfare is itself worthy of serious study. This should, indeed, be the first task of the social scientists hired to participate in it. I have no doubt that the scientists who are engaged in foreign propaganda will become aware of this and that they will sooner or later come to redirect and remodel it with a fuller appreciation of the problems involved.

The planning of hostile propaganda naturally also raises the ethical problem of its direct and ancillary effects as well as that of the values pursued. So also does the work of social scientists assisting various interest organizations and businesses to manipulate public opinion and to sell products.[1] In fact, all these new functions of applied social sciences are apt to raise emphatically the general value problem. As a problem of logic and scientific methodology I have already referred to it

---

[1] "All too often there is a dubious quality about the usually short-run policies implemented by such research. They are mainly method-policies designed to sell goods at the highest possible profit; to get elected; to promote a vested interest; to control quality; to measure costs; to explore and control the market; or to get public support for some ill-defined policy which may be detrimental to public welfare. Research is seldom used to ascertain or influence the long-run effects of the policy on the welfare of the community or even the organization that is sponsoring the programme. This would require intensive value-policy research." Read Bain, " Natural Science and Value Policy", *Philosophy of Science*, vol. 16, no. 3, July, 1949.

in the introduction and I shall come back to it towards the end of my lecture. But the value problem has certain aspects bearing on personal morality and institutional conditions which I should like to touch upon at this stage.

Let me start by pointing to the fact that the development I have sketched provides us as social scientists with a wider scope for our urge, inherited from the period of the Enlightenment, to the promote rationality in collective behaviour. Many of us will for shorter or longer periods have a measure of direct influence upon actual social developments. The general direction of this influence is given and determined by the essential character of science and by the ethos of our profession: to make policy more rational by ascertaining relevant facts and bringing them into their true perspective and by clarifying the causal relations between means and aims. In principle, this holds true irrespective of whether the immediate employer is a government, a group of governments co-operating in an international organization, an interest organization or an individual business firm.

It is true that as we move closer to the helm, the limitations of this influence will be ever more apparent. Policies will hardly ever follow the scientists' prescriptions but will be decided by a political process. Dependent upon where—i.e., at what strategic point—in this process our scientific contribution is applied and, of course, dependent on our skill and luck, our influence towards greater rationality will be greater or smaller. The perfectionist will always be disappointed by what it is possible to achieve in the world of practical affairs. Even reasonable men will often feel frustrated.

In addition there is, however, the question of the fundamental policy values actually pursued in the political process within which the contribution of the social scientist is applied. The methodological recognition of the fact that values are extra-scientific and that it is not possible to determine them by logical procedure, does not free the social scientist from his duty to make them explicit in his reasoning. To this I shall revert when I come to discuss the methodological value problem. The personal value problem arises from the fact that the social scientist's conscience may revolt against the value

35

premise. There is then no other way to keep his personal moral accounts in balance than by availing himself of the only reliable freedom a man engaged in practical affairs has, namely the freedom to leave, which to a competent social scientist should mean nothing worse than his retreat to the university reserve. Again, this holds true whoever is the immediate employer of the practising social scientist, whether a government, a group of governments, an interest organization or a business firm. But, naturally, the problem of conscience usually tends to become more acute as we descend from the larger units of organized society to special interest groups.

There is one particular value problem which deserves to be mentioned separately. A special interest group—a business firm or an organization—may want to be aided in deceiving the public: in spreading false beliefs, blurring true beliefs, and making people's attitudes towards something less rational than they were. Much propaganda and advertising are notoriously of this character. Even a government—which in a democratic state is nothing more respectable than a hierarchical body based on a political party or several co-operating parties —and its various bureaucratic ancillaries might at times want to deceive the people.

Personally I feel that such attempts are always unethical. In other words, I cannot conceive of any aim—and certainly not the simple profit motive—which should be permitted to give it a covering excuse. It violates a central value premise of democracy. In any case, it goes absolutely against all the inner urges of science, which are to find truth and spread true knowledge. A social scientist cannot co-operate in such attempts but is, on the contrary, under an obligation to expose them publicly whenever he becomes aware of their existence.

The employment to an ever-increasing extent of social scientists in all sort of practical tasks, and particularly, the coming into existence of a commercialized branch of social science raise, as I see it, the demand for a code of professional ethics for the guidance of social science practitioners. For many generations such rules have been codified for two other groups of practising scientists who make their skills available for remuneration, namely doctors and lawyers. In both cases also—in different ways depending upon the varying institutional set-up in different countries—authorities set up and controlled by the profession itself have come into existence to supervise individual practitioners' compliance with the established code of professional ethics. The practice has recently shown a certain tendency to spread to other professions, for instance, to accountants. The fact that practice takes place under such a code has generally been regarded as giving more, and not less, prestige to a profession and securing a greater public trust in its members.

The principle that the duty of a social scientist is to attempt to find truth and spread true knowledge and that he is under no circumstances permitted to co-operate in spreading false beliefs and making people's attitudes less rational corresponds, in my opinion, to the public interest in a democracy, and it should in such a code take the same dominant place as the basic principles of the medical and the legal professions: in the doctors' case the public interest that ills be cured and life preserved, in the lawyers' case the public interest that every citizen's lawful rights be defended. The fact that in practical life, human beings and society being what they are, the public interest in rationality is not under all conditions such a clear and definite guide as it appears to be, merely implies that the code will have to be worked out in greater detail to take account of the varying circumstances under which the practitioner operates. In this respect this principle is not different from the two principles quoted as basic for the code of professional ethics for doctors and lawyers which also have to be specified considerably in order to become definite.

I venture further to suggest that in the working out of such a code for practising social scientists provision should be made for a rather exhaustive publicity, making it possible for disinterested colleagues to challenge not only the practical conclusions reached but also the methods used and, perhaps most important, the value premises implied. In cases where there are valid reasons for not giving full and immediate publicity to a study, a routine procedure should be laid down by which all the information would be made available to the authority for professional self-control which the enforcement of the code requires. These might all seem very harsh requests, but it is my sincere conviction that they are in the interest of our profession and that a continuance of the present development will make them urgently needed.

I have only one additional point to make. Now that the social sciences are being applied to practical problems and that therefore a rapidly growing profession of practising social scientists, catering to special interests, is becoming established, it is necessary to stress most emphatically the paramount importance of the continued existence and the strengthening of independent university institutions, where the activity of the social scientists employed by the government, the interest organizations and business can be continuously followed and criticized. I should also like to emphasize that what is needed to preserve a healthy atmosphere around our attempts in social technology is not only a persistent and incisive methodological scrutiny but also an uninhibited public discussion on the highest academic level of the broad issues involved.

4. EFFECTS ON SCIENCE

The effects on working conditions in the social sciences of the rising demand from society for our services for practical tasks are bound to be of paramount importance, though they are as yet difficult to discern.

One effect will be to enhance the prestige of our work and our profession. It is true that the hurried and unprepared application of social science methods to practical problems of all sorts will often in the short run lead to disillusionment. Occasionally, there may occur such an accumulation of experiences of deficiencies in our attempts to be of practical service that among a smaller or larger group of people and, perhaps, more generally, the respect for social sciences might for a time drop lower than it was in their pre-practical epoch. But, as I have already stressed, in the present trend of social development it is unlikely that the demand for our aid will not steadily increase. As social scientists we have certainly a definite interest in furnishing from our own ranks the most unsparing criticisms of shortcomings in the attempts to apply our scientific methods to practical problems. One result of our self-criticism will be the gradual realization that we shall have to be awarded time and adequate resources to be able to base our advice on more extensive and penetrating research.

Now that the social sciences are becoming applied to an ever wider range of practical problems new research techniques are being developed. This represents a permanent enrichment of our scientific resources. Without any doubt, many of the scientific advances in recent years have originated in this way. Even the commercialization of certain branches of social sciences has not been entirely sterile. I am thinking, for instance, of opinion and market research, which very definitely would not have developed so rapidly, had there not existed a commercial demand.

More generally, we are learning a lot about our subject matter, which is the social facts. For the opportunity which we are given of being 'participating observers' of actual social processes must increase our knowledge and give us new perspectives and constructive ideas. Furthermore, the activity of the interest organizations, the interventions of the state and, in general, the practice of planning and control produce and organize for us huge masses of statistical data for which we could not otherwise hope. The integrated and planned society of to-day and still more of to-morrow will not only raise the demand for social scientists in engineering functions but will also make the social sciences much better founded upon empirical records of the social processes and will press for more intensive analysis of social relations.

One very wholesome effect of the increasing use of social scientists in practical tasks will be the progressive demolition of the boundaries between the several traditional disciplines. For a generation this has anyhow been the trend of thinking of the best brains among the social scientists. Fewer and fewer of us have written books about the 'Concept', the 'Principles', the 'Scope and Methods', the 'Significance' of a particular discipline as distinct from the others. And it has become recognized that the most promising field for research is the 'no man's land' between the traditional disciplines. There is one concept which the economist or the sociologist can keep blurred,

39

namely the concept of 'economics' or 'sociology'; for it can never be a premise for a rational inference. In reality, what exists are merely problems to be solved, theoretical or practical; and the rational way of attacking them is to use the methods which are most adequate for solving each particular problem.

The truth of this is most forcibly brought home when we are asked to handle practical and policy problems which, of course, never organize themselves according to the traditional academic formulae and disciplines. This is one of the reasons why I expect large-scale scientific progress as a result of the new demands upon the social scientists. Gradually social science will become a unity of assembled knowledge and of scientific methods, as medicine already is.

For practical reasons there will, of course, always remain the necessity for a certain amount of specialization. But there will be a stress on the need for a general social science training at the bottom, the demarcation of the fields of specialization will be kept flexible, and many roads held open for moving from one specialization to another. The demand for the highest expertness in scientific work must always be preserved; but I see no reason why a social scientist should be tied to only one speciality and for his whole life. There has been, and is, much intellectual inbreeding in our traditional academic disciplines. The confrontation with practical tasks, the co-operation with scientists from other disciplines, and the constant transgressions of the old boundary lines will feed us all with new ideas, make us relate the part to the whole, and fructify scientific thought over the entire field.

The universities will feel great strain in meeting the new demand for social scientists and will for periods be severely hurt by the depletion of their teaching staff. But as social scientists are becoming increasingly important to society, the universities will undoubtedly in time get the means to maintain academic work in the social sciences and even to increase it. Universities will have the very important functions not only of training the growing army of social scientists needed for practical tasks but also of taking the main responsibility for carrying on research, particularly in general and methodological questions, a responsibility which will tend to be recognized as ever more important the greater our policy functions become. It will remain a problem to find how public and quasi-public research institutions serving the practical needs of the administration and the interest organizations can most effectively be related to the old academic system, and what sort of division of labour and responsibilities should be sought. This is a practical matter of organization which in an environment of general expansion of the demand for and supply of social scientists will gradually be solved between the interested parties by trial and experience.

Many of our best brains will, permanently or for long periods, be taken from purely academic work to perform policy functions. Many will be lost to politics and business. But our basic supply of brains will grow so much larger. At the same time, policy tasks have so many frustrations and disappointments of their own that we shall see a constant stream of seasoned talent returning to the universities. Those returning will bring with them experience and aptitudes which were not so easily at hand when social scientists were mainly restricted to an academic existence.

This all tends to spell out one of the sweetest day-dreams a social scientist could indulge in. Is it perhaps too good to be true? Or are there in this development also other, less favourable changes affecting the conditions under which the social sciences will be preserved and developed? One crucial question arises immediately: whether the increased policy importance of the social sciences may impair the academic freedom which has sheltered their growth up till now. Science is criticism, and social sciences imply criticism of society. The question is whether the integrated state, when once our work has come to have this immediate practical importance for social policy, will be willing to grant us the great freedom which we have hitherto enjoyed and which we need.

It is true, and I shall return to this question, that with all individual variations we shall always—whether we want it or not and whether we know it or remain naïve—be working, as we always have been working, under the impact of the social *ethos* of the culture and the society of which we are a part. A careful sociological and psychological investigation of any social scientist and his work would be able to lay bare how the interests he has pursued and the positions he has taken are the outcome of a causal process. It is, indeed, part of our general intellectual approach to social reality that everything that happens, even within our own minds, has its causes as it has its effects. But this general assumption of determinism has never fettered anybody in his enjoyment of academic freedom. In the peculiar human activity which we call the study of social science the fullest amount of freedom is, we believe, a necessary condition for progress. We need only to consider the products of social science which now and then reach our desks from non-democratic countries to realize how fundamental freedom is for the quality of our work.

One danger in the new situation is, naturally, plain corruption. Such very great economic interests are often at stake in the questions of policy in which we are becoming active that there might be high pecuniary rewards for a social scientist who was willing to tamper with truth and his conscience. Personally I do not believe that this danger is very great in the countries where social research has always had its centres. Professional pride and tradition are too powerful with us. Our group is a small community of its own and we know each other fairly well. The academic grape-vine is highly developed. The social controls are therefore strong. As a matter of fact, I believe that the number of cases of such plain corruption are negligible in our society. Should somebody slip, his reputation would be ruined, and he would lose that very importance for policy which he was selling.

Commercialized social science raises a special problem to which I have already referred. In so far as the social science practitioner is himself a high-level scientist and aspires to preserve the respect of the profession he will be as careful as or more so than his colleagues at the universities or in government service. He will also be particularly interested in the development of an ethical code for the practitioners.

There are, of course, more subtle forms of corruption or let us rather say adjustment to what is opportune for personal advancement. This has, however, always been the situation. The very fact by itself that social scientists are in greater demand will not necessarily increase the incidence of such irrational influences upon science. Rather, the opposite can well be expected. Since the increased demand stems not only from governments but also from interest groups and since the market for social scientists is becoming international, we can increasingly choose our employers according to our policy predilections. And the universities will, as before, remain a refuge for anyone who wants to withdraw from direct policy responsibilities.

Thus if the present development of Western society should imply dangers for the freedom of social scientists, it can scarcely be a result simply of the fact that we are in greater demand and that our work has become of increasingly immediate importance to society. It must be because this development at the same time contains other elements which have dangerous effects. In some circles it is believed that the deeper social changes which at the beginning of this lecture I pointed to as causes of the increased demand for social scientists in policy functions, and particularly the growth of interest organizations and the broadening scope for state intervention, are themselves endangering democracy.

As democracy had a great development during the historical era characterized by economic liberalism, some economists have drawn the conclusion by analogy that the end of the liberal era will also be the end of democracy. Another glib analogy which is utilized is the association, and occasionally even the identification, of 'free enterprise society' with 'free society'. State economic planning is said to take us straight on the road to thraldom. Some of my fellow economists have recently shown such a naïvety concerning the historical and sociological problems of the social processes involved that there would be ample justification for an attempt to clarify this issue. But again I shall have to restrain myself to a few *obiter dicta*.[1]

I would begin by expressing my agreement that there is a kernel of truth and realism in the fear of what social planning might do to our society. It is my conviction, too, that our culture is approaching a grave crisis and that in this crisis

[1] "The Trend towards Economic Planning", the *Manchester School of Economic and Social Studies*, January 1951, pp. 40–2.

democracy itself is at stake. But the usual analysis of the causes of the crisis is in my opinion superficial and totally faulty.

The causes are not to be sought in the cumulative waves of economic and other emergencies. We can take care of them as they come. Britain stood up to the immense dislocations and disturbances caused by the last war without seeing its democracy falter. She has been standing up to a series of economic emergencies after the war. A new serious depression would hit Britain very hard and necessitate a whole system of policy measures; but no Englishman believes in his heart that it would endanger democracy.

Nor are the causes the secular trend towards a growing volume of state interventions and social planning and the increasing strength and importance of civic and economic interest organizations. These developments have rather the very opposite effect of making organized society increasingly concerned with the welfare of all the citizens and of calling for an ever wider participation of everybody in the responsibility for society, thereby giving democratic government deeper roots and wider scope.

The danger for democracy stems, in fact, not from causes working from within our society, from factors indigenous to our culture and our politics. The causes spring from the cold war or, rather, from the methods we are choosing to meet the revolutionary challenge of our time; they express themselves in fear and ideological confusions.

And so much is true: if Western society should be scared into gradually giving up the basic tenets of democracy, if it should retreat into adopting totalitarian methods, then, of course, the increase of controls and planning, and the availability of social scientists able and willing to handle them, would enhance the effectiveness of this retreat from democracy.

In the social sciences this danger is already visible in the disloyalty-phobia, so strange, and indeed, perverse when viewed in the light of our great tradition. As our nations feel themselves in danger, subjective and social pressures develop for loyalty to the state. This development, if not combated, will of course emasculate science which, I repeat, can recognize no other loyalty than to truth. The very essence of totalitarianism is, in the field of ideas, the preposterous claim by a state to set bounds to what it is permissible to think and to teach.

The present state of public hysteria becomes the more dangerous for the social sciences as there are, undoubtedly, certain long-range effects of their changing role in society to make the social scientists more pliable to social pressure and more reluctant to participate in the general policy debate, which is so important to democracy.

To begin with, it is very natural for social scientists to feel less of an urge to express themselves on the broader issues nowadays when increasingly they are finding themselves in a situation where they are given an opportunity to assist in planning and effectuating actual social policy. The availability of much more detailed factual data will at the same time encourage them to move on a lower level of generality and to refrain from the broad synoptical view which is necessary in discussions of major alternatives in social policy.

Another line of long-range effects stems from the very fact that social scientists are given policy responsibilities. In so far as they become regular civil servants, they come, of course, under the same obligations as other civil servants: to accept the policy valuations as determined by the political process, to work out the technical implications, and to keep silent. Very much the same rules easily come to apply to those who are from time to time more temporarily drawn upon for policy responsibilities. If they wish to be consulted in the future, they may feel it advantageous to remain reticent even during their academic interludes. This amounts to saying that not only social scientists who are actually used for policy tasks but all candidates for such assignments are becoming tempted to caution in dealing with policy issues and to seek to win their merits in less dangerous scientific endeavours.

When, furthermore, as at present in America, the government and its various political and military agencies become interested in a rapidly enlarging range of social science fields and start to sponsor and finance 'projects' of all sorts in the universities, one certain effect is a growing tendency to secretiveness, motivated by real or alleged security reasons. From the government's point of view it is often felt appropriate to keep secret even the fact that it is interested in a particular problem. And already the normal tradition of bureaucracy to protect as many of their brain-products as possible from public criticism by stamping them 'classified', must work in this direction.

From what little an outsider can know of this proliferation of government projects in social science, made possible by all the public money which now like a Jovian gold rain is descending upon the universities, one gathers an impression that common knowledge about many of these 'projects' and about the fact that they are kept secret would invite public amusement. But from the point of view of science this matter is really not amusing at all. If this practice should continue, if the academic institutions should acquire a vested interest in its continuance, if a growing number of young social scientists should become dependent on it for their livelihood and their advancement, one of the most important traditions of our old craft could easily be broken, namely that we produce for publication and for public scrutiny.

All these tendencies converge into the common resultant that social scientists are beginning to abstain from carrying on academic public discussion of broad policy issues. The social scientists are either employed by the government in such responsibilities that they have neither the right nor the time and interest for this task; or they do not want to prejudice their acceptability for such assignments in the future. Those who work for big business and the organizations in the commercialized sections of applied social sciences will also often feel it advantageous not to get into too deep water. The special interests who employ and pay them will usually want to have results published that are favourable to them; but, apart from this, they will want to see their scientists remain so far as possible uncommitted and uncompromised.

And for the social scientists who continue independent work within the universities, there are boundless opportunities to make respectable contributions to science without becoming involved in the broader issues. There is a tendency, visible to any reflecting reader of our learned journals, that more and more effort is devoted to less and less important problems.

To my present audience I should not conceal my impression that this is particularly evident in sociological journals. This is not simply a result of the increase of the total labour force in the social sciences. The fact is that less and less labour is being applied to major problems. Certain critical problems are entirely bypassed; it so happens that many of them are 'hot cargo' in the present political situation.

If I am right in assigning a capital importance for our democracy to the continuation of a rich, full, and free academic discussion of broad policy issues, it inevitably follows that the present trend towards the use of social scientists for policy tasks raises a serious problem and involves a grave danger because of the effects I have just mentioned. The solution of this problem must be sought in creating incentives for a considerable number of social scientists to stay aloof, for life or for large parts of their lives, from direct participation in practical tasks. It will require a strengthening of the universities in their power to compete for brains. This would be highly desirable for another reason too: as a means of assuring a balanced growth of the social sciences and a training ground of the highest fertility for all the other social scientists, destined to go out into practical fields.

Under the impact of our growing cultural crisis, both the need for a high-level discussion of the broader issues and the difficulties in finding those who will take part in it have grown immensely. As the impact of the cold war is closing down upon us, so many issues, and not only the international ones, become inopportune to the weak-hearted. If the cold war should last for a long time, our very status, which is the basis for our freedom and therefore also for our influence, may be at stake, not only in America but also here in our old world where the social sciences were born and reared.

I have no other advice to give than that we should now demonstrate the courage which is part of our great tradition. I realize fully that this advice is hard when directed to our young disciples, who do not have the inner security of age and recognized accomplishments and who have before them a long life to live and a career to establish. This is also the reason why I should feel most pessimistic about the future of free social sciences if the cold war should be for a long time the condition of Western civilization. The sequence of generations would then most probably imply a cumulative deterioration of status and freedom for the social scientists. But to the older generation, who have experienced the tradition and who represent it, and who usually have also so much less to risk because of their position and their shorter life expectation, the advice becomes a moral imperative that they should now stand up and be counted.

5. THE VALUE PROBLEM

This brings me to the last section of my lecture, where I should like to make some observations on the general value problem. I have stressed that the increasing role of social scientists in social policy and the drive to transform social sciences into social technology emphasized dramatically the reality and the importance of this problem. I have expressed my views on certain aspects of the problem which relate to personal morality and institutional conditions. I have left the logical and methodological value problem to be treated here at the end of my lecture. There can be no question of an exhaustive treatment at the end of this lecture.[1] I will attempt only to draw the very broadest outline of my position.

I have mentioned that for more than a century most social scientists have agreed that a sharp distinction must be drawn between *what is* and *what ought to be*. Science is concerned only with establishing the facts and the causal relations between facts. On this basis valid prognosis can be made about the future development which is probable on given assumptions. If we are faced with the task of advising on policy, a value premise has to be chosen and inserted. This value premise is extra-scientific; it does not emerge from the analysis itself. When the value premise is chosen and defined, it will, in combination with the analysis of the facts, permit rational policy conclusions. These conclusions are rational because they

[1] Cf. *An American Dilemma. The Negro Problem and Modern Democracy*, New York, 1944, Chap. 1 and Appendices 1–3; reprinted below, chapter III; also the Preface to the English edition of *The Political Element in the Development of Economic Theory*, London, 1953.

48

are in this sense hypothetical. They only spell out the logical policy implications of the selected value premise in a known context of reality.

This familiar view, which I shall take as the starting point in my brief exposition of the value problem, is often expressed thus: though it is not possible for science to pronounce on the *ends* of social policy, it is a scientific problem which can be scientifically solved to establish what *means* are most appropriate for reaching an end which is postulated. This way of reasoning presumes that the means are not themselves objects for human valuation, except indirectly for their efficiency as instruments in achieving an end. This, incidentally, should be recognized as a reminiscence of a central thesis of Utilitarianism. To this moral philosophy it was a basic principle that nothing was good or bad in itself but only because of its good or bad effects (and the effects were judged according to their tendency to increase or decrease the total sum of 'happiness' in society or the 'general welfare' which was the end of all ends). We may also recall in passing that this thesis was one of the main objects of the Intuitionalists' attack on utilitarian philosophy and was also a reason why economics in particular brought upon its head censure for being 'the dismal science'.

But leaving all these old doctrinal quarrels aside, it is simply not true that only ends are the object of valuations and that means are valued only as instrumental to ends. In any human valuation means have, in addition to their instrumental value, independent values as well. The value premise which has to be introduced in order to allow policy conclusions to be reached from factual analysis has therefore to be a valuation of means as well as ends.

Furthermore, in reality, of course, a desired end, if reached, is never attained in purity. The dynamic social process initiated by the means results in many other changes besides the positive achievement of the end. These accessory effects of the means have also to be taken into account in the chosen value premise.

All this makes the matter of introducing a value premise in social research considerably more complicated than is usually recognized. It implies, in effect, that the extra-scientific value premise needed for reaching policy conclusions from scientific research must contain valuations of every single element in the great number of different processes of future development which, as possibilities corresponding to various modifications of policy, ramify from a given situation assumed to be ascertained and analysed with respect to these possibilities.

Now, the secret of all science is the principle of generalization. But in this case generalizations do not only make things simpler. It is true that by courageous use of our scientific intuition we can manage to exclude a number of policies as unfeasible or in some other sense unrealistic. We can also invent certain instrumental common denominators for measuring—in terms of aggregates, averages, and indices of all sorts—the various characteristics of ends, means, and accessory effects in such a way as to make the value premise simpler and easier to formulate. (These and similar tricks of our craft imply that our research is given direction; I will return to this problem in a moment.) But at the same time a generalizing analysis will also make the needed value premise more complicated and difficult to formulate and handle. For such an analysis is not being related only to one concrete initial situation; it will aspire to a much more general judgment on the policies, corresponding to the postulated value premise, appropriate to different initial situations.

Finally, even if the value premise is now openly assumed to be extra-scientific, deliberately chosen, and made explicit —which is the great advance in method compared with the old practice, where the valuation was most of the time kept implicit and often made to emerge out of the analysis itself— the value premise cannot be arbitrarily chosen. It must be relevant, even significant, and it must be practicable. This means that it must correspond to the real valuations of existing groups in society, large enough or for other reasons having power enough to make it realistic. An author's beliefs about reality are of interest and importance if they are founded upon good analysis of factual data; as we are not poets, our own valuations of reality are not important and interesting if they an extravagant in relation to the society in which we live.

In most situations there are, furthermore, not one but several sets of relevant and significant valuations. Therefore, if the policy analysis of a practical social problem is not to be one-sided and therefore inadequate, the analysis will have to be worked out with several sets of co-existing value premises.

To be founded in reality, in the sense of not being arbitrary, the value premises should not be taken out of the air by intelligent guesswork but be the result of careful empirical opinion studies—of a perfected type which does not yet exist —concerning the 'true' attitudes of the different social groups. Particular difficulties in utilizing even the most perfected opinion studies for constructing the sets of co-existing value premises needed for the practical application of social analysis are: first, that the valuations should, as far as possible, be 'rational', in the sense that they represent the valuations people would have if they had a better knowledge about reality; second, that they must be valuations not only of the elements in the present situation but also of elements in all the possible future developments.

And yet I have not touched upon the greatest difficulty of all in this type of practical analysis, the difficulty Immanuel Kant struggled with in his criticism of metaphysics. It concerns a problem already hinted at from one particular aspect: the direction of research. Up till now I have assumed that, before we came to the problem of practical application by introducing a value premise, we had already carried out a purely factual analysis which was independent of any valuations. This assumption is naïve empiricism: the idea that if we observe, and continue to observe, reality without any preconceptions, the facts will somehow organize themselves into a system which is assumed to pre-exist. But without questions there are no answers. And the answers are preconceived in the formulation of the questions. The questions express our interests in the matter. The interests can never be purely scientific. They are choices, the products of our valuations. 'Without valuations we have no interest, no sense of relevance or of significance and, consequently, no object,' my late friend Louis Wirth once wrote to me when we corresponded about this problem. This is, indeed, the principal paradox of science: the value premise, as I pointed out, cannot be even formulated except in relation to all elements in all the alternatively possible development processes laid bare by factual analysis: the factual analysis cannot be carried out except when guided by the value premise.

This concentrated analysis of the logical relation between social theory and social policy will make understandable why I must now confess that I have not read any major work, or written any myself, which fully satisfies me as really meeting the demands of how properly to deal with facts and valuations in social science. But this situation where we all fall short of the ideal provides no reason why we should not continuously strive to approach it by perfecting our working methods. In any case, the old hedonistic and utilitarian method does not offer a substitute in any real sense. For it cannot be seriously suggested that we should continue to conceal our introduction of valuations into our research by forced interpretations of empty formulae, i.e., by logical errors. These defects are inherent in the old metaphysical method and its basic philosophy; they cannot be eradicated by any econometric rejuvenation.

Let me try in one paragraph to formulate the main rules we should attempt to apply to social analysis. Value premises should be introduced openly. They should be explicitly stated and not kept hidden as tacit assumptions. They should be used not only as premises for our policy conclusions but also to determine the direction of our positive research. They should thus be kept conscious and in the focus of attention throughout the work. This is our only protection against bias in research, for bias implies being directed by unacknowledged valuations. The value premises should be formulated as specifically and concretely as possible. They cannot be *a priori* self-evident or generally valid. They should be chosen, but not arbitrarily, for the choice must meet the criteria of relevance and significance to the society in which we live. Since as a matter of fact conflicting valuations are held in society, the value premises should ideally be given as a number of sets of co-existing valuations.

If we know the actual power coefficients of the different value premises—dependent, among other factors, upon the weight of the groups which hold the corresponding valuations

—and if the value premises are really worked into our analysis as they should be, we should be able to present as the result of our research what I have once called an abstract 'war game', a sociological equivalent of the drawing-board strategy before the battle. We should be able to form opinions both about the policies different groups should rationally attempt to pursue (taking into account their own valuations and all other pertinent facts in society) and about the probable outcome of the social process (taking into account also the power co-efficients). Programmes and prognoses may in this way be logically correlated, because the programmes are founded upon estimates of what would happen (under different policies) and prognoses take into account the effect of the different policies employed in the programmes.

There are two sets of difficulties we shall meet in any attempts to realize this method in social research. We have first the difficulties originating from the fact that our knowledge about actual value preferences in society falls far short of our knowledge about the other data which we are accustomed to deal with in social research. This implies, in turn, that our hopes for future advance in social research depend upon progress in studies which could aid us in learning more about the content and processes of social valuations and their political expression. This calls for a very much modernized political science which has learned to utilize an improved and fully relativistic sociology and social psychology, not as formerly an absolutistic moral philosophy based on a hedonistic, i.e., rationalistic and individualistic, psychology.

The other set of difficulties is of a more technical, not to say mechanical character. To deal properly with a value premise is, as I have pointed out, a very complicated procedure, and it becomes particularly complicated when we operate with the number of co-existing valuations that is needed for objectivity. We cannot assume a convergence of interests. We stand continuously before research tasks where a clash of interests and valuations is part of the problem. Nor, of course, can the institutional frame be treated as a constant, except in short-range problems. Changing this frame is regularly the long-range object of policies.

Permit me finally to stress again one main point. Quite apart from drawing any policy conclusions from social research or forming any ideas about what is desirable or undesirable, we employ and we need value premises in making scientific observations of facts and in analysing their causal interrelation. Chaos does not organize itself into cosmos. We need viewpoints and they presume valuations. A 'disinterested social science' is, from this viewpoint, pure nonsense. It never existed, and it will never exist. We can strive to make our thinking rational in spite of this, but only by facing the valuations, not by evading them.

For about a century the historical and institutional criticisms of abstract theorizing—of, for instance, economic theory in the classical tradition—have, of course, made this point that social theory was conditioned by its material and cultural setting. But as the critics were either deeply engulfed in metaphysical thinking themselves—though of a different kind: usually organic and juridical—or else just naïvely empirical like the social theorists they criticized, they never developed a clear methodology from their criticism. The thesis that social science like every other branch of human endeavour is, as a matter of fact, conditioned by the valuations prevalent in society which form its cultural environment was, however, developed into a sociology of science by two great German social scientists, Max Weber and Karl Mannheim. It is for social science itself to draw the rational consequences of this insight for its methods of observation and analysis. The most important thing is to make this unavoidable conditioning a conscious and deliberate situation, to change an uncontrolled general bias into a set of explicit and specific viewpoints.

PART 2

CHAPTER THREE

INTRODUCTION TO THE STUDY OF THE NEGRO PROBLEM[1]

1. THE NEGRO PROBLEM AS A MORAL ISSUE

THERE is a 'Negro problem' in the United States and most Americans are aware of it, although it assumes varying forms and intensity in different regions of the country and among diverse groups of the American people. Americans have to react to it, politically as citizens and, where there are Negroes present in the community, privately as neighbours.

To the great majority of white Americans the Negro problem has distinctly negative connotations. It suggests something difficult to settle and equally difficult to leave alone. It is embarrassing. It makes for moral uneasiness. The very presence of the Negro in America;[2] his fate in that country through slavery, Civil War and Reconstruction; his recent career and his present status; his accommodation; his protest and his aspiration; in fact his entire biological, historical, and social existence as a participant American represent to the ordinary white man in the North as well as in the South an anomaly in the very structure of American society. To many, this takes on the proportion of a menace—biological, economic, social, cultural, and, at times, political. This anxiety may be mingled with a feeling of individual and collective guilt. A few see the problem as a challenge to statesmanship. To all it is a trouble.

These and many other mutually inconsistent attitudes are

---

[1] From the Introduction to *An American Dilemma.*

[2] The word *America* will be used in this book as a synonym for the continental United States.

blended into none too logical a scheme which, in turn, may be quite inconsistent with the wider personal, moral, religious, and civic sentiments and ideas of the Americans. Now and then, even the least sophisticated individual becomes aware of his own confusion and the contradiction in his attitudes. Occasionally he may recognize, even if only for a moment, the incongruity of his state of mind and find it so intolerable that the whole organization of his moral precepts is shaken. But most people, most of the time, suppress such threats to their moral integrity together with all the confusion, the ambiguity, and inconsistency which lurks in the basement of man's soul. This, however, is rarely accomplished without mental strain. Out of the strain comes a sense of uneasiness and awkwardness which always seems attached to the Negro problem.

The strain is increased in democratic America by the freedom left open—even in the South, to a considerable extent—for the advocates of the Negro, his rights and welfare. All 'pro-Negro' forces in American society, whether organized or not, and irrespective of their wide differences in both strategy and tactics, sense that this is the situation. They all work on the national conscience. They all seek to fix everybody's attention on the suppressed moral conflict. No wonder that they are often regarded as public nuisances, or worse—even when they succeed in getting grudging concessions to Negro rights and welfare.

At this point it must be observed that America, relative to all the other branches of Western civilization, is moralistic and 'moral-conscious'. The ordinary American is the opposite of a cynic. He is on the average more of a believer and a defender of the faith in humanity than the rest of the Occidentals. It is a relatively important matter to him to be true to his own ideals and to carry them out in actual life. We recognize the American, wherever we meet him, as a practical idealist. Compared with members of other nations of Western civilization, the ordinary American is a rationalistic being, and there are close relations between his moralism and his rationalism. Even romanticism, transcendentalism, and mysticism tend to be, in the American culture, rational, pragmatic and optimistic. American civilization early acquired a flavour of enlightenment which has affected the ordinary American's whole personality and especially his conception of how ideas and ideals ought to 'click'. He has never developed that particular brand of tired mysticism and romanticism which finds delight in the inextricable confusion in the order of things and in ineffectuality of the human mind. He finds such leanings intellectually perverse.

These generalizations might seem venturesome and questionable to the reflective American himself, who, naturally enough, has his attention directed more on the dissimilarities than on the similarities within his culture. What is common is usually not obvious, and it never becomes striking. But to the stranger it is obvious and even striking. In the social sciences, for instance, the American has, more courageously than anyone else on the globe, started to measure, not only human intelligence, aptitudes, and personality traits, but moral leanings and the 'goodness' of communities. He is a rationalist; he wants intellectual order in his moral set-up; he wants to pursue his own inclinations into their hidden haunts; and he is likely to expose himself and his kind in a most undiplomatic manner.

In hasty strokes we are now depicting the essentials of the American *ethos*. This moralism and rationalism are to many of us—among them the author of this book—the glory of the nation, its youthful strength, perhaps the salvation of mankind. The analysis of this 'American Creed' and its implications have an important place in our inquiry. While on the one hand, to such a moralistic and rationalistic being as the ordinary American, the Negro problem and his own confused and contradictory attitudes toward it must be disturbing, on the other hand, the very mass of unsettled problems in his heterogeneous and changing culture, and the inherited liberalistic trust that things will ultimately take care of themselves and get settled in one way or another, enable the ordinary American to live on happily, with recognized contradictions around him and within him, in a kind of bright fatalism which is unmatched in the rest of the Western world. This fatalism also belongs to the national *ethos*.

The American Negro problem is a problem in the heart of the American. It is there that the interracial tension has its focus. It is there that the decisive struggle goes on. This is the central viewpoint of this treatise. Though our study includes economic, social, and political race relations, at bottom our problem is the moral dilemma of the American— the conflict between his moral valuations on various levels of conscious- ness and generality. The 'American Dilemma', referred to in the title of this book, is the ever-raging conflict between, on the one hand, the valuations preserved on the general plane which we shall call the 'American Creed', where the American thinks, talks, and acts under the influence of high national and Christian precepts, and, on the other hand, the valuations on specific planes of individual and group living, where personal and local interests, economic, social, and sexual jealousies, considerations of community prestige and conformity, group prejudice against particular persons or types of people, and all sorts of mis- cellaneous wants, impulses and habits dominate his outlook.

The American philosopher John Dewey, whose immense influence is to be explained by his rare gift for projecting faith- fully the aspirations and possibilities of the culture he was born into, in the maturity of age and wisdom has written a book on *Freedom and Culture*, in which he says :

Anything that obscures the fundamentally moral nature of the social problem is harmful, no matter whether it proceeds from the side of physical or of psychological theory. Any doctrine that eliminates or even obscures the function of choice of values and enlistment of desires and emotions in behalf of those chosen weakens personal responsibility for judgment and for action. It thus helps create the attitudes that welcome and support the totalitarian state.[1]

We shall attempt to follow through Dewey's conception of what a social problem really is.

2. VALUATIONS AND BELIEFS

The Negro problem in America would be of a different nature, and, indeed, would be simpler to handle scientifically, if the moral conflict raged only between valuations held by different persons and groups of persons. The essence of the moral situation is, however, that the conflicting valuations are also held by the same person. *The moral struggle goes on within*

[1] (1939), p. 172.

people and not only between them. As people's valuations are conflicting, behaviour normally becomes a moral compromise. There are no homogeneous 'attitudes' behind human behaviour but a mesh of struggling inclinations, interests, and ideals, some held conscious and some suppressed for long intervals but all active in bending behaviour in their direction.

The unity of a culture consists in the fact that all valuations are mutually shared in some degree. We shall find that even a poor and uneducated white person in some isolated and backward rural region in the Deep South, who is violently prejudiced against the Negro and intent upon depriving him of civic rights and human independence, has also a whole compartment in his valuation sphere housing the entire American Creed of liberty, equality, justice, and fair opportunity for everybody. He is actually also a good Christian and honestly devoted to the ideals of human brotherhood and the Golden Rule. And these more general valuations—more general in the sense that they refer to all human beings—are, to some extent, effective in shaping his behaviour. Indeed, it would be impossible to understand why the Negro does not fare worse in some regions of America if it were not constantly kept in mind that behaviour is the outcome of a compromise between valuations, among which the equalitarian ideal is one. At the other end, there are few liberals, even in New England, who have not a well-furnished compartment of race prejudice, even if it is usually suppressed from conscious attention. Even the American Negroes share in this community of valuations: they have eagerly imbibed the American Creed and the revolutionary Christian teaching of common brotherhood; under closer study, they usually reveal also that they hold something of the majority prejudice against their own kind and its characteristics.

The intensities and proportions in which these conflicting valuations are present vary considerably from one American to another, and within the same individual, from one situation to another. The cultural unity of the nation consists, however, in the fact that *most Americans have most valuations in common* though they are arranged differently in the sphere of valuations of different individuals and groups and have different intensities.

59

This cultural unity is the indispensable basis for discussion between persons and groups. It is the floor upon which the democratic process goes on.

In America as everywhere else people agree, as an abstract proposition, that *the more general valuations—those which refer to man as such and not to any particular group or temporary situation— are morally higher.* These valuations are also given the sanction of religion and national legislation. They are incorporated into the American Creed. The other valuations—which refer to various smaller groups of mankind, or to particular occasions— are commonly referred to as 'irrational' or 'prejudiced', sometimes even by people who express and stress them. They are defended in terms of tradition, expediency, or utility.

Trying to defend their behaviour to others, and primarily to themselves, people will attempt to conceal the conflict between their different valuations of what is desirable and undesirable, right or wrong, by keeping away some valuations from awareness and by focusing attention on others. For the same opportune purpose, *people will twist and mutilate their beliefs of what social reality actually is.* In our study we encounter whole systems of firmly entrenched popular beliefs concerning the Negro and his relations to the larger society, which are blatantly false and which can only be understood when we remember the opportunistic *ad hoc* purposes they serve. These 'popular theories', because of the rationalizing function they serve, are heavily loaded with emotions. But people also want to be rational. Scientific truth-seeking and education are slowly rectifying the beliefs and thereby also influencing the valuations. In a rationalistic civilization it is not only that the beliefs are shaped by the valuations, but also that the valuations depend upon the beliefs.[1]

Our task in this inquiry is to ascertain social reality as it is. We shall seek to depict the actual living conditions of the American Negro people and their manifold relations to the larger American society. We must describe, in as much detail as our observations and space here allow, who the American

---

[1] The theory of human behaviour and its motivation, which is sketched in the text and is basic to our approach to the Negro problem, is explained in Chapter V on 'Valuations and Beliefs'.

Negro is, and how he fares. Whenever possible, we shall present quantitative indices of his existence and of the material conditions of his existence. But this is not all and, from our point of view, not even the most important part of social reality. We must go further and attempt to discover and dissect the doctrines and ideologies, valuations and beliefs, embedded in the minds of white and Negro Americans. We want to follow through W. I. Thomas's theme, namely, that when people define situations as real, they *are* real.[1] We shall try to remember throughout our inquiry that material facts in large measure are the product of what people think, feel and believe. The actual conditions, as they are, indicate from this point of view the great disparities between the whites' and the Negroes' aspirations and realizations. The interrelations between the material facts and people's valuations of and beliefs about these facts are precisely what make the Negro a social problem.

It is sometimes assumed to be the mark of 'sound' research to disregard the fact that people are moral beings and that they are struggling for their conscience. In our view, this is a bias and a blindness, dangerous to the possibility of enabling scientific study to arrive at true knowledge. Every social study must have its centre in an investigation of people's conflicting valuations and their opportune beliefs. They are social facts and can be observed by direct and indirect manifestations. We are, of course, also interested in discovering how these inclinations and loyalties came about and what the factors are upon which they rest. We want to keep free, however, at least at the outset, from any preconceived doctrine or theory, whether of the type making biological characteristics, or economic interests, sexual complexes, power relations, or anything else, the 'ultimate' or 'basic' cause of these valuations. We hope to come out with a type of systematic understanding as eclectic as common sense itself when it is open-minded.

When we thus choose to view the Negro problem as primarily a moral issue, we are in line with popular thinking. It is as a moral issue that this problem presents itself in the daily life of ordinary people; it is as a moral issue that they brood over it in

[1] William I. Thomas and Florian Znaniecki, *The Polish Peasant in Europe and America* (1918).

61

their thoughtful moments. It is in terms of conflicting moral valuations that it is discussed in church and school, in the family circle, in the workshop, on the street corner, as well as in the press, over the radio, in trade union meetings, in the state legislatures, the Congress, and the Supreme Court. The social scientist, in his effort to lay bare concealed truths and to be useful in guiding practical and political action, is prudent when, in the approach to a problem, he sticks as closely as possible to the common man's ideas and formulations, even though he knows that further investigation will carry him into tracts uncharted in the popular consciousness. There is a pragmatic common sense in people's ideas about themselves and their worries, which we cannot afford to miss when we start out to explore social reality. Otherwise we are often too easily distracted by our learned arbitrariness and our pet theories, concepts, and hypotheses, not to mention our barbarous terminology, which we generally are tempted to mistake for something more than mere words. *Throughout this study we shall constantly take our starting point in the ordinary man's own ideas, doctrines, theories and mental constructs.*

In approaching the Negro problem as primarily a moral issue of conflicting valuations, it is not implied, of course, that ours is the prerogative of pronouncing on *a priori* grounds which values are 'right' and which are 'wrong'. In fact, such judgments are outside the realm of social science, and will not be attempted in this inquiry. Our investigation will naturally be an analysis *of* morals and not *in* morals. In so far as we make our own judgments of value, they will be based on explicitly stated value premises, selected from among those valuations actually observed in the minds of the white and Negro Americans and tested as to their social and political relevance and significance. Our value judgments are thus derived and have no greater validity than the value premises postulated.

3. FURTHER NOTES ON THE SCOPE AND DIRECTION OF THIS STUDY

This book is an analysis, not a description. It presents facts only for the sake of their meaning in the interpretation. Since, however, an attempt at a comprehensive analysis was made, the scope of the facts, even when compressed into outline form, is extensive, though, we hope, selective. The author had available not only the vast existing published literature, but also some specially prepared research memoranda, a portion of which is being published, and all of which are made available to the inquiring reader.

On the theoretical[1] side, the aim of this book is to formulate tentative generalizations on the basis of known facts. A corollary of this scientific task is to indicate gaps in our knowledge. These gaps will be noted in passing, and in some respects positive suggestions for investigation will be offered. Undoubtedly, we shall sometimes be found to have overlooked existing sources. In view of the scope of the investigation this is inevitable but, nevertheless, regrettable.

As the known and verified facts are scarce, a courageous use will be made of the writer's own observations. Their conjectural character will always be made explicit. They are the author's best judgments, when published data are insufficient, as to what is the truth, and they should be taken only for what they are. For the outlining of further research they may serve as the projection of plausible hypotheses.

On the practical side, the aim of this book is to throw light on the future, and to construct, in a preliminary way, bases for rational policy. This is one reason why the theoretical analysis will stress interrelations and trends. Even though reliable prognoses cannot be made in many respects, various possibilities can be presented and their probabilities estimated.

Explicit value premises will be introduced, usually in the beginning of each main part of the inquiry. As a source for the value premises, the relatively comprehensive and definite body of political ideals contained in the 'American Creed' will be used; we shall sketch the historical origin of the American Creed in the first chapter. The use of explicit value premises serves three main purposes: (1) to purge as far as possible the scientific

---

[1] The terms *theoretical* and *practical* (or *political*) are used in this book as in the discipline of philosophy. The former word implies thinking in terms of causes and effects; the latter words imply thinking in terms of means and ends. (See Chapter VII, Section 4.)

investigation of distorting biases which are usually the result of hidden biases; (2) to determine in a rational way the statement of problems and the definition of terms for the theoretical analysis; (3) to lay a logical basis for practical and political conclusions.[1]

---

[1] The problem of bias, of theoretical and practical research, and of the utilization of the scientific technique of explicit value premises are treated in Chapter VII on Facts and Valuations.

CHAPTER FOUR

AMERICAN IDEALS AND THE AMERICAN CONSCIENCE

1. THE AMERICAN CREED[1]

IN spite of, or perhaps because of, the heterogeneity of the American nation, there is a strong unity and basic stability in its valuations. America has a more explicit political creed than any other Western nation. The discovery of what we shall call the American Creed transforms the cacophony into a melody.

Not only is the American system of ideals the most explicitly formulated, but all vehicles of communication are mobilized to indoctrinate everyone with its principles. The schools teach them, the churches preach them, the courts announce them in their decisions. The Supreme Court pays its homage when it declares what is constitutional. Editorials, articles, and public addresses all reflect this idealism.

The Negro people share this creed and are under its spell, not merely pleading with it for their rights, but half believing, as do many whites, that it actually guides America. The ideals of the dignity of the individual, fundamental equality, and certain inalienable rights to freedom, justice, and fair opportunity, were written into the Declaration of Independence, the Preamble of the Constitution, the Bill of Rights, and the constitutions of the states.

The American Creed is identified with America's peculiar brand of nationalism, and it gives the American his feeling of the historical mission of his country in the world. American nationalism carries an international message. This national feeling of pride, and responsibility for the world, has been

[1] This section is a brief summary of Chapter 1 of *An American Dilemma*.

frequently expressed, amongst others, by historians like George Bancroft and Frederick J. Turner, and more recently by Wilson's fourteen points and Roosevelt's four freedoms. In the past, political revolutionaries of other countries were approved of even by conservatives in America. Just as the Western frontier country challenged the East to remove the barriers that prevented the full development of men and women, so America challenged the world at large to create a better society.

Although the Constitution was conceived in suspicion of democracy and fear of 'the people', and designed as a defence of property against the democratic spirit of the Revolution, what emerged was a triumph of the American Creed. America has had gifted conservative statesmen and national leaders, but with few exceptions only the liberals have gone down in history as national heroes. America is conservative in fundamental principles, but hopefully experimental in practical social arrangements. Even the principles conserved by American conservatism seem liberal, in some cases even radical.

One of the historical roots of the American Creed is the philosophy of Enlightenment, with its belief in reason, the perfectibility of man, and his endowment with certain natural, inalienable, rights; its belief in the existence of a harmony between equality of opportunity and liberty, and its faith in education. Another root is Christianity, particularly in the form which it took in various Protestant sects. Democracy had been envisaged in religious terms long before it assumed a political expression. The presence of many denominations and of competition between them forces American churches to greater tolerance and humanism, and an interest in social problems. A third influence is English law, and the idea of government as the rule of law, not man. This concept contains certain fundamental aspects of both equality and liberty. The philosophical ideas of eighteenth century liberalism would not have struck root as they did, had it not been for a soil cultivated by English law.

The combination of Christian faith and English law explains why America has so doggedly stuck to her high ideals; why she has been so conservative in adhering to liberalism as her creed, even if not as her way of life. This conservatism has, to some extent, been perverted into a nearly fetishistic cult of the Constitution, ill-suited to modern conditions, and opposed to the American Creed, which is experimental.

While Americans believe in the Creed and express it in their laws, they do not live up to it in practice. To understand this we have to consider the American attitude to law, which is highly ambivalent. The heritage of the natural law philosophy sees in the individual conscience the ultimate legislator and judge, commanding disobedience whenever the law violates the natural order. Against and together with this in effect anarchistic streak, there is also a desire to regulate human conduct tyrannically by decree, another heritage of early Puritanism, which could be fanatical and dogmatic, and was strongly inclined to mind other people's business. The conjunction of '*I* obey only *my* conscience; but there ought to be a law against *your* sins', together with badly prepared and inefficiently administered laws often led to disappointment in attempts to legislate for social change. (Negroes' Civil Right, Anti-Trust, and Prohibition legislation are examples.) This in turn has encouraged defeatism amongst American social scientists. In other respects, too, there is a moral tension between American ideals and practice, sometimes decried as hypocrisy, particularly by Americans themselves. But it is not hypocrisy. The sins are not committed secretly, nor hushed up, but are widely and loudly proclaimed. In spite of some division of labour between those who do the sinning and those who do the muckraking, preaching, and lamenting, there is a muck-raker, preacher and lamenter in every American. The consciousness of sins committed, and of the devotion to high ideals, contribute to the formation of the cultural unity of a nation of idealists, accusing themselves of materialism, of reformers, charging themselves with paying only lip service to morality.

2. Value Premises in This Study[1]

For the study of a national problem which cuts so sharply through the whole body politic as does the Negro problem, no other set of valuations could serve as adequately as the norm

---

[1] From *An American Dilemma*, pp. 23–25.

for an incisive formulation of our value premises as can the American Creed. No other norm could compete in authority over the people's minds. 'The American democratic faith is a pattern of ideals providing standards of value with which the accomplishments of realistic democracy may be judged,' observes an author surveying the historical trends of American thinking[1].

And there is no doubt that these ideals are active realities. The student of American history must be professionally nearsighted or blinded by a doctrinal belief in a materialistic determinism if he fails to see the significance of tracing how the Creed is gradually realizing itself. *The American Creed is itself one of the dominant 'social trends.'* 'Call it a dream or call it vision,' says John Dewey, 'it has been interwoven in a tradition that has had an immense effect upon American life.'[2] Or, to quote a distinguished Negro thinker, the late Kelly Miller:

> In this country political, social and economic conditions gravitate toward equality. We may continue to expect thunderstorms in the political firmament so long as there exists inequality of political temperature in the atmosphere of the two regions. Neither Massachusetts nor Mississippi will rest satisfied until there is an equality of political condition in both states . . . . Democratic institutions can no more tolerate a double political status than two standards of ethics or discrepant units of weight and measure.[3]

But apart from trends, the American Creed represents the national conscience. The Negro is a 'problem' to the average American partly because of a palpable conflict between the status actually awarded him and those ideals.

The American Creed, just because it is a living reality in a developing democracy, is not a fixed and clear-cut dogma. It is still growing. During the Revolutionary epoch the interests of statesmen and philosophers and of the general public were focused on the more formal aspects of freedom, equality, and justice. After a long period of material expansion but not rapid

---

[1] Ralph H. Gabriel, *The Course of American Democratic Thought* (1940), p. 418.

[2] *Freedom and Culture* (1939), p. 55. Dewey is here referring to the theory of human freedom that was developed in the writings of the philosophers of the American Revolution, particularly Jefferson.

[3] *Out of the House of Bondage* (1914), pp. 134–135.

spiritual growth, the American Creed is in this generation again in a formative stage. It is now discovering its ideals in the social and economic sphere and in the realm of international organization.

While this is going on, there are great disparities in opinions even on fundamentals in these new fields of valuation—as there were during the Revolution concerning the ideals which then became crystallized. Some Americans see in trade unions a denial of the rights to human liberty; others see in the unions an expression of the common man's right to reach for greater quality and freedom. Some Americans want to tax property and nationalize public utilities in order to defend equality of opportunity for the masses of the people and to preserve their liberties; others see in such attempts an assault upon American principles of liberty. In the international field American ideals in recent decades and even to-day seem divided and rambling in the wide space of the triangle marked by the three points: absolute isolation, an organized world democracy, and American world imperialism.

These great disparities of opinion would, in any other social problem, considerably increase the technical difficulties of using the Creed as a set of specified and definite value premises for research. When in later chapters we face the task of defining our value premises specifically, we shall find that this is not the case in the Negro problem. The Creed is expressive and definite in practically all respects of importance for the Negro problem. Most of the value premises with which we shall be concerned have actually been incorporated for a long time in the national Constitution and in the constitutions and laws of the several states.

The deeper reason for the technical simplicity of the value aspect of the Negro problem is this: from the point of view of the American Creed the status accorded the Negro in America represents nothing more and nothing less than a century-long lag of public morals. In principle the Negro problem was settled long ago; in practice the solution is not reached. The Negro in America has not yet been given the elementary civil and political rights of formal democracy, including a fair opportunity to earn his living, upon which a general accord w..s already won when the American Creed was first taking form. And this anachronism constitutes the contemporary 'problem' both to Negroes and to whites.

If those rights were respected, many other pressing social problems would, of course, still remain. Many Negroes would, together with many whites, belong to groups which would invoke the old ideals of equality and liberty in demanding more effective protection for their social and economic opportunities. But there would no longer be a *Negro* problem. This does not mean that the Negro problem is an easy problem to solve. It is a tremendous task for theoretical research to find out why the Negro's status is what it is. In its unsolved form it further intertwines with all other social problems. It is simple only in the technical sense that in America the value premises —if they are conceived to be the ideals of the American Creed —are extraordinarily specific and definite.

Finally, in order to avoid possible misunderstandings, it should be explained that we have called this Creed 'American' in the sense that it is adhered to by the Americans. This is the only matter which interests us in this book, which is focused upon the Negro problem as part of American life and American politics. But this Creed is, of course, no American monopoly. With minor variations, some of which, however, are not without importance, the American Creed is the common democratic creed. 'American ideals' are just humane ideals as they have matured in our common Western civilization upon the foundation of Christianity and pre-Christian legalism and under the influence of the economic, scientific, and political development over a number of centuries. The American Creed is older and wider than America itself.

CHAPTER FIVE

VALUATIONS AND BELIEFS[1]

1. THE MECHANISM OF RATIONALIZATION

PEOPLE have ideas about how reality actually is, or was, and they have ideas about how it ought to be, or ought to have been. The former we call '*beliefs*'. The latter we call '*valuations*'. A person's beliefs, that is, his knowledge, can be objectively judged to be true or false and more or less complete. His valuations—that a social situation or relation is, or was, 'just', 'right', 'fair', 'desirable', or the opposite, in some degree of intensity or other—cannot be judged by such objective standards as science provides. In their '*opinions*' people express both their beliefs and their valuations. Usually people do not distinguish between what they think they know and what they like or dislike.

There is a close psychological interrelation between the two types of ideas. In our civilization people want to be rational and objective in their beliefs. We have faith in science and are, in principle, prepared to change our beliefs according to its results. People also want to have 'reasons' for the valuations they hold, and they usually express only those valuations for which they think they have 'reasons'. To serve as opinions, specific valuations are selected, are formulated in words and are motivated by acceptable 'reasons'. With the help of certain beliefs about reality, valuations are posited as parts of a general value order from which they are taken to be logical inferences. This value hierarchy has a simple or elaborate architecture, depending mainly upon the cultural level of a person. But independently of this, most persons want to present to their fellows—and to themselves—a trimmed and polished sphere of

[1] Appendix 1 in *An American Dilemma*.

valuations, where honesty, logic, and consistency rule. For
reasons which we shall discuss, most people's advertised
opinions are, however, actually illogical and contain conflicting valuations bridged by skewed beliefs about social reality.
In addition, they indicate very inadequately the behaviour
which can be expected, and they usually misrepresent its
actual motivation.

The basic difficulty in the attempt to present a logical order of
valuations is, of course, that those valuations actually are conflicting. When studying the way in which the valuations clash,
and the personal and social results brought about by the conflicts, we shall, moreover, have to observe that the valuations
simply cannot be treated as if they existed on the same plane.
They refer to different levels of the moral personality.[1] The
moral precepts contained in the respective valuations correspond to different degrees of generality of moral judgment.
Some valuations concern human beings in general; others
concern Negroes or women or foreigners; still others concern a
particular group of Negroes or an individual Negro. Some
valuations have general and eternal validity; others have validity only for certain situations. In the Western culture people
assume, as an abstract proposition, that the more general and
timeless valuations are morally higher. We can, therefore, see
that the motivation of valuations, already referred to, generally
follows the pattern of trying to present the more specific
valuations as inferences from the more general.

In the course of actual day-to-day living a person will be
found to focus attention on the valuations of one particular
plane of his moral personality and leave in the shadow, for the
time being, the other planes with their often contradicting
valuations. Most of the time the selection of this focus of
evaluation is plainly opportunistic. The expressed valuations
and beliefs brought forward as motives for specific action or
inaction are selected in relation to the expediencies of the
occasion. They are the 'good' reasons rather than the 'true'
reasons; in short, they are 'rationalizations'.

The whole 'sphere of valuations'—by which we mean the
entire aggregate of a person's numerous and conflicting

[1] This hypothesis is presented more fully in Chapter III (Sections 1 and 2).

valuations, as well as their expressions in thought, speech and behaviour—is thus never present in conscious appreciation. Some parts of it may even be constantly suppressed from awareness. But it would be a gross mistake to believe that the valuations temporarily kept in the shadow of subjective inattention —and the deeper-seated psychic inclinations and loyalties represented by them—are permanently silenced. Most of them rise to consciousness now and then as the focus of apperception changes in reaction to the flow of experiences and impulses. Even when submerged, they are not without influence on actual behaviour. They ordinarily bend behaviour somewhat in their direction; the reason for suppressing them from conscious attention is that, if obeyed, they would affect behaviour even more. In this treatise, therefore, behaviour is conceived of as being typically the outcome of a moral compromise of heterogeneous valuations, operating on various planes of generality and rising in varying degrees and at different occasions to the level of consciousness. To assume the existence of homogeneous 'attitudes' behind behaviour would violate the facts, as we must well know from every-day introspection and from observation and reflection. It tends to conceal the moral conflicts which are the ultimate object of our study in this book.

The individual or the group whose behaviour we are studying, moreover, does not act in moral isolation. He is not left alone to manage his rationalizations as he pleases, without interference from outside. His valuations will, instead, be questioned and disputed. Democracy is 'government by discussion', and so, in fact, are other forms of government, though to a lesser degree. Moral discussion goes on in all groups from the intimate family circle to the international conference table. Modern means of intellectual communication have increased the volume and the intensity of such moral interrelations.

When discussion takes the form of moral criticism by one person or group of another, it is not that the one claims to have certain valuations that the other does not have. It is rather an appeal to valuations which the other keeps in the shadow of inattention, but which are assumed, nevertheless, to be actually held in common. This assumption, that those with opposing opinions have valuations in common, is ordinarily correct. As we observed in the Introduction,[1] cultural unity in America consists in the fact that most Americans have most valuations in common, though they are differently arranged and bear different intensity coefficients for different individuals and groups. This makes discussion possible and secures an understanding of, and a response to, criticism.

In this process of moral criticism which men make of each other, the valuations on the higher and more general planes— referring to *all* human beings and *not* to specific small groups— are regularly invoked by one party or the other, simply because they are held in common among all groups in society, and also because of the supreme prestige they are traditionally awarded. By this democratic process of open discussion there is started a tendency which constantly forces a larger and larger part of the valuation sphere into conscious attention. More is made conscious than any single person or group would on his own initiative find it advantageous to bring forward at the particular moment. In passing, we might be allowed to remark that this effect—and in addition our common trust that the more general valuations actually represent a 'higher' morality —is the principal reason why we, who are convinced democrats, hold that public discussion is purifying and that democracy itself provides a moral education of the people.

When thus even the momentarily inopportune valuations are brought to attention, an element of indecision and complication is inserted. A need will be felt by the person or group, whose inconsistencies in valuations are publicly exposed, to find a means of reconciling the inconsistencies. This can be accomplished by adjusting one of the conflicting pairs of valuations. If the valuation to be modified is on the less general plane, a greater moral harmony in the larger group is brought about. Specific attitudes and forms of behaviour are then reconciled to the more general moral principles. If, on the other hand, an attempt is made to change or reinterpret valuations which are more general in scope and most of the time consciously shared with all other groups in society, the deviating group will see its moral conflict with other groups becoming

[1] Chapter II, Section 2.

74

increasingly explicit (that is, if the other groups are not themselves prepared to change their general valuations toward a moral compromise). This process might go on until discussion is no longer feasible. In the extreme case such a moral isolation, if the dissenting group is powerful enough, may break the peace and order of society and plunge a nation into civil war.

In the short-run day-to-day conflicts, usually no abrupt changes of valuations will occur. The need for reconciling conflicting valuations brought into the open through public discussion will, for the time being, result only in quasi-logical constructions. In the very nature of things, these constructions must be fantastic, as they represent an attempt to reconcile the illogicalities by logical reasoning.

The temptation will be strong to deny the very existence of a valuation conflict. This will sometimes bring in its wake grossly distorted notions about social reality. There is a sort of social ignorance which is most adequately explained as an attempt to avoid the twinges of conscience. It is, for instance, an experience of every social scientist who has been working on problems of social policy and has taken some interest in people's reactions, that the strongest psychic resistance is aroused when an attempt is made to teach the better situated classes in a society about actual lower class standards of living, and what causes them. This particular type of moral escapism works, sometimes with extraordinary effectiveness, in the American Negro problem.

The feeling of need for logical consistency within the hierarchy of moral valuations—and the embarrassed and sometimes distressed feeling that the moral order is shaky—is, in its modern intensity, a rather new phenomenon. With less mobility, less intellectual communication, and less public discussion, there was in previous generations less exposure of one another's valuation conflicts. The leeway for false beliefs, which makes rationalizations of valuations more perfect for their purpose, was also greater in an age when science was less developed and education less extensive. These historical differentials can be observed to-day within our own society among the different social layers with varying degrees of education and communication with the larger society, stretching all the way from the tradition-bound, inarticulate, quasi-folk-societies in isolated backward regions to the intellectuals of the cultural centres. When one moves from the former groups to the latter, the sphere of moral valuations becomes less rigid, more ambiguous and also more translucent. At the same time, the more general valuations increasingly gain power over the ones bound to traditional peculiarities of regions, classes, or other smaller groups. One of the surest generalizations is that society, in its entirety, is rapidly moving in the direction of the more general valuations. The speed stands in some relation to, and can be gauged by, geographical mobility, the development of intellectual communication, the decrease of illiteracy and the funds spent on education.

During this process of growing intellectualization, people's awareness of inconsistencies in their own spheres of valuations tends to be enhanced. At the same time—if moral cynicism does not spread, a possibility which we shall consider presently —they are increasingly reconditioned to demand consistency in their own valuations and, particularly, in those of other people. They learn to recognize and to avoid the use of illogical-ities and misconceptions of social reality for overcoming the incongruities in their valuations. The impatient humanitarian might find this process exasperatingly slow, and the results meagre. The perspective of decades and generations, however— if moral catastrophes do not interrupt the process—yields a more optimistic impression.

We have already mentioned the fact that valuations are seldom overtly expressed except when they emerge in the course of a person's attempts to formulate his beliefs concerning the facts and their implications in relation to some section of social reality. Beliefs concerning the facts are the building stones for the logical hierarchies of valuations into which a person tries to shape his opinions. When the valuations are conflicting, as they normally are, beliefs serve the function of bridging illogicalities. The beliefs are thus not only determined by available scientific knowledge in society and the efficacy of the means of its communication to various population groups but are regularly 'biased', by which we mean that they are systematically twisted in the one direction which fits them best for purposes of rationalization.

There are in the Negro problem whole systems of popular beliefs concerning the Negro and his relations to the larger society which are crudely false and can only be understood in this light. These 'popular theories' or ideologies are themselves important data in our study, as they represent strategic social facts in the practical and political problems of race relations. A legitimate task of education is to attempt to correct popular beliefs by subjecting them to rigorous examination in the light of the factual evidence. This educational objective must be achieved in the face of the psychic resistance mobilized by the people who feel an urgent need to retain their biased beliefs in order to justify their way of life.

If this educational effort meets with success, the illogicalities involving valuations become exposed to the people who hold them. They are then pressed to change their valuations to some degree. For if popular beliefs depend upon valuations, as we have shown, the valuations also depend upon the beliefs in our civilization bent upon rationalism. When supporting beliefs are drawn away, people will have to readjust their value hierarchies, and eventually their behaviour. As the more general norms in our culture are given supreme moral sanction, this means—if we assume that this 'valuation of the valuations' is upheld, and moral cynicism counteracted—that the valuations on a more specific level (often called 'prejudices') will yield to them. This is the reason, and the only reason, why we generally assume that improved knowledge will make for 'better' citizens. Facts by themselves do not improve anything.

There is a question of terminology which should be touched upon, as it is not without importance for our scheme of thinking. The term 'value' has, in its prevalent usage, a loose meaning. When tightened it is generally taken to refer to the object of valuations, rather than to the valuations themselves. Unfortunately it has a connotation of something solid and homogeneous while our hypothesis is that the valuations are conflicting. We shall avoid using the term 'value'. The term 'attitude' has the same connotation of solidity. It is also often used to denote beliefs as well as valuations. When used in this book 'attitude' should be understood as simply a convenient synonym for valuation.[1]

2. THEORETICAL CRITIQUE OF THE CONCEPT 'MORES'

We must voice our grave scepticism toward the simple explanatory scheme concerning the role of valuations in social life typified by William Graham Sumner's concepts 'folkways' and 'mores'.[2] Since his time these concepts—or one of their several synonyms—have been widely used by social scientists and have, in particular, determined the approach to the Negro problem. The formula will be found to be invoked with some regularity whenever an author expresses his attitude that changes will be slow, or, more particularly, that nothing practical can be done about a matter. It is closely related to a bias in social science against induced changes, and especially against all attempts to intervene in the social process by legislation. The concept of mores actually implies a whole social theory and an entire *laissez-faire* metaphysics,[3] and is thus used.

Leaving aside for the present the political connotations of Sumner's construction, and focusing our interest only on its usefulness as a scientific tool, our main criticism is the following: By stowing the commonly held valuations into the system of mores, conceived of as a homogeneous, unproblematic, fairly static,[4] social entity, the investigator is likely to underestimate the actual difference between individuals and groups and the actual fluctuations and changes in time. He is also likely to lose sight entirely of the important facts, that even within a

[1] This paragraph will, perhaps, explain why the author has not been able to avoid the term "valuation" though knowing well that it is not widely used in America. The term has been used, however, by John Dewey in several of his works, by Charles H. Cooley in his *Social Process* (1918), by Robert M. MacIver in his *Social Causation* (1942), and probably by others.

[2] William Graham Sumner, *Folkways* (1911, first edition 1906).

[3] See Chapter VII, Section 3, and Chapter IV.

[4] Sumner recognized a 'strain toward consistency' within the mores because of conflicting principles, but his main emphasis—and the same is true when the concept is used by contemporary writers—is always upon stability, inertia, and resistance against induced change. Compare Chapter VII, Section 3.

single individual valuations are operative on different planes of generality, that they are typically conflicting, and that behaviour is regularly the outcome of a moral compromise.

It might be that Sumner's construction contains a valid generalization and offers a useful methodological tool for studying primitive cultures and isolated, stationary folk-communities under the spell of magic and sacred tradition. It might even be that the most convenient definition of such a folk-culture is the applicability of the theory of folkways and mores. The theory is, however, crude and misleading when applied to a modern Western society in process of rapid industrialization, moving in swift trends rippled by indeterminate cyclical waves: a society characterized by national and international mobility, by unceasing changes and differentiations of all valuations and institutions, by spreading intellectualization, by widening intellectual communication and secularization, by ever more daring discussion even of fundamentals and intimacies, and by a consequent virtually universal expectation of change and a firm belief in progress. If Sumner's construction is applied to such a society, except as a contrast to mark off some remaining backward elements of cultural isolation which are merely dragged along and do not themselves contain the active factors of social dynamics, it is likely to conceal more than to expose. It conceals what is most important in our society: the changes, the conflicts, the absence of static equilibria, the lability in all relations even when they are temporarily, though perhaps for decades, held at a standstill. The valuation spheres in a society such as the American more nearly resemble powder-magazines than they do Sumner's concept of mores.

3. VALUATION DYNAMICS

In our view, changes in valuations—of the type known as 'revolutions', 'mutations', or 'explosions'—are likely to occur continuously in modern society. 'Stability', or rather lack of change, when it reigns, is the thing which requires explanation. Individual persons in modern society are in the same sort of labile equilibrium as the molecules of explosives. Their valuations are inconsistent, and they are constantly reminded of the inconsistency. Occasionally the moral personalities of individuals burst, and a modification and rearrangement of the valuations in the direction of a more stable equilibrium is accomplished.

Since similar influences work upon all individuals in the society, the cumulative results include continuous changes of 'public opinion'. Such changes are 'intentional', in a sense, and part of a democratic development. The trend of opinions and changes in institutions in a democracy—the 'reforms'— usually have their core in the cumulation of such explosions of valuations in the minds of people. When the inconsistency between people's valuations is large and has effectively been exposed, the change might occasionally be sudden and quite big, and we speak then of a social revolution. But the more evolutionary social changes, if they are dissected into their elements, are not very different except in magnitude.

The history of every nation and of every community, in fact of every group, is, in one sense, the record of the successive waves of such explosions of opinions. Even societies have their catharses and, like individuals, they have them almost all the time. It is the weakness, not only of the static and fatalistic traditions in social science attached to the great names of Marx and Sumner, but of our common tendency to look for explanations in terms only of natural forces and material trends,[1] that we blind ourselves to the dynamics of opinion as it develops from day to day; or, in any case, we become inclined to deal with human opinions more as the result of social change than as part of the cause of it.

By stressing that opinions are not passive elements in the social process, we do not mean to make them altogether independent of material forces. The very fact that opinions to an extent are opportunistic implies that they will change as a result of every other change in social environment. Changes in the technique of production, of communication and of consumption force individual and group revaluations. But so, also, does spread of knowledge, as well as moral discussion and political propaganda. Ideas have a momentum of their own; they are partly primary causes in the social process;

[1] See Chapter VII, Section 3, page 134.

or rather, they are integral factors in an interdependent system of causation.

In a catharsis of opinions—of an individual or a group—a new, temporary, and labile equilibrium of conflicting valuations is established. The direction in a normal and peaceful process of popular education is toward decreasing inconsistency. We said that ordinarily the new balance gives greater weight to the more general valuations. But our reason for the conclusion was that those valuations were generally agreed to be morally 'higher' and to have supreme social sanction, and we added the reservation that our conclusion assumes that moral cynicism does not spread. If moral cynicism should spread, however—that is, if people became willing to throw aside even their most cherished general valuations, such as their faith in democratic liberty, equality, and Christian brotherhood—the situation would permit almost any type of reconstruction. Instead of a rebirth of democracy and Christianity such that those terms acquire new personal meanings for every individual, there may be a revulsion to fascism and pagan gods.

When a sudden and great catharsis of opinions occurs in society, customs and social trends seem to the participants to be suspended or radically changed, as they actually are to a certain extent. In this sense history is indeterminate; it can take several courses. Ideological forces take on a greater importance. Leaders—whom we call either 'statesmen', 'thinkers' and 'prophets' or 'demagogues' and 'charlatans', depending upon our valuation of their aims and means—capture the attention of the masses and manage to steer the upheaval in one direction or the other. On a smaller scale the same occurs in every group at all times, and the 'leaders' are legion; in a sense we are all 'leaders'. In the explanation of this type of process, where ideological factors, together with all other factors, are active forces within an interdependent system of causation, the materialistic conception of history breaks down. Indeed, any mechanical philosophy of human dynamics is inadequate— except when looking backwards, because in looking backwards, *any* development can be organized into *any* scheme, if it is general enough.

Before leaving the subject of social dynamics, we must

qualify our remarks to recognize the existence of social statics. By stressing the instability of valuations we do not deny that there is an enormous amount of resistance to change. There *is* a great deal of practically mechanistic causation in human life, almost completely divorced from valuations. People do strive to keep their valuation conflicts under control. They want to keep them off their minds, and they are trained to overlook them. Conventions, stereotypes, and convenient blind spots in knowledge about social reality succeed in preserving a relative peace in people's conscience. Even more important, perhaps, is the fact that there are only a few hours a day free from the business of living, and that there are so many 'pleasant' things to do during these few hours. Most people, most of the time, live a routine life from day to day and do not worry too much. If it could be measured, the amount of both simple and opportune ignorance and unconcernedness about social affairs would undoubtedly be greater than the amount of knowledge and concern.

But to stress these things is not to invalidate the dynamic theory we have presented. Modern people *do* have conflicting valuations, and the spread of knowledge and the increase of interrelations *are* more and more exposing them. Changes in the material environment also keep minds from becoming settled. If we call the relative absence of change in modern society 'stability', we must recognise that it is not such as is envisaged in the theory of the folkways and mores. There is *instability* at bottom, a *balancing of forces in conflict with each other*, and there is continuously the possibility of rapid, and even induced, change, the direction of which is not altogether predetermined by trends and natural forces.

4. THE EMPIRICAL STUDY OF VALUATIONS AND BELIEFS[1]

The paramount importance attached to observing and measuring valuations and beliefs in the Negro problem by means of scientifically controlled research must be clear from the Introduction to this book. Unfortunately the results of quantitative studies of opinions and attitudes regarding this aspect of

[1] From *An American Dilemma*, Appendix 10.

the Negro problem are meagre. The most general conclusion from a survey of the existing studies regarding the relation between valuations and beliefs is that they have not added anything significant to our knowledge. They have not yet succeeded in quantifying our general common-sense notions on the subject. The main explanation is undoubtedly that, until now, not much work has been done in this particular field.[1]

Another general defect is that the studies which have been made usually have been planned in isolation from both the general social study of the Negro and the political battle about his status. They have, therefore, not had a perspective which gives relevance to the questions asked, and they have not been prepared by the working out of consistent schemes of scientific hypotheses. This is the more natural and, indeed, the more defensible, since the studies carried out have usually had an experimental character and have been more concerned with perfecting the tools of measurement than with the conclusions to be obtained. In the main this holds true also of the mass public opinion polls. Particularly when asking Negroes for their opinions—but also when asking whites for theirs on the Negro problem—there are a number of purely technical difficulties which have not yet been overcome.

Instead of indulging in further negative criticism, we shall develop briefly certain positive suggestions for opinion research as they have arisen in our study of the Negro problem. At the outset it should be remembered that an average opinion in regard to the Negro problem, as does every other opinion, contains two elements which are of different character: (1) beliefs concerning reality which can be true or untrue, complete or incomplete; (2) valuations of an actual or hypothetical reality which can vary in intensity, clarity, and homogeneity but in themselves are neither complete nor incomplete, neither true nor untrue. There are, of course, opinions which are only

[1] It should be clear that our statement does *not* apply to the whole range of attitude and public opinion measurement, but solely to this activity regarding the Negro problem. The measurement of attitudes and public opinion has contributed much both to scientific and to practical knowledge outside the Negro problem, and is now showing amazingly rapid advancement in present achievement and tremendous possibilities for future achievement.

beliefs or only valuations. But more usually, opinions are combinations of both: on the one hand, beliefs are, as we have seen, nearly always influenced by the valuations for which they serve as rationalizations (which in logical terms means that they are 'biased'), and, on the other hand, beliefs influence valuations.

Reacting to the earlier schools of rationalistic psychology, several decades ago we became so impressed by the fact that people did not act and think rationally that a tradition became established not to split opinions into two components relating to the cognitive and to the volitional sides of mental processes. This is part of the background for the present loose usage of the word 'attitude' as a scientific term.[1] In many questionnaires one can find questions concerning knowledge, concerning almost pure valuations, and concerning both combined—all these three types mixed together without distinction. The subsequent analysis does not take into account the difference between them. Such a differentiation is of great importance, however, since a study of people's beliefs throws light not only on what they know or do not know but, in addition, on the structure of their entire sphere of valuations.

The fact that people's beliefs, unlike their valuations, can be directly judged by the objective criteria of correctness and completeness offers us a clue for analysing scientifically the complexes of struggling valuations that exist in the minds of people. It is a sound hypothesis that, since the beliefs of men serve an opportunistic function, both the direction and the degree of their deviation from 'objective' knowledge will tell us how people are trying to reconcile their valuations on a lower plane, implicit in their daily behaviour, with the more general valuations which are recognized as morally higher in our society. From this point of view, it becomes of great importance to chart quantitatively people's knowledge and ignorance on controversial subjects. For this purpose the questions to be utilized in certain types of opinion studies should be purged as far as possible of all valuations; they should test only the respondent's conception of this particular

---

[1] As used by Thomas and Znaniecki in *The Polish Peasant*, the term ' attitude ' was a part of the reaction against the complete irrationalism emphasized by the instinctivist and behaviourist schools.

part of reality. It is fairly easy to prepare a standard norm of what represents objective knowledge; in the many problems where we are still ignorant or hesitant, consciousness of our ignorance constitutes true knowledge. For testing knowledge as to its degree of completeness, some sort of graduated scale can be worked out with the help of available techniques.

If properly carried out, such a study of factual knowledge regarding the Negro problem—differentiated in relation to certain main axes: white-Negro, North-South, urban-rural, social class, education, sex, age—would be revealing. Its practical importance for education is obvious. It will also have great theoretical importance in explaining white people's behaviour with respect to Negroes. The hypothesis is that we are not facing a question merely of more or less meagre and incorrect knowledge. There is an emotional load of valuation conflicts pressing for rationalization, creating certain blind spots—and also creating a desire for knowledge in other spots— and in general causing conceptions of reality to deviate from truth in determined directions. If such an analysis of the degree of knowledge and ignorance and also of their localization and concrete character is carried out, the valuations and their conflicts can be recorded indirectly but quantitatively—just as the heat of distant stars is measured by observing their spectra. From our inquiry into the Negro problem we are convinced that ignorance is *not* always simple; it is often opportune.[1]

But the valuations should, of course, also be studied directly.

[1] As examples of how opportune ignorance and knowledge may be, it might be pointed out that Negroes are amazingly sophisticated with respect to the incidence of indirect taxation and the environmental influences on intelligence test scores. Even ordinary Negroes with little formal schooling can explain to the satisfaction of the economist just how taxes on real estate are passed on to the tenant, and can often do better than the trained psychologist in revealing just how lack of incentive and intellectual stimulation can keep intelligence tests from revealing 'innate ability'. It is apparent that the reason Negroes know these things is that they have been victimized by indirect taxation and the intelligence tests—that is, it is claimed that Negroes pay practically no taxes, because they pay practically no *direct* taxes, and that they are biologically inferior because their I.Q. scores are lower. It is apparent, too, that whites—especially the dominant ones, the ones who pay direct taxes and who have, or think they have, high I.Q. scores—have an opportune ignorance with respect to these things. Even when simple facts are presented to ruffle their ignorance, they reject them.

For this purpose questions should be selected which relate to opinions that do not contain any reference to reality. A main consideration in the analysis of answers to such questions should be that valuations are complex and ordinarily conflicting, and that an individual's focusing of attention in the valuation sphere may be opportune. In most cases the indirect analysis of the valuation sphere, through the study of the deviations of beliefs from true knowledge, is likely to reach deeper than does the direct analysis. An individual continually tends to arrange his valuations so that they may be presented in an acceptable form. But in his beliefs concerning social reality— which are shaped to give the appearance of rational organization to his morals—he reveals himself.

5. 'PERSONAL' AND 'POLITICAL' OPINIONS

When studying valuations there is another distinction the observance of which is of utmost significance in the Negro problem as in other problems where human valuations are sharply conflicting, namely, the distinction between a person's 'private', or 'personal', opinion and his 'public', or 'political', opinion on the same question.[1] They do not need to agree; in fact they seldom agree. This, in itself, is a reason for a clear distinction to be upheld, since otherwise a major source of systematic error is contained in the observations. A further reason is that the very registration and measuring of this difference is an important part of an opinion analysis.

A man's opinion as to the desirable size of a normal family might be totally different, on the one hand, when he faces the problem as a citizen taking a stand on the population issue

---

[1] There has been much discussion about the distinction between 'opinion' and 'attitude', with the assumption that the former is measurable while the latter is not and that the former is a mere verbalization while the latter directs action. Our distinction between personal and political opinions is different, and should not be confused with the distinction between opinion and attitude. It is no easier to measure political opinions than personal opinions; both direct action—although different kinds of action; and one is no more a mere verbalization than is the other.

Schanck has attempted to investigate statistically the distinction between public and private attitudes, although without relation to the Negro. (R. L. Schanck, 'A Study of a Community and Its Groups and Institutions Conceived of as Behaviours of Individuals,' *Psychological Monographs* (1932).)

if this is brought to the political forefront, and, on the other hand, when he faces his own family limitation problem.[1] Exactly the same thing is true in the Negro problem. Many white people would be prepared to stand for and practise changed relations to Negroes *if* they were made the common rule in society, while they are not prepared to practise them as exceptions to the rule. Some of the apparent confusion and contradiction in nearly every individual's attitude to the Negro problem becomes explainable by applying this distinction.[2]

Part of the actual differences between personal and political attitudes is *rational*. The very aim of a person's political opinion is to ask for and, eventually, to cause such institutional changes in society that the circumstances under which he lives and forms his personal opinions are modified, and, consequently, to change his personal behaviour and attitudes also. A positive stand on the political population question—say a demand that the average non-sterile marriage produce four children—may be the centre of a complex of political opinions demanding legal and economic changes in the family institution. There is no contradiction between a four-child norm in one's political opinion and, say, a two-child norm in one's personal opinion and actual family limitation behaviour.

[1] See Gunnar Myrdal, *Population : A Problem for Democracy* (1940), Chapter 5, 'People's Opinions,' particularly pp. 106 ff. and 115 ff.

[2] The distinction between public and private attitudes also comes out with regard to what one will or will not admit with respect to the Negro. Baker tells a story which illustrates this aspect of the distinction. It is from '. . . the discussions of the Alabama legislature then in session. A compulsory education bill had been introduced; the problem was to pass a law that would apply to white people, not to Negroes. In this connection I heard a significant discussion in the state senate. I use the report of it, for accuracy, as given the next morning in the *Advertiser:*

' "Senator Thomas said . . . he would oppose any bills that would compel Negroes to educate their children, for it had come to his knowledge that Negroes would give the clothing off their backs to send their children to school, while too often the white man, secure in his supremacy, would be indifferent to his duty.

' "At this point Senator Lusk arose excitedly to his feet and said:

' " 'Does the Senator from Barbour mean to say that the Negro race is more ambitious and has more aspirations than the white race ? '

' " 'The question of the gentleman . . . is an insult to the senate of Alabama,' replied Senator Thomas deliberately. 'It is an insult to the great Caucasian race, the father of all the arts and sciences, to compare it to that black and kinky race which lived in a state of black and ignorant savagery until the white race seized it and lifted it to its present position.' " ' (Ray Stannard Baker, *Following the Colour Line* (1908), p. 248.)

Value in Social Theory

Similarly in the Negro problem. In numerous conversations with white Americans in the North and in the South, the observer is informed by the man he talks to that he himself would be prepared to act in such and such a way different from his ordinary behaviour *if* society, the local community, or 'public opinion' did not react in such and such a way; and, second, that he would favour this and this social change implying such and such alterations of the caste relations in society, although he is not prepared to live up to those alterations as an individual *unless* the social changes are first carried out. It should be noticed that political opinions are thus regularly of a conditional character and that they usually refer to a more distant future. There are few white Americans even in the South who do not declare themselves in favour of much more equality for the Negro in politics, education, and everything else—but they want them far in the future when certain conditions are changed. (The inconsistency in their attitudes often consists only in their being unwilling to do anything—even in the political sphere and often least of all there—to change those conditions.) Generally, it can be assumed that being able to keep more of a rational and conscious distinction and relation between one's personal and political opinions is a function (1) of education and intelligence on the part of the individual, (2) of his identification with society (being a 'good citizen'), and (3) of his training to think of himself as a would-be legislator, that is, as a participant in inducing the social change.

But part of this difference between personal and political opinions is *irrational*, and there is then inadequate intellectual connection between the two. In many countries, again to use an illustration from the population problem, it is possible to prove statistically that a large number of people who publicly condemn birth control as immoral and who back legislative measures to prohibit it, must practise it privately. In the Negro problem there are equally flagrant contradictions between people's opinions about how society ought to be and the opinions whereby they defend their own daily behaviour.

CHAPTER SIX

ENCOUNTERING THE NEGRO PROBLEM[1]

1. On the Minds of the Whites

WHEN we say that there is a Negro *problem* in America, what we mean is that the Americans are worried about it. It is on their minds and on their consciences. To begin with, the Negro is a problem to himself. If a multitude of first-hand random observations, such as we have made over the whole country, are any evidence, the contented Negro, whose mind is at peace on the race issue, is a rare phenomenon. As a generalization he is definitely a myth. Whether the myth was ever wholly true in the past, I cannot say. It is evident, however, that for a long time the Negro protest has been rising. This trend became sharply accentuated during the First World War. The present War will, in all probability, increase the Negroes' discontent with their status in America.

The Negro problem is working on the white man's mind too, even, and not least, when he wants to convince himself and others that it is settled for all time. The problem has varying degrees of importance in different regions, depending partly on their historical backgrounds and on the relative proportion of Negroes in their populations, as also in different social classes and under different religious, educational and ideological influences. Over large areas of America where there are few or no Negroes, the Negro problem is of minor importance to the people living there. To these ordinary white Americans, the only reason why the Negro problem has a higher salience than, say, the problem of British imperialism in India, or, earlier, the Irish question, is their citizenship in the United States, and consequently, their feeling of national responsibility. The

[1] From *An American Dilemma*, Chapter 2.

frequent reminders in the press and in public discussions of the practice of lynching and the agitation around the proposed anti-lynching legislation, the reports of Negro criminality, the continuous recollections of discrimination in education and in the labour market, and just now the public discomfort around the racial angle of both the larger world conflict and the war efforts at home—all constantly actualize to some degree this feeling of responsibility.

This national participation in the Negro problem should not be exaggerated. Neither should it be minimized. It is the writer's conclusion that even in those Northern states with few Negroes, the Negro problem is always present though relatively quiescent. Nearly everybody in America is prepared to discuss the issue, and almost nobody is entirely without opinions on it. The opinions vary. They may be vague and hesitating or even questioning, or they may be hardened and articulate. But few Americans are unaware of the Negro problem.

So it seems always to have been. Wandering around the stacks of a good American library, one is amazed at the huge amount of printed material on the Negro problem. A really complete bibliography would run to several hundred thousand titles.[1] Nobody has ever mastered this material exhaustively, and probably nobody ever will. The intellectual energy spent on the Negro problem in America would, if concentrated in a single direction, have moved mountains.

This does not imply that the Negro problem approaches the status of a dominant issue. It is not now a main divider of opinions in national politics, although it was so in the decades before and after the Civil War. There were other periods in American history, however, when it was in the background, perhaps never so much as in the decades before the First World War. But as a secondary problem and as a peculiar influence on all the dominant national issues, it has always held a rank among the most conspicuous. Through the generations, it has disturbed the religious moralists, the political philosophers, the

---

[1] It is interesting to note that the first books having the term 'sociology' in their titles were almost exclusively concerned with the Negro problem: (1) George Fitzhugh, *Sociology for the South* (1854); (2) Henry Hughes, *Treatise on Sociology: Theoretical and Practical* (1854).

statesmen, the philanthropists, the social scientists, the politicians, the businessmen and the plain citizens.

A number of factors underlie the present trends—such as the danger of continued and, after the Second World War, intensified economic dislocation with its serious effects on Negro employment; the rising tension around democracy as a form of government and a way of life; and, finally, the rising educational level and intensified group consciousness and discontent of the Negro people themselves. All this makes it probable that the Negro problem in America is again going to mount high in relative importance among national issues.

2. TO THE NEGROES THEMSELVES

To the Negro himself, the problem is all-important. A Negro probably seldom talks to a white man, and still less to a white woman, without consciousness of this problem. Even in a mixed white and Negro group of closest friends in Northern intellectual circles, and probably even in an all-Negro group, the Negro problem constantly looms in the background of social intercourse. It steers the jokes and the allusions, if it is not one of the dominant topics of conversation. As an inescapable overtone in social relations, 'race' is probably just as strong as sex—even in those most emancipated American environments where apparently sex is relatively released and 'race' is suppressed.

The Negro leader, the Negro social scientist, the Negro man of art and letters is disposed to view all social, economic, political, indeed, even æsthetic and philosophical issues from the Negro angle. What is more, he is expected to do so. He would seem entirely out of place if he spoke simply as a member of a community, a citizen of America or as a man of the world. In the existing American civilization he can grow to a degree of distinction, but always as a representative of 'his people', not as an ordinary American or an individual in humanity. He might protest; if he does it for the proper audience and in the proper forms, he is allowed to protest: but he protests as a Negro. He can criticize, but only as a Negro defending Negro interests. This is the social role awarded him, and he cannot step out of it. He is defined as a 'race man' regardless of the role he might wish to choose for himself. He cannot publicly argue about collective bargaining generally in America, the need of a national budgetary reform, monetary schemes for world organization, moral philosophies and æsthetic principles.

Even if originally he should have had the interests and the aptitudes for wider knowledge and a broader career, the pressure of this expectancy on the part of society conditions his personality and forces him, willy-nilly, into the role of a Negro champion. This expectancy is entrenched in all institutions in American society, including universities, learned societies and foundations. It animates even the staunchest friends and protectors of the Negro minority, often, indeed, for the reason that the Negroes sorely need their leadership. The same expectancy of their leaders is shared by the Negro people. The Negro leader, sensing that his own people need him and conscious that his racial origin offers him an easy opportunity for a role in life, thus acquires his characteristic direction. Even women in modern times do not have their souls so pressed into one single narrow furrow of human interests by the tyrannic expectancy of society, although the women's lot in this, as in many other respects, offers the nearest analogy. The Negro genius is imprisoned in the Negro problem. There is throughout the entire history of the United States no single example of an exception to this rule important enough to be cited.[1]

[1] Possible exceptions are a few natural scientists, such as Ernest E. Just, and a few celebrities, such as Joe Louis. But even they, when they reach national top standards, and probably before that, are forced to become representatives of their 'race'.

George S. Schuyler, a prominent columnist, gives the Negro point of view in his recent criticism of the white press for its 'sinister policy of identifying Negro individuals as such':

'This is a subtle form of discrimination designed to segregate these individuals in the mind of the public and thus bolster the national polity of bi-racialism. Thus Paul Robeson is not a great baritone, he is a great "Negro" baritone. Dr. Carver is not just a great scientist, he is a great "Negro" scientist. Anne Brown is not merely a great soprano, she is a great "Negro" soprano. Langston Hughes is not a poet merely, he is a "Negro" poet. Augusta Savage is a "Negro" sculptor, C. C. Spaulding is a "Negro" insurance executive, R. R. Wright, Sr., is a "Negro" banker, J. A. Rogers is a "Negro" historian, Willard Townsend is a "Negro" labour leader, etc., etc., *ad infinitum* . . . No other group in this country is so singled out for racial identification, and no one can tell me that there is not a very definite reason for it.

The difference in this respect between the Negro and other 'racial' minorities—the Jews, for example—is notable. The difference is not explainable simply in terms of differences in natural and cultural abilities between the two groups. A Jewish economist is not expected to be a specialist on Jewish labour. A Jewish sociologist is not assumed to confine himself always to studying the Ghetto. A Jewish singer is not doomed eternally to perform Jewish folk songs. A Jew is not out of place either as a governor of a state or as a planner of world reconstruction. The Jew is discriminated against in America, but there is a quantitative difference between this and the discrimination against the Negro which is so great that it becomes qualitative. On the intellectual level, which we are now discussing, the fettering of the Negro spirit within the Negro problem is not accomplished so much by simple discrimination as by the prejudice inherent even in the most friendly but restrictive expectancy, including the expectancy of the Negro people.

So far we have been commenting on the fate of those rare persons with extraordinary talents who, if any, should have both the intellectual strength and the opportunities to break out of the prison of the Negro problem. To the ordinary members of the Negro upper and middle class, even the window shutters of the prison are closed. It will be the theme of following

No daily newspaper refers to Mr. Morgenthau as "Jewish" Secretary of the Treasury, or New York's Herbert H. Lehman as the "Jewish" governor, or Isador Lubin as a "Jewish" New Dealer. Mayor Rossi is never identified as the "Italian-American" executive of San Francisco, nor is the millionaire Giannini called an "Italian" banker. There would be considerable uproar if Senator Robert F. Wagner were termed "New York's able German-American Solon," or Representative Tenerowicz dubbed "Detroit's prominent Pole". When has a Utah legislator in Washington been labelled "Mormon"?

'One could go and on, but the point is that "our" daily newspapers carefully avoid such designations except in the case of so-called Negroes. I cannot recall when I have seen a criminal referred to as a Jew, an Italian, a German or a Catholic, but it is commonplace for coloured lawbreakers or suspects to be labelled "Negro".

'Personally, I shall not be convinced of the sincerity of these white editors and columnists who shape America's thinking unless and until they begin treating the Negro in the news as they do other Americans. Those who continue this type of journalism are the worst sort of hypocrites when they write about democracy and national unity.' (Pittsburgh *Courier*, June 13, 1942.

Schuyler's point is perfectly clear and his description of the situation correct—except that he does not care to mention that Negro newspapers are, if possible, more unfailing in giving prominent Negroes their 'race label.'

chapters to show in some detail how Negro preachers, teachers, professionals, and businessmen have had to build their whole economic and social existence on the basis of the segregation of their people, in response to the dictates of the white society. To state the situation bluntly: these upper class Negroes are left free to earn their living and their reputation in the back-water of discrimination, but they are not free to go into the main current of the river itself. On the one hand, they are kept fully aware of the wider range of opportunities from which they are excluded by segregation and discrimination. On the other hand, they know equally well how they are sheltered by the monopoly left to them in their little world apart. In their whole outlook on life and society they are forced into an impossible and tragic dilemma.

The masses of the Negro people, however, unlike the more advantaged leaders, professionals, and businessmen, derive almost none of the compensatory gains from the caste system. They sense how they are hampered and enclosed behind the walls of segregation and discrimination more acutely than might be expected.

They do not usually spend too much of their mental energy on theorizing over the Negro problem. Their days are filled with toil and more personal troubles and pleasures. But, as we shall find, in most of these varied activities, the Negro problem enters as a loud overtone. It is heard in church, in school, in the work place, in the play yard and on the street. They, too, are imprisoned in the Negro problem.

The broad masses of Negroes are also enclosed in the prison as effectively by the restrictive expectancy of their friends as by the persecutions of their enemies.

The patronising attitude is really more damning than the competitive struggle. The stone wall of calm assumption of his inferiority is to the Negro a keener hurt and a greater obstacle than the battle which admits an adversary worth fighting against. It is hard to keep ambition alive and to maintain morale when those for whom you have fondness and respect keep thinking and saying that you are only children, that you can never grow up, that you are cast by God in an inferior mould.[1]

[1] E. R. Embree, *Brown America* (1931), p. 205.

The late James Weldon Johnson sums up this situation of the Negro people in the following way:

And this is the dwarfing, warping, distorting influence which operates upon each and every coloured man in the United States. He is forced to take his outlook on all things, not from the view-point of a citizen, or a man, or even a human being, but from the view-point of a *coloured* man. It is wonderful to me that the race has progressed so broadly as it has, since most of its thought and all of its activity must run through the narrow neck of this one funnel.[1]

3. Explaining the Problem Away

To the white Americans the possibilities of keeping the Negro problem out of their minds are, naturally, greater and, in addition, they have certainly good selfish reasons for keeping it below the level of consciousness. To be sure, it was a not unusual experience of the writer to be told confidently sometimes by the learned, but most often by the laity, that there is 'no Negro problem' in America and that, if there ever was one, it is solved and settled for all time and to the full satisfaction of both parties. Everything is quiet on the racial front. We think the Negroes are all right in their place; and they on their part do not want things changed. In fact, they are the happiest lot on earth. Just look at them: how they laugh and enjoy themselves; how they sing and praise the Lord.

This attitude was met most frequently and expressed most emphatically in the Deep South. It was often maliciously added that there was surely a Negro problem in the North, but only because the Yankees have not yet learned to know the Negro and how to keep him in his proper place. The situation, if true, would certainly deserve to be called paradoxical: The Negroes would be least of a problem to the whites in the regions where they are most numerous. They would show up among the human and national worries, though certainly not as a principal one, of a Minnesota farmer who never sees

---

[1] James Weldon Johnson, *The Autobiography of an Ex-Coloured Man* (1927; first edition, 1912), p. 21.

Negroes, but be no problem at all to the Southern planter who works them in scores and is always surrounded by them.

All this is not true, of course. A contrary statement, that the white South is virtually obsessed by the Negro problem, that the South has allowed the Negro problem to rule its politics and its business, fetter its intelligence and human liberties, and hamper its progress in all directions, would be nearer the truth.[1] A brilliant Northerner, Frank Tannenbaum,[2] has taken up this thought and, presumably fully in earnest, suggested, as the only hope of solving the Southern problem, that the Southerners get other worries to keep their minds off the Negro: they should get labour troubles, try to get immigrants and develop a complex at home against white 'foreigners', and generally get some real issues into their petty politics. This might be carrying an idea to an extreme for educational purposes, but certainly there is a kernel of sense in it.

Apart from the few intellectuals of pronounced liberal leanings, however, statements to the effect that there really is no Negro problem have become part of the common stock of stereotyped opinions in the South, and they are not entirely absent from the North. But such statements cover a volcanic ground of doubt, disagreement, concern, and even anxiety—of moral tension and need for escape and defence. To furnish such a covering is, from a psychological point of view, their very 'function'. The prevalence of such opinions and the intensity with which they are expressed might serve as an index of the latent inter-racial tension felt in the white world.

The usefulness of this escape rationalization has a limit, however. The limit is reached when overt inter-racial struggles appear. The notion of 'no Negro problem' is then suddenly transformed into an alarming awareness that the contrary is so. This contrary reaction can be invoked experimentally, simply by directing attention to the potentialities of conflict. Particularly when talking to people among the poorer classes

[1] See Edgar G. Murphy, *Problems of the Present South* (1909; first edition, 1904), especially pp. 188 ff. and Chapter 8; also Jonathan Daniels, *A Southerner Discovers the South* (1938), Chapter 35; and Thomas P. Bailey, *Race Orthodoxy in the South* (1914), especially pp. 341 ff., pp. 368 ff. and p. 380, also William Jenkins, *Pro-Slavery Thought in the Old South* (1935), pp. vii-viii.

[2] *Darker Phases of the South* (1924), pp. 157 ff.

of whites with less intellectual control over their thoughts and feelings, the writer has repeatedly observed the most flagrant contradictions on this point, sometimes appearing within the same sentence. A white Southerner can defend, for instance, the suppression of the Negroes by saying that they are satisfied with their status and lack a desire for change. Without any intermediate remarks, he can then proceed to explain that suppression is necessary, that Negroes must be kept down by all means, and that Negroes have an ineradicable craving to be like white people. Attempts on the part of the interlocutor to draw attention to the contradiction have seldom succeeded.

Some light might be thrown on this state of mind of many American whites by observing the different state of mind of the Negroes. The Negroes cannot, of course, feel an equivalent need for this special type of self-defence, that there is 'no Negro problem', which in the white world is a defence against one's own thoughts and feelings and the opinions of other whites. Actually, it often happened that the writer was told by Negroes in the South that race relations in their part of the country offered no particular difficulties and were not much of a problem. White people present at such pronouncements took great pleasure in the corroboration of their own statements. It would seem that such statements from Negro leaders are part of the moral tribute expected from those leaders at all public inter-racial affairs, such as school festivals, programmes of entertainment centred around Negro singers, inter-church meetings, and other occasions where white representatives are present. That the Negroes should be allowed to voice complaints, even though only in a cautious tone, constituted the radical departure in the innovation of inter-racial commissions after the First World War. Their meetings are between the 'best people of the two races', and are typically not open to the general public.

Statements that inter-racial relations are good thus belong in the South to the etiquette of Negro college presidents, principals and teachers of Negro schools, and all other Negroes enjoying upper or middle class status under the sanction of the power of appointment and dismissal in the hands of white boards or officials. They are also widely accepted as a way of getting along

97

by a considerable number of Negro preachers and by the handful of thriving and successful Negro businessmen. In return, these persons are allowed much leeway, particularly in the Upper South. These sentiments are sometimes also expressed by Negro professionals who are aware of the local requirements for successful leadership.

But, even in these cases, the statements that there is 'no Negro problem' have an easily detected difference in tone when pronounced by Negroes. To begin with, they are usually restricted expressly to the local community, and often qualified by certain reservations as to this or that which might need improvement, while the corresponding white pronouncements are mostly broad and absolute in character. They are, further, as a defence mechanism, primarily directed against provoking the suspicions of the other group. They are, finally, not to be taken too seriously. The writer repeatedly made the observation, both in the Deep South and in the Upper South, as well as in the North, that a Negro seldom took this position when talking freely and when there was no point in hiding his real feelings.

The difference between the two groups, with respect to the recognition of the Negro problem, corresponds, of course, to the fundamental fact that the white group is above and the Negro group is below, that the one is intent upon preserving the *status quo*, while the other wants change and relief from the pressure of the dominant group. The one group is tempted to convince itself and others that there is 'no problem'. The other group has a contrary interest to see clearly and even make visible to others the existence of a real problem. This latter group may be hushed by fear or opportunistic calculations. These calculations can, of course, be of the most respectable character; indeed, they often are part of the cautious Negro patriot's wise policy of trying to safeguard his people from needless sufferings and to gain favours for them from the dominating white group. But, in any case, the explanation is not to be sought in such deep-seated internal tensions as with the white people. The Negro's rationalization, when it is articulated, is likely to be much more overt and, indeed, sometimes cynically so. It has not the same character of a self-deceiving defence construction against one's own moral feelings.

4. EXPLORATIONS IN ESCAPE

In a big city in the Deep South I was once taken by a friend
to an upper class club for a social luncheon party. The conversation turned around world affairs, the business trend, art,
literature and some personal gossiping; the tone was most
congenial and free, perhaps even carefree, and had the dis-
tinctive mark of sceptical open-mindedness which accompan-
ies social confidence and a lifelong experience of unhampered
cultural opportunities. Near the intended end of the party,
my friend announced the peculiar reason for my being in
America at the present time and invited the company to
tell me their frank opinions on the Negro problem.

For a moment a somewhat awkward silence descended
upon our party, a queer feeling that our relation of human
understanding was broken. An illusion was shattered. Here
we had all been behaving on the understanding that we were
men of the world, members of that select cosmopolitan
fellowship which senses no strong local ties and whose minds
meet in most broad topics of general and human interest;
and then suddenly my friend had violated this understanding
by addressing all the others as a local fraternity sharing a
dark secret together, while I was marked off as the stranger
peeping in on them and their secret, the Negro problem.

The situation most urgently had to be redefined. The responsibility was shouldered by an elderly, very distinguished
doctor. He made a short speech (the discussion had suddenly
turned very formal) to the effect that in the South there was
'no Negro problem'; a static equilibrium had been reached,
and was going to remain, and it fitted the situation as a glove
fits the hand. More particularly, he went on, the relations
between the two races in the South corresponded to their inherited abilities and aptitudes. A long time ago those relations
had been stratified into 'folkways and mores', known and
respected by both races and taken for granted, or rather as
self-evident, in view of the inferior endowments of the African
race and the superior qualities of the Anglo-Saxon master
race. The doctor ended up by pointing out that it was, in
fact, inherent in this very notion of 'mores', that they could
never be questioned or disputed or even consciously analysed.

There could, indeed, by definition, never be a 'problem' concerning the mores of society. The very question was nonsensical. The mores were the ground everybody walked upon, the axioms of social life, even more unquestioned than the religious truths and for more substantial psychological reasons.

The doctor finished. Everybody agreed, and there was really nothing in the issue to discuss. The few moments' stress was eased, and a measure of congeniality again restored. I then reflected that the South was, as I was finding out, now on the way to giving the Negroes a real chance in education. I referred to the continuous improvement of public schools even for Negroes and to the growing number of Negro youths who were permitted to acquire a higher education of a kind, even in the South. It had occurred to me, I continued, that this trend in education—leaving many other primary causes of change unmentioned—represented a dynamic factor of cumulative importance. If it was given time, and if the direct and indirect effects in all spheres of life were allowed to accumulate, the resultant social change might finally attain a momentum where it could seriously challenge, or at least move quite a bit, the 'folkways and mores' our doctor had rooted so firmly, not only in tradition, but in the very nature of things and particularly in the biology of the races. Yes, it might make it difficult to keep the Negro in his place. It might, for instance, make it much less easy to hold him disfranchised; in all certainty it would soon render obsolete one of the principal arguments and constitutional instruments for denying him the ballot— namely, his illiteracy.

After this remark, I did not need to say anything more for the next hour or two but could lean back and listen to one of the most revealing and most ably performed, though sometimes heated, intellectual debates on the Negro problem in America I had heard up till then, or even heard thereafter. This was not a theatre performance staged for my benefit; the arguments were too well considered and reasoned to be suspected of being improvised for the occasion; I was, indeed, happily forgotten most of the time. There was genuine concern, and there was serious disagreement. Professor Sumner's theory of folkways and mores had evaporated into the thinnest nothing; even the doctor never said a word more about the mystically unproblematic 'mores'. At the end I had the opportunity to restore good feeling between the debaters in a roar of understanding laughter when I closed my thanks for Southern hospitality with the observation that apparently they seemed to have a most disturbing Negro problem on their minds down in the Old South.

A situation in the Negro world parallel to this experience showing how the problem burns under the cover of a placid stereotype was given me in one of the very first weeks of my study of the Negro problem in America. When I and my Swedish associate (accompanied on this occasion by a white friend of the Negro people, a professor at a Southern university) visited a Negro leader prominent in banking and insurance in a city of the Upper South, he had kindly arranged for a gathering in his office of a group of about thirty Negro gentlemen of upper class status, representing business, church, university and professions. One of his subordinates had been given the function of relating statistics on the progress of Negro business in America. He fulfilled his task with much ability and eloquence. The figures sometimes rose to millions and hundreds of millions and, nevertheless, were presented to the last unit; they marched along solemnly and created an illusion of greatness and success. The lecture ended up in a cheerful and challenging mood. All had listened as to a sermon and felt duly elevated.

This spirit prevailed until I happened to touch off some of the unfortunate realities so guardedly concealed within the statistical house of cards that had just been erected. I referred to the facts that one of the white companies alone had more Negro insurance business than all the Negro companies together, while the latter had practically no white business at all; that Negro banking had a rather serious record of bankruptcies; that Negroes were practically excluded from all production and wholesale trade; that they controlled only an inconsiderable fraction of retail trade even in the Negro consumers' market and practically none in the white market.

My remarks were formulated as questions, and I was hoping for some discussion. But I had never expected the tumultuous and agitated controversy which, much to the embarrassment of our dignified host, broke loose. The comforting unanimity a few minutes before was suddenly decomposed into the wide and glaring spectrum of American Negro ideologies, bearing not only on business but on all other aspects of life as well. All possible opinions were vented in a debate where seldom one spoke at a time, ranging from an old-fashioned revolution demanding violent resistance and aggression by force against the white suppressors, on the infra-red end, to a pious religious plea, voiced by an elderly preacher, for endurance, forbearance, and patience under the sufferings, on the ultra-violet end.

As these two occurrences exemplify, the artificially constructed escapist consensus is liable to crash if pushed from the outside. It is inherent in the situation, however, that such pushes do not originate from inside, or, if they do, that an attempt is made to canalize them safely. An unstable equilibrium is retained and actually believed to be stable.

I once visited an art exhibition in one of the cultural centres of the Old South where everything from the city plan to the interests and manners of the people carries the cherished memories of the romantic, glorious past. Among the exhibits was a man-sized sculpture in terra cotta called 'Soldier in Rain', representing a Negro man lynched by hanging. The piece was forcefully done; and, as I thought, a real masterpiece. The hanging man was clothed only in a shirt and a pair of trousers tightly stretched around the body by the rain. On the chest there was a medal affixed to the shirt; a raindrop was suspended under the medal. I was absorbed in admiring the sculpture with two ladies who were supervising the exhibition. They were true experts in art appreciation, and had kindly followed me around and told me many things which I could not otherwise have seen for myself.

Quite unintentionally I happened to refer to the sculpture as representing a lynching. My hostesses immediately reacted as to a shock and explained eagerly that I was totally mistaken. The sculpture represented a soldier being hanged, probably behind the front for some offence, a soldier *in abstracto*, 'just any soldier'. It had nothing to do with the Negro problem. They were bent on convincing me that I was wrong; they mentioned that none of all the thousands of visitors to the exhibition had ever hinted at the possibility that the sculpture represented a lynched Negro and eagerly showed me newspaper clippings with reviews where the sculpture was discussed in terms of 'a soldier', 'a simple soldier', 'a soldier behind the line'. I answered that soldiers were never anywhere executed by hanging either at or behind the line, and that in the whole world hanging was, in the popular conception, which is the important thing for an artist, usually associated with the English custom of hanging petty thieves and with American lynching parties. I was even brought to point out that the sculptor had endowed the hanged man with the long limbs and facial characteristics commonly ascribed to the Negro race. But no arguments had any weight. I am convinced that they sincerely believed they were right, and I preposterously wrong. The visit ended with some mutually felt embarrassment.

As my curiosity was awakened, I went to see the sculptor. He is an immigrant from one of the republics of Latin America and is of nearly pure Indian descent. I was told later that because of his slightly dark colour, he sometimes had met some difficulties when he was not personally recognized. On one occasion, quite recently, he had been beaten by the police when he had appeared on the street one night with a white woman. I now told him about my experience at the exhibition and asked him to clear up the matter for me. His first answer was that there was nothing to clear up: his sculpture was an abstract piece of art and represented a soldier being hanged, 'any soldier'. We discussed the matter for a while on this line. But gradually, I must confess, I came to feel slightly exasperated, and said, 'If you, the artist, do not know what you have created, I know it as an art spectator. You have depicted a lynching, and more particularly, a lynching of a Negro.' The sculptor then suddenly changed personality, became intimate and open, and said:

'I believe you are right. And I have intended it all the time.'
I asked, 'Don't you think everybody must know it?' He said
'Yes, in a way, but they don't want to know it.' I asked again,
'Why have you spent your time in producing this piece?
You understand as well as I that, even if it is admirable
and is also being greatly admired by the whole public, nobody is actually going to buy it. Personally, I would not dare
to have it in the cellar of my house, still less in a room where
I lived'. He answered, 'I know. I suppose that I have made
this for myself. I am going to keep it in a closet. This is the
"American Skeleton in the Closet". That would be the right
name of my sculpture. "Soldier in Rain" is only a fake, a
deception between me and the public down here.'

The situation described is a beautiful crystallization of moral
escape. A sculptor, with so much colour in his skin and such
experiences because of his colour that a degree of identification with the American Negro people has been established,
is living out his aggression in a piece of art which, in reality,
is meant as an accusation against society. In the layer of
his mind where his artistic imagination works and directs his
skilful hands, he is clear and bent on his purpose; and the result
is forceful and exact. In the layer where he meets the community, there is twilight. He gave me two contradictory
statements as to what the sculpture actually represented, and
he was, as I believe, serious and honest both times. The art
appreciative public in this refined old city shares in his twilight.
They accept his fake with grace and gratitude. To some extent
they also share in the deep meaning of the sculpture to its
creator. They probably even 'get a kick' out of an obvious
association which, however, they suppress. Probably none of
the visitors to the exhibition would ever take part in a lynching
or have anything but regret for its occurrence. But they par-
take in a national and regional responsibility. Lynching,
further, stands only as a symbol for a whole system of suppres-
sions in which they daily are participants. Their valuations
are in conflict. Art, particularly when presented in such a
tactful way, has a function of releasing the tension of suppressed
moral conflicts.

Encountering the Negro Problem

5. THE ETIQUETTE OF DISCUSSION

Generally the form of a matter becomes important when the matter itself is touchy. Explosives must be handled with care. Educators, reformers, and journalists with liberal leanings in the South have a standard text which they recite to please one another and the visitor. Everything can be said in the South if it is said 'in the right way'. Criticisms and even factual statements should be phrased in such a manner that they do not 'offend' or create 'embarrassment'. I have listened again and again to the pronouncements of this theory of Southern indirectness from liberal white Southerners who have been most eager that I should understand, not only the æsthetics, but also the pragmatic purpose of this escape machinery. I have been told countless examples, where, as my interlocutor confided to me, he was able to 'get by' in saying so and so to such and such a person because he phrased it in this or that way, or how this or that change for the better in inter-racial relations was 'put over' on the public by letting it appear in a euphemistic light. I have sensed the high subjective pleasure of this persistent balancing on the margins and the corresponding pleasures of the less liberal audience in being merely teased but never affronted by the sore points. I have come to understand how a whole system of moral escape has become polite form in the South. This form is applicable even to scientific writings and, definitely, to public discussion and teaching on all levels. It is sometimes developed into an exquisite and absorbing art.

It renders the spoken or written word less effective. It is contrary to the aims of raising issues and facing problems; it makes difficult an effective choice of words. It represents an extra encumbrance in intellectual intercourse. At the same time as it purposively opens a means of escape, it also fetters everything to the very complex suppressed by this means: the Negro problem on their minds.

This form has even crystallized into a peculiar theory of induced social change. It has become policy. There is nearly common agreement in the South that reforms in inter-racial relations should be introduced with as little discussion about them as possible. It is actually assumed that the race issue is a

105

half dormant, but easily awakened, beast. It is a complex which is irrational and uncontrollable, laden with emotions, and to be touched as little as possible.

When talking about the Negro problem, everybody—not only the intellectual liberals—is thus anxious to locate race prejudice outside himself. The impersonal 'public opinion' or 'community feelings' are held responsible. The whites practically never discuss the issue in terms of 'I' or 'we' but always in terms of 'they', 'people in the South', 'people in this community', or 'folks down here will not stand for . . .' this or that. One can go around for weeks talking to white people in all walks of life and constantly hear about the wishes and beliefs of this collective being, yet seldom meeting a person who actually identifies himself with it. But he follows it.

In the more formal life of the community the Negro problem and, in fact, the Negro himself, is almost completely avoided. 'In effect the Negro is segregated in public thought as well as in public carriers ", complains Robert R. Moton.[1] The subject is only seldom referred to in the church. In the school it will be circumvented like sex; it does not fit naturally in any one of the regular courses given. Sometimes, but rarely, the topic will be taken up for ostentatious treatment as part of an effort toward inter-racial good-will. The press, with remarkable exceptions, ignores the Negroes, except for their crimes. There was earlier an unwritten rule in the South that a picture of a Negro should never appear in print, and even now it is rare. The public affairs of community and state are ordinarily discussed as if Negroes were not part of the population. The strange unreality of this situation becomes apparent when one comes to realize that for generations hardly any public issue of importance has been free from a heavy load of the race issue, and that the entire culture of the region—its religion, literature, art, music, dance, its politics and education, its language and cooking—are partly to be explained by positive or negative influences from the Negro.

If the Negro is a shunned topic in formal intercourse among whites in the South, he enters all informal life to a disproportionate extent. He creeps up as soon as the white Southerner

[1] *What the Negro Thinks* (1929), p. 55.

is at ease and not restraining himself. He is the standard joke. It is interesting to notice the great pleasure white people in all classes take in these stereotyped jokes and in indulging in discussions about the Negro and what he does, says and thinks. It is apparently felt as a release. Ray Stannard Baker, surveying the South and the Negro problem a generation ago, told a story, which the present writer has encountered several times and which seems to define the situation properly.[1]

A Negro minister I met told me a story of a boy who went as a sort of butler's assistant in the home of a prominent family in Atlanta. His people were naturally curious about what went on in the white man's house. One day they asked him:

'What do they talk about when they are eating?'
The boy thought a moment; then he said:
'Mostly they discusses us cullud folks.'

As Baker adds, the same consuming interest exists among Negroes. A large part of their conversation deals with the race question. One gets the feeling that the two groups are sitting behind their fences, publicly ignoring each other but privately giving free rein to a curiosity emotionalized to the highest degree.

The stories and the jokes give release to troubled people. It is no accident that Americans generally are a story-telling nation, and that jokes play a particularly important role in the lives of the Southerners, white and black, and specifically in race relations. It should not surprise us that sex relations are another field of human life with a great proliferation of jokes. There is much of human brotherhood in humour—a sort of fundamental democracy in a plane deeper than the usual one. It usually conveys a notion that we are all sinners before the Lord. When people are up against great inconsistencies in their creed and behaviour which they cannot, or do not want to, account for rationally, humour is a way out. It gives a symbolic excuse for imperfections, a point to what would otherwise be ambiguous. It gives also a compensation to the sufferer. The

[1] *Following the Color Line* (1908), p. 26.

'understanding laugh' is an intuitive absolution between sinners and sometimes also between the sinner and his victim. The main 'function' of the joke is thus to create a collective surreptitious approbation for something which cannot be approved explicitly because of moral inhibitions. To the whites the Negro jokes further serve the function of 'proving' the inferiority of the Negro. To the Negroes the function of anti-white jokes is partly to pose the whites in a ridiculous light, which to them is a compensation. Partly it is a mechanism of psychological adjustment; they 'laugh off' their misfortunes, their faults, their inferiority.

In this situation the minds of people are, however, likely to show signs of deep-seated ambivalence. White Southerners like and love individual Negroes and sometimes Negroes in general; they apparently also hate them. I have often witnessed how the feeling tone can pass from the one emotional pole to the other abruptly as a result of a remark changing the imagined type of inter-relation toward which the person reacts.

What applies to the emotional level may also be found on the intellectual level. Thus a Southerner, while extolling the virtues of the 'good old Negroes' he used to know and deploring the vices of the young who go to school and are recalcitrant, may suddenly turn an intellectual somersault and bemoan the ignorance and backwardness of the older group and become enthusiastic about the intelligence and progressiveness of the young. I have come to know how fundamental and common this ambivalence of Southern white people is toward the relative value of the different Negro generations and how strategically important it is for policy, educational policy particularly.

Sometimes mental contradictions are elaborated into theories and find their way into learned treatises and documents of state policy. An example is the theory that Negroes have 'lower costs of living', which defends—in the writers' minds— lower salaries for Negroes against the equalitarian principles of the Constitution. The all-embracing Jim Crow doctrine 'equal but separate' belongs to the same category of systematized intellectual and moral inconsistency. A partial blinding of a person's knowledge of reality is sometimes necessary. There are plenty of people in the South who will tell you, honestly and sincerely, that Negroes have equal educational opportunities with whites. I think they believe it—for a moment, in a way, and with a part of their minds. Their conviction rests on two contradictory principles between which they shift.

This mental training of the Southerner, which makes him shift between principles according to momentary change or stimulus, spreads from the Negro problem to other issues. The Negro problem is unique only in intensity. But in most of the other issues, the Negro problem is, directly or indirectly, involved. One meets it in the attitude toward trade unionism, factory legislation, social security programmes, educational policies, and virtually all other public issues.

I once went to see the director of the Department of Labour in a Southern capital. The discussion started by his asking me if trade unions were strong in Sweden, to which I answered, 'Yes.' Without any initiative from my side, he then told me how the trade union movement in this region had the great sympathy of the state and municipal authorities, and how it was favoured in all ways. I said to him, 'Look here, I am an economist. I know that this state is not rich. Your infant industry has to overcome a ruthless competition from the North where industry is long established. Trade unions mean higher production costs. Is it really a wise policy to lay this extra burden upon your young industry?' My interlocutor immediately changed mood. 'Now you hit the point. And this is the reason why we try to keep the unions out of this state.' Then he started to tell me the techniques used to keep out labour organizers from the state.

I changed the subject of conversation and told him I had been visiting some mills and felt that there was too little interest shown for security measures to protect the workers against accidents. The official started out to give me a vivid impression of factory legislation and factory inspection as being the very thing nearest to the legislators' hearts in this state. Again I invoked my profession as an economist, emphasized the cost factor and the competitive situation; and again I got the answer, 'You hit the point' and the totally different story about the attitude of the state.

These inconsistencies and contradictions should not be taken as indicating simply personal insincerity. They are, rather, symptoms of much deeper unsettled conflicts of valuations. The absorbing interest in the form of a matter; the indirectness of approach to a person, a subject, or a policy; the training to circumvent sore points and touchy complexes—which we consider as symptoms of escape—are developing into a pattern of thinking and behaviour which moulds the entire personality. People become trained generally to sacrifice truth, realism and accuracy for the sake of keeping superficial harmony in every social situation. Discussion is subdued; criticism is enveloped in praise. Agreement is elevated as the true social value irrespective of what is to be agreed upon. Grace becomes the supreme virtue; to be 'matter of fact' is crude. It is said about the Southern Negro that he is apt to tell you what he thinks you want him to say. This characteristic ascribed to the Negro fits, to a considerable extent, the whole civilization where he lives.

This escape mechanism works, however, only to a point. When that point is reached, it can suddenly be thrown out of gear. Then grace and chivalry, in fact, all decent form, is forgotten; criticism becomes bitter; opinions are asserted with a vehemence bordering on violence; and disagreement can turn into physical conflict. Then it is no longer a question of escape. The conflict is raging in the open.

6. The Convenience of Ignorance

In this connection the remarkable lack of correct information about the Negroes and their living conditions should at least be mentioned. One need not be a trained student of the race problem to learn a lot in a couple of days about the Negroes in a community which is not known by even its otherwise enlightened white residents. To an extent this ignorance is not simply 'natural' but is part of the opportunistic escape reaction.

It thus happens that not only the man in the street, but also the professional man, shows ignorance in his own field of work. One meets physicians who hold absurd ideas about the anatomical characteristics of the Negro people or about the frequency of disease among the Negroes in their own community; educators who have succeeded in remaining wholly unaware of the results of modern intelligence research; lawyers who believe that practically all the lynchings are caused by rape; ministers of the gospel who know practically nothing about Negro churches in their own town. In the North, particularly in groups where contacts with Negroes are lacking or scarce, the knowledge might not be greater, but the number of erroneous conceptions seems much smaller. The important thing and the reason for suspecting this ignorance to be part of the escape apparatus is that knowledge is constantly twisted in one way—toward classifying the Negro low and the white high.

The ignorance about the Negro is the more striking as the Southerner is himself convinced that he 'knows the Negro', while the Yankee is supposedly ignorant on the subject. The insistence on the part of the Southern whites that they have reliable and intimate knowledge about the Negro problem is one of the most pathetic stereotypes in the South. In fact, the average Southerner 'knows' the Negro and the inter-racial problem as the patient 'knows' the toothache—in the sense that he feels a concern—not as the diagnosing dentist knows his own or his patient's trouble. He further 'knows' the Negro in the sense that he is brought up to use a social technique in dealing with Negroes by which he is able to get them into submissive patterns of behaviour. This technique is simple; I have often observed that merely speaking Southern dialect works the trick.

Segregation is now becoming so complete that the white Southerner practically never sees a Negro except as his servant and in other standardized and formalized caste situations. The situation may have been different in the old patriarchal times with their greater abundance of primary contacts. Today the average Southerner of middle or upper class status seems to be just as likely as the typical Northerner to judge all Negroes by his cook, and he is definitely more disposed than the Northerner to draw the widest conclusions from this restricted source of information. I have also found that the white participants in the work of the local inter-racial commissions— who are not typical Southerners because they are extraordinarily friendly to the Negro and are looked upon as local

experts on the race problem—regularly stress the importance
of those meetings in bringing together representatives of the
two races so that they can 'come to know each other'. They
often confess how vastly their own knowledge of the Negro
has increased because they, in these meetings, had a chance to
talk to Reverend So-and-so. These testimonies are the more
telling when one has been present at a few of these inter-racial
meetings and observed how strictly formal and ruled by mental
inhibitions they are. It is also astounding to observe that at
such meetings Negro members, by relating simple and obvious
facts in the local situation, can reveal things unknown to the
whites present. Even when true friendliness is the basis for the
approach, the awkwardness and anxiety shown in these inter-
racial contacts is often apparent.

The ignorance about the Negro is not, it must be stressed,
just a random lack of interest and knowledge. It is a tense and
highstrung restriction and distortion of knowledge, and it
indicates much deeper dislocations within the minds of the
Southern whites. The blind spots are clearly visible in stereotyped opinions. The 'function' of those stereotypes is, in fact, to
serve as intellectual blinds.[1] Thinking and talking in terms of
stereotypes appear to be more common in the Negro problem
than in other issues and more dominant in the regions of
America where the race problem is prominent.

The stereotypes are ideological fragments which have been
coined and sanctioned. They are abstract and unqualified, as
popular thinking always tends to be. They express a belief that
'all niggers' are so and so. But, in addition, they are loaded
with pretension to deep insight. It is because of this emotional
charge that they can serve to block accurate observation in
everyday living and detached thinking. They are treated as
magical formulas. It is amazing to see the stern look of even
educated people when they repeat these trite and worn ban-
alities, inherited through the generations, as if they were pointing out something new and tremendously important, and also

[1] The important problem of opportune distortion of knowledge has been dealt
with by some outstanding writers in American literature. See, for example,
William James' two essays 'The Will to Believe' in *The New World: A Quarterly
Review of Religion, etc.* (June 1896), pp. 327–347, and 'On a Certain Blindness in
Human Beings' in *On Some of Life's Ideals* (1912), pp. 3–46.

to watch their consternation and confusion when one tries to disturb their conventional thoughtways by 'outlandish' questions.

7. THE NORTH AND THE SOUTH

In the North the observer finds a different mental situation in
regard to the Negro problem. The South is divergent from the
rest of the country not only in having the bulk of the Negro
population within its region but also in a number of other
traits and circumstances—all, as we shall find, directly or
indirectly connected with the Negro problem.

There has been less social change in the South. Industrialization has lagged until recently. The South is more agricultural
and rural. Parts of it are isolated. There has been relatively
little immigration from foreign countries or from the North;
practically all migration has been internal or outward. The
South is poorer on the average: it is true both that there are
more poor people in the South and that they are poorer than
in the North.[1] Farm tenancy is common in the South but
rarer in the North. The tradition of the 'independent farmer' is
largely a Northern tradition. On the other hand, the tradition
of aristocracy is much stronger in the South; 'the Southern
gentleman', 'the Southern lady', and 'Southern hospitality' are
proverbial, even if stereotyped.

Because of this tradition and because of the relative lack of
industrialization, a main way to get and remain rich in the
South has been to exploit the Negroes and other weaker
people, rather than to work diligently, make oneself indispensable and have brilliant ideas. The South has been relatively
intolerant of reform movements of any sort. Circumstances
connected not only with the Negro problem but also with such
traditions as state's rights make change seem more hazardous
than in the North. Education for all groups and on all levels
has been inferior in the South. The trauma of the Civil War is

[1] Contrary to the general impression, however, the well-to-do whites in the
South are in about the same proportion in the population as are the well-do-do
whites in the North. (We except here the very few tremendous fortunes in the
North which are more numerous than in the South.) Also, the Southern whites *as a
whole* have about the same income as do Northern whites: a large proportion of the
poor in the South are Negroes (See Chapter 16, *An American Dilemma*).

still acute. The observer finds many Southerners still 'fighting' the Civil War. In the North it is forgotten.

The mere existence of a more rapid tempo of life in the North, the constant changes, and the feeling of progress push the Negro problem into the background. And the human capacity for interesting oneself in social problems is crowded by many other worries. There have been more frequent clashes of political opinions in the North. The North has been made to feel labour problems. The Northern farmers have been more restless and articulate in their demands. The continuous mass immigration of foreigners has created local problems of exploitation and poverty, maladjustment and cultural assimilation. Placed beside these problems a local Negro problem, where it existed in the North, became robbed of its singularity and shrank in significance.

The Negro problem has nowhere in the North the importance it has in the South. 'Too often we find', complained a Southern student of the Negro problem long ago, 'that when our Northern journalism discusses wrongs at the North or at the West, it criticizes the *wrongs*, but when it discusses wrongs at the South, it criticizes the *South*.'[1] This is a correct observation. But the explanation and, we must add, the justification of this fact is, first, that the Negro problem is a main determinant of all local, regional, and national issues, whether political, economic, or broadly cultural, in the South, while this is not true in the North; and, second, that there is a 'Solid South' backing the 'wrongs' in the one region, while opinions are much more diversified in the North.

There are few Negroes living in most of the North. This is especially true of the rural regions. Where Negroes live in small cities, particularly in the New England states, they are a small element of the population who have never been much of a problem. In the big cities where the greater part of the total Northern Negro population lives, the whites are protected from getting the Negro problem too much on their minds by the anonymity of life and the spatial segregation of racial, ethnic, and economic groups typical of the metropolitan organization of social relations.

[1] Murphy, *op. cit.*, p. 23.

The Northern whites have also been able to console themselves by comparing the favourable treatment of Negroes in
the North with that in the South. Negroes have votes in the
North and are, on the whole, guaranteed equality before the
law. No cumbersome racial etiquette in personal relations is
insisted upon. The whole caste system has big holes in the
North, even if prejudice in personal relations is pronounced,
and the Negroes are generally kept out of the better jobs.
Reports of how Negroes fare in the South tend to make the
Northerners satisfied with themselves, if not smug, without, in
most cases, making them want to start again to reform the
South. We fought a Civil War over the Negroes once, they will
say; it didn't do any good and we are not going to do it again.

The mass migration of Southern Negroes to the North since
the beginning of the First World War leads naturally—especially
in periods of economic depression—to the reflection on the
part of the Northerners that improvement of conditions for
Negroes in their own communities is dangerous as it will
encourage more Southern Negroes to come North. Most white
Northerners seem to hold that the Negroes ought to stay on
Southern land, and that, in any case, they cannot be asked to
accept any responsibility for recent Negro migrants. Few
Northerners have any idea that the Negroes are being pushed
off the land in the South by the development of *world* competition against Southern agricultural products in combination
with a *national* agricultural policy discriminating severely
against the Negroes. This argument that Negroes should not
be encouraged to come North—which is in the minds of many
Northern city authorities—is a chief factor in hampering a
sound welfare policy for Negroes.

This 'passing the buck' is, of course, not only a device of
Northerners to quiet their conscience. It is prominently displayed also by Southerners. The latter get satisfaction out of
every indication that Negroes are not treated well in the North
and, indeed, that groups other than Negroes are living in
distress in the North. Such things help to assuage their own
conscience. They need a rationalization against their sympathy
for the underdog and against their dislike of the caste pressure
inflicted upon the Negro. This situation has prevailed since

before the Civil War. The horrors of Northern free-labour slavery and Northern city slums have never left the Southerner's mind. The victim of this maltreatment, namely, the poor Negro in both South and North, is the loser. Meanwhile each of the two guilty regions points to the other's sins—the South assuaging its conscience by the fact that 'the Negro problem is finally becoming national in scope' and the North that 'Negroes are much worse off in the South'.

The Civil War, even if it does not figure so highly in Northern consciousness as the corresponding memories in the South, is a definite source of historical pride in the North. Many families, particularly in the higher social classes which contain 'Old Americans', have ancestors who fought in the War, the recollection of which carries emotional identification with the Northern cause. The teaching in the schools of the North spreads an identification and a vicarious pride even to the Northerners whose ancestors were Europeans at the time of the Civil War. The liberation of the slaves plays an important part in this idealization. But, paradoxically enough, it turns against the Negro in his present situation: 'We gave him full citizenship', the Northerner will say. 'Now it is his own funeral if he hasn't the guts to take care of himself. It would be an injustice in the opposite direction to do more for him than for people in general just because of his race. The Negro shouldn't be the ward of the nation. Look at all other poor, hardworking people in America. My grandfather had to sweat and work before he got through the mill.'

This rationalized political valuation, which can be heard anywhere in the North, goes back to the Northern ideological retreat and the national compromise of the 1870's. It still, in disguised forms, creeps into even the scientific writings of Yankee authors. Donald Young, for example, writes :

With the Civil War came emancipation, enfranchisement, and guarantees of equal rights for black and white. If anything, Northern politicians did their best to give the Negro a favoured status which in effect would have made him almost a ward of the government. . . . Although a reaction to slavery was naturally to be expected, it would have been a mistake to give the freedman any more protection from private or public persecution than is afforded a citizen of any other colour. Fortunately, the United States Supreme Court and the post-Civil War decline in emotionalism and increase in political sanity prevented the consummation of such attempts at special Negro legislation protection as the Fourteenth and Fifteenth Amendments and Sumner's Civil Rights Bill originally intended.[1]

The logic of this argument is weak. From the basic equalitarian assumption, it could not, of course, be deemed to be an unjust favouring of the Negro people on account of their race, if they were protected from the specific discriminations which are inflicted upon them just because of their race. Guaranteeing them civil liberties as citizens could not be said to be making them the wards of the nation in this particular sense. But even if this Northern rationalization is, in fact, an escape notion like many others we have found in the South, it is not charged with much emotion. The Northerner's social conscience and his political thinking is not permeated with the Negro problem as the Southerner's is.

Rather, he succeeds in forgetting about it most of the time. The Northern newspapers help him by minimizing all Negro news, except crime news. The Northerners want to hear as little as possible about the Negroes, both in the South and in the North, and they have, of course, good reasons for this. The result is an astonishing ignorance about the Negro on the part of the white public in the North. White Southerners, too, are ignorant of many phases of the Negro's life, but their ignorance has not such a simple and unemotional character as that in the North. There are many educated Northerners who are well informed about foreign problems but almost absolutely ignorant about Negro conditions both in their own city and in the nation as a whole.

[1] *American Minority Peoples* (1932), pp. 205-206. The author, thereafter, describes the subsequent disfranchisement, condones the Southern election laws—without any explicit value premises—criticizes the white primary and generally the unfair administration of the laws, leaving the reader, however, with the impression that measures to enforce the Constitution and the state laws are out of the discussion. There is no other interpretation than that such interferences would mean making the Negro 'a ward of the nation'.

This has great practical importance for the Negro people. A great many Northerners, perhaps the majority, get shocked and shaken in their conscience when they learn the facts. The average Northerner does not understand the reality and the effects of such discriminations as those in which he himself is taking part in his routine of life. *To get publicity is of the highest strategic importance to the Negro people.* The Negro protection and betterment organizations and many white liberals see this clearly and work hard to articulate the sufferings of the Negroes.

There is no doubt, in the writer's opinion, that a great majority of white people in America would be prepared to give the Negro a substantially better deal if they knew the facts. But to understand the difficulty the Negroes have to overcome in order to get publicity, we must never forget the opportunistic desire of the whites for ignorance. It is so much more comfortable to know as little as possible about Negroes, except that there are a lot of them in Harlem, the Black Belt, or whatever name is given to the segregated slum quarters where they live, and that there are still more of them in the South; that they are criminal and of disgustingly, but somewhat enticingly, loose sexual morals; that they are religious and have a gift for dancing and singing; and that they are the happy-go-lucky children of nature who get a kick out of life which white people are too civilized to get.

Just one note more should be added: the Southerners are not entirely different on this last point from the Northerners. I have become convinced also that a majority even of Southerners would be prepared for much more justice to the Negro if they were really brought to know the situation. The younger generations of Southern whites are less indoctrinated against the Negro than their parents were. But they are also farther away from him, know less about him and, sometimes, get more irritated by what little they see. We do not share the scepticism against education as a means of mitigating racial intolerance which recently has spread among American sociologists as a reaction against an important doctrine in the American Creed. *The simple fact is that an educational offensive against racial intolerance, going deeper than the reiteration of the 'glittering generalities' in the nation's political creed, has never seriously been attempted in America.*

CHAPTER SEVEN

FACTS AND VALUATIONS[1]

1. Biases in the Research on the American Negro Problem

THE biases in popular beliefs about social reality and the deeper conflicts of valuations rationalized by these popular theories can be made apparent through comparison with 'objective' truth as this is revealed by scientific research.[2] But the scientist himself is not necessarily immune to biases. In the light of the history of scientific writings on the American Negro problem, the biased notions held in previous times and the opportunistic tendencies steering them stand out in high relief against the better controlled scientific views of to-day. Our steadily increasing stock of observations and inferences is not merely subjected to continuous cross-checking and critical discussion but is deliberately scrutinized to discover and correct hidden preconceptions and biases. Full objectivity, however, is an ideal toward which we are constantly striving, but which we can never reach. The social scientist, too, is part of the culture in which he lives, and he never succeeds in freeing himself entirely from dependence on the dominant preconceptions and biases of his environment.

Race problems, generally, and the Negro problem in America, particularly, are to an extraordinary degree affected by conflicting valuations of high emotional tension. Keeping in mind the actual power situation in the American nation and observing the prevalent opinions in the dominant white group, we are led, even by a superficial examination, to expect that even the scientific biases will run against the Negroes most of the

---

[1] Appendix 2 in *An American Dilemma.*   [2] See Chapter V, Section 1, page 71

time. This expectation has been confirmed in the course of our study.[1]

The underlying psychology of bias in science is simple. Every individual student is himself more or less entangled, both as a private person and as a responsible citizen, in the web of conflicting valuations, which we discussed in Chapter V. Like the layman, though probably to a lesser extent, the scientist becomes influenced by the need for rationalizations. The same is true of every executive responsible for other people's research and of the popular and scientific public before which the scholar performs, and whose reactions he must respect. Against the most honest determination to be open-minded on the part of all concerned and, primarily, on the part of the scientists themselves, the need for rationalization will tend to influence the objects chosen for research, the selection of relevant data, the recording of observations, the theoretical and practical inferences drawn and the manner of presentation of results.

The method of detecting bias also is simple. As the unstated premises are kept hidden, the inferences drawn from them and from the factual data contain logical flaws. The general method of detecting biases is, therefore, to confront conclusions with premises and find the *non sequitur* which must be present if inferences are biased. If all premises are not stated explicitly, the inferences must be inconclusive. This method works as long as the biases are restricted to the plane of inferences. If the biases have influenced the very observations, so that the observed data are wrongly perceived and recorded, the method is to repeat the observations. If they have influenced the selection of data collected, the viewpoint and hypotheses applied, or the demarcation of the field of study, the check consists in the application of alternative hypotheses and the widening of the scope of research to embrace the neglected fields. Awareness of the problem of bias is a most important general protection.

Certain tendencies toward scientific bias are apparent on

---

[1] The fact that most of the literature on the Negro problem is biased one way or the other is commonly understood in America and often stated; see, for example, E. B. Reuter, *The American Race Problem* (1938; first edition, 1927), pp. 17 and 27; John Dollard, *Caste and Class in a Southern Town* (1937), pp. 33–41.

the surface.[1] These biases may be classified into groups, each of which may be regarded as a continuum along which the specific biases fall.[2]

(a) *The scale of 'Friendliness' to the Negro.* Various authors show a different degree of 'friendliness' to the Negro people and to the Negro cause. It will often be visible in the very style of presentation, but its more important locus is, of course, in approaches and conclusions. This applies not only to general books on the Negro problem but to special researches and to researches primarily centred on other topics but involving some aspect of the Negro problem.

White scholars until the last two or three decades worked more or less consistently in the interests of the dominant white group's need for rationalization or justification of the system of colour caste. Even the friends of the Negro people were moved by the dominant public opinion to assume, without much questioning, views which were unduly unfavourable to the Negroes. They were, in other words, 'friendly' to the Negroes only when compared with the very unfriendly general public opinion, but not when compared with what disinterested scholarship should have demanded. This general bias is most easily detected in the question of the Negro's racial traits, but it also operates in other fields, for instance in the writing of history.

In the course of a general movement in the American social sciences toward increasing emphasis upon the 'environment' as a cause of differences between social groups the scientific treatment of the Negro problem has, during the last few decades, become vastly more friendly to the Negroes. Without any doubt many white scientists in the field, perhaps the majority, have attached their research interests to the Negro problem or to various aspects of it because of a primary reform interest. In the national *ethos* there is traditionally, as we

[1] In a more penetrating analysis all tendencies to bias will be found to have involved relations among themselves and with deeper ideological tendencies which have even shaped our main conceptional tools in social science; see Section 3 below. These ideological tendencies are biased in a static and do-nothing (*laissez-faire*) conservative direction, which, in the main, works against a disfavoured group like the American Negroes.

[2] The statements made in the following paragraphs grew out of the author's reflections upon the literature on the Negro problem. For further explanation and substantiation the reader is referred to the specific chapters of our inquiry.

often have occasion to point out, a strong demand for 'fair play' and for consideration toward 'the underdog'. Since Negroes are severely suppressed, even to-day, and since by virtue of that fact they often fall below the mark in conduct and accomplishments, and since public opinion is still prejudiced against the Negroes, even a friendliness which stands out as exceptional may allow views which are rather on the unfriendly side of true objectivity. The range of scientific opinions, therefore, does not even to-day necessarily include the unbiased opinion.

Negro social scientists can be assumed, naturally, to have been biased in the friendly direction. Generally speaking, they have most of the time reached results more favourable to their group. Public and academic opinion in the dominant majority group, the Negro scientists' desire to lean backwards and be strictly scientific, and other reasons, may often cause even the Negro scientist to interpret the facts in a way which is actually biased against his own people.

(b) *The Scale of 'Friendliness' to the South.* Most Negroes still live in the South, and, what is more important, all economic, social, and political problems of this region are connected with the Negro problem to a degree without comparison in other regions. The historical tradition through slavery, Civil War, Reconstruction, and Restoration also ties together the judgments on the South and on the Negro. The same is true of the caste restrictions to which the Negro in the South is subjected. In general, a friendly attitude toward the South carries with it unfavourable views toward Negroes or at least a tendency to minimize the fact that they are a substantial proportion of the South's people. Conversely, a sympathetic attitude toward Negroes, their shortcomings, their grievances, and their problems, and especially the attempt to explain them on any basis other than racial inferiority, will be taken as a criticism of the social and moral order of the South.

The first tendency is conspicuous in practically all writings on the Negro problem by Southern writers—at least until recently. The natural interest to defend the white South will be reflected in adverse biases in the discussion about the Negro. Because of the present trend in social sciences toward fewer adverse biases against the Negro, Southern social scientists have increasingly taken a critical attitude toward Southern institutions and morals. This second tendency runs parallel to, and supports, Southern liberalism.

A pro-Southern bias, is, however, not restricted to Southern writers. Ever since the great national compromise of the 1870's, when Reconstruction was liquidated, the need for rationalization of the anomalous position and treatment of the Negro has been national in scope. Contrary to the belief commonly held in the South, the present writer has reached the conviction that not only the general public in the North but also Northern social scientists are rather pro-Southern in their biases.[1] Because the existence of the Negro problem is so widely held to be a blot upon Southern civilization, this common tendency in favour of excusing or explaining the South gives rise to biases adverse to the Negro. The recent trend toward increased friendliness to the Negro has been connected with rising criticism against the South.

Negro writers have naturally never shared much in the pro-Southern bias.

(c) *The Scale of Radicalism-Conservatism.* The place of the individual scientist in the scale of radicalism-conservatism has always had, and still has, strong influences upon both the selection of research problems and the conclusions drawn from research. *In a sense it is the master scale of biases in the social sciences.* It can be broken up into several scales, mutually closely integrated: equalitarianism-aristocratism, environmentalism-biological determinism, reformism–*laissez-faire*, and so forth. There is a high degree of correlation between a person's degree of liberalism in different social problems. Usually the more

[1] This impression is based upon the writer's comparative studies of the literature on the Negro problem. The more precise significance of the statement is the belief that if a statistically reliable sample from Northern scientific literature were made of statements which twisted truth somewhat in one direction or the other, there would be a considerable preponderance of twists in favour of the South. Usually those twists are in the nature of avoidance of facts and conclusions which would be embarrassing to the South; sometimes the avoidance takes the form of understatements, euphemistic expressions or concealment of such data and conclusion in unduly abstract and complicated formulations. Pro-Southern biases in the studies of Southerners, when they occur, take the same expression; in addition, their presentations of facts will often be softened by tributes to the regional romanticism. This bias is more prevalent in the fields of history and sociology than in the other social sciences.

radical a scientist is in his political views, the more friendly to the Negro cause he will feel and, consequently, the more inclined he will be to undertake and carry out studies which favour the Negro cause. The radical will be likely to take an interest in refuting the doctrine of Negro racial inferiority and to demonstrate the disadvantages and injustices inflicted upon the Negro people.

The tendency toward increased friendliness to the Negro people, already referred to, is undoubtedly related to a general tendency during the last few decades, in American society and its social science, toward greater liberalism. In a particular problem where public opinion in the dominant white group is traditionally as heavily prejudiced in the conservative direction as in the Negro problem, even a radical tendency might fail to reach an unprejudiced judgment; whereas under other circumstances or in other problems the objective truth might lie beyond the most extreme conservative position actually held. The prevalent opinion that a 'middle-of-the-road' attitude always gives the best assurance of objectivity is, thus, entirely unfounded.

(d) *The Scale of Optimism-Pessimism.* Without doubt most social scientists are under the influence of the general tendency of any man or any public not to want to be disturbed by deeply discouraging statements about the social situation and impending trends or by demands for fundamental changes of policy.[1] In the Negro problem, which has extremely disturbing prospects indeed, this tendency to defend the 'happy ending' for white America and the Negro people will generally make for a soft-pedalling of such adverse facts in the inter-racial situations as offer little prospect of being changed within a reasonable time. This minimization or suppression of discouraging facts may occur when they refer to either the white or the

---

[1] This tendency can be illustrated from many other fields. When an economic depression turns into a prolonged stagnation of industry as in America during the 'thirties, economists are likely to begin to talk about 'maturity' of the economy, and to direct their interests to minor waves of ups and downs within the stagnation. When the industrialization process is checked for a time, some agricultural economists will always be found to give themselves and the general public consolation in a new enthusiasm for self-sustaining farming or even an American peasantry. When sound forecasts of the reproduction trend point to a cumulatively declining future population, the statisticians in all countries turn out for a time to talk about the approach of a 'constant population'.

Negro group. At the same time encouraging signs will be unduly played up. Practically the whole literature on the Negro,
as on all other social problems, is influenced by this tendency.[1]

This optimistic bias may work against the Negro or for him.
It may be connected with a radical or a conservative inclination. In some respects this tendency will gain strength as
people's interest in reforms increases; they do want to believe
in them. A sceptical conservative is, sometimes, more likely
to face facts as they are, than is a fervent liberal. On the other
hand, a conservative is interested in presenting actual conditions in a favourable light, while the reformer reveals unfavourable facts. The tendencies here cross each other in a
complicated pattern.

The majority of people resist having matters which they
regard as unfortunate depicted as hopelessly closed. They
usually do not want, either, to be confronted with demands for
fundamental reforms in deeply ingrained social usages. The
reluctance on the part of many Negro and white social scientists
to accept the term 'caste' to describe the white-Negro relationship—and the remarkable charge of emotion invested in this
minor terminological question—apparently has part of its
explanation in the common dislike of a term which carries
associations of permanency to an institution incompatible
with the American Creed and in the unwillingness to face a
demand for fundamental reforms.

The optimistic bias becomes strengthened, paradoxically
enough, by the scientist's own critical sense and his demand for
foolproof evidence. The burden of proof is upon those who assert
that things are bad in our society; it is not the other way around.
Unfortunate facts are usually more difficult to observe and
ascertain, as so many of the persons in control have strong

---

[1] An illustration on a high level of an adjustment to the general demand for a
'happy end' is Lord Bryce's famous study of American local and national politics,
The American Commonwealth, published in 1893 and republished in 1910 and 1919.
Bryce had to engage in a close investigation of many deeply disturbing phases of
American public life, and the greatness of his work is due largely to his successful
effort never to shun the facts and never to present his conclusions in uncertain
terms. But in short paragraphs sprinkled throughout his text he played up the
reform tendencies somewhat. This became visible when, in later editions, he could
retain most of his text unchanged—including the optimistic forecasts about
'impending' reforms.

interests in hiding them. The scientist in his struggle to detect truth will be on his guard against making statements which are unwarranted. His very urge to objectivity will thus induce him to picture reality as more pleasant than it is.

(e) *The Scale of Isolation-Integration.* In the Introduction we pointed out the opportune interests and factual circumstances which must make both white and Negro scientists inclined to treat the Negro problem in isolation from the total complex of problems in American civilization. The maximum integration represents absence from bias along this line. Objectivity is reached the more completely an investigator is able to inter-relate the Negro problem with the total economic, social, political, judicial and broadly cultural life of the nation.

(f) *The Scale of Scientific Integrity.* The degree to which a scientist is prepared to study unpopular subjects and to state plainly and clearly unpopular conclusions derived from his findings depends, naturally, on his own political inclinations, his personal courage, and the relative freedom awarded him by society. These factors, however, are not independent of each other. In communities where academic freedom is low, the scientist normally will, in adjustment to the environment in which he works, develop, on the one hand, a dislike for con-troversial matters and for clear and bluntly scientific state-ments concerning them, and, on the other hand, an unduly high valuation of agreement and conformity as such. Quite independent of the favourable or unfavourable judgment society passes upon such an attitude, it is, of course, detrimental to scientific clarity and objectivity and to scientific progress.

It is apparent that the social and political situation in the South, and particularly in the Deep South, is still not very favourable to a disinterested and objective study of the Negro problem. Until recently this problem, in spite of its supreme importance to the region, was avoided as an object for re-search. Even at present, and even at the academic fortresses where a considerable amount of academic freedom has been realized, it requires personal courage on the part of a scientist to investigate objectively such aspects of the Negro problem as are heavily loaded with emotions; for example, those con-nected with sex or religion. Similar influences work upon the

Negro scientist in the South. He will often have to become an artist in inter-racial diplomacy, which, on the whole, will tend to make him rather diplomatic even in his scientific research. The inter-racial situation in the South will thus tend to lay political inhibitions on both white and Negro scientists.

In the North, and particularly at the great and famous institutions, such inhibitions are not found. Where there are remnants of inhibitions in social research they will rather be applied to other fields—economic and political—more important to the social forces in control of universities and other research institutions, than to the Negro problem.

Quite generally it must be remembered, however, that the Negro problem is something of a skeleton in the American cupboard. Objective studies are liable to show up situations which are scandalous, not only to the community but also to the nation. A certain apprehension is natural. On the whole, *however, the American public is remarkably scandal-proof.*[1] But it seems as if the cupboard has first to be opened, and the scandal, so to speak, be publicly 'established'. Certain scandals are public, as a matter of tradition and convention, and investigations of them do not meet with violent protest. Lynching, for example, is such a public scandal in connection with the Negro problem. The phenomenon can be investigated and written about rather freely everywhere, even in the South. The same is true, to a great extent, of the seamy sides of politics. These scandals have become notorious and recognized. The national conscience has dissociated itself from them, even if it has not been possible to stamp them out of existence. There are, however, other scandals which are not, at least not as yet, 'established'. It seems to be rather accidental and, to some extent, a result of private initiative on the part of an investigator who originally opens the issue, which scandals are, and which are not, established enough to move the national conscience and leave the scientists free for their work.[2]

[1] The extraordinarily high degree of openness to criticism which characterizes American culture above every other national culture in the Western world is discussed in Chapter VI.

[2] There are other scales along which biased views fall, such as the scales of dogmatism—eclecticism, long-run—short-run perspective, practicality—impracticality. They have been taken up in the various chapters of *An American Dilemma.*

2. METHODS OF MITIGATING BIASES

Since Benjamin Franklin's day, American science has quite distinctly leaned toward a healthy trust in 'hard facts'. The inclination to stress empirical 'fact-finding' has characterized the magnificent rise of American social sciences. As a trend it has become accentuated during the last generation by the huge funds made available for research, the unprecedentedly rapid growth of universities and research institutions, the equally rapid increase of the number of persons engaged in scientific pursuits, and the specialization thereby made possible.

By subjecting popular beliefs and scientific assumptions to the test of facts, specific biases in the research on the Negro have time and again been unmasked. The recent history of research on racial differences offers excellent examples. Incidentally, it also gives a clue as to the direction in which the biases in the Negro problem would tend to go if unchecked. Generally speaking, our attempts to eradicate biases by stress on factual research have been the more fruitful, the simpler the problems involved are from a methodological point of view and the more successfully we have been able to utilize controlled research methods such as have been developed in the natural sciences.

It must be maintained, however, that *biases in social science cannot be erased simply by 'keeping to the facts' and by refined methods of statistical treatment of the data*. Facts, and the handling of data, sometimes show themselves even more pervious to tendencies toward bias than does 'pure thought'. The chaos of possible data for research does not organize itself into systematic knowledge by mere observation. Hypotheses are necessary. We must raise questions before we can expect answers from the facts, and the questions must be 'significant'. The questions, furthermore, usually have to be complicated before they reach down to the facts. Even apparently simple concepts presume elaborate theories. These theories—or systems of hypotheses—contain, of necessity, no matter how scrupulously the statements of them are presented, elements of *a priori* speculation. When, in an attempt to be factual, the statements of theory are reduced to a minimum, biases are left a freer leeway than if they were more explicitly set forth and discussed.

Neither can biases be avoided by the scientists' stopping short of drawing practical conclusions. *Science becomes no better protected against biases by the entirely negative device of refusing to arrange its results for practical and political utilization.* As we shall point out, there are, rather, reasons why the opposite is true.

When perhaps a majority of the foremost social scientists in America have an ambition toward, and take pride in, keeping entirely free from attempting to reach practical and political conclusions from their research, part of the explanation is their high professional standards. The quest for scientific objectivity is, I believe, more lively, and kept more explicit, in America than elsewhere. The position is also more understandable when considered from an historical perspective. Social science in America in its modern form developed as a conscious reaction to an earlier highly normative and teleological doctrine. Monumental theories were built without resort to the observation of social facts, and radical changes in social life were demanded without due consideration of the actual forces and processes through which social life exists and changes. The reaction against reformism and philosophical system-building has been particularly violent in American sociology where a concerted drive to build a social science on the model of the natural sciences is clearly apparent. This tremendous reaction is so recent that many of the older generation of present-day sociologists took part in it.[1] Among the less influential social scientists, the old-fashioned 'practical' doctrine is actually still alive.

In seeking to explain why American social science avoids conclusions that are practical, we must also recall its high degree of specialization. Practical conclusions must always

[1] In a significant sense this advance in social knowledge was part of the general modern trend toward secularization of thought. Many of the earlier sociologists—against whose teachings contemporary sociologists are still reacting—were clergymen, as were the fathers of some of our outstanding contemporary sociologists. The recent trend toward facts and naturalistic explanations is, therefore, a movement toward emancipation. In both the radical wing of previous social speculation —represented by such reform movements as Perfectionism, Positivism, and Telesis —and the conservative do-nothing (*laissez-faire*) wing—Utilitarianism, Malthusianism, and Social Darwinism—there was an assumption of the freedom and rationality of the individual. The reaction of modern sociologists has been against this assumption as well as against the similar 'freedom of the will' doctrine of their clerical predecessors. Such a reaction alone would tend to make social science less interested in the practical sphere of its subject matter.

draw on a much more comprehensive range of insights into many fields than is necessary for good work in most specialities. Many excellent social scientists honestly feel incompetent before the broader practical tasks.[1] Finally, there has been in America, until the New Deal at least, a great personal and institutional isolation of the scholars from the political agencies of the nation. In America the general public has not developed a strong tradition of looking to its academicians for leadership of national thought in the broader issues. It has not given them the ear and prestige—and especially in the earlier period, not even the freedom—which was due to them.[2]

This attempt at explanation of the fact that most outstanding social scientists want to keep strictly to the principle of avoiding practical conclusions does not weaken the present author's conviction that the principle is arbitrary as a methodological rule and is detrimental to true scientific objectivity in its application. The main reasons for this conviction are the following:

Although the social scientist attempts to make his initial observation of a phenomenon as factual as possible, he finds it difficult to adhere strictly to this principle. Our whole literature is permeated by value judgments despite prefatory statements to the contrary. To the knowledge of the present writer, there is no piece of research on the Negro problem which does not contain valuations, explicit or implicit. Even when an

---

[1] Specialization and the handling of the larger research funds and of the correspondingly large personnel resources also make co-operative work more possible and more necessary. Serving on committees of all sorts usually belongs to the responsibilities of the best men in every field. American social scientists have broken new paths and carried out huge tasks, which earlier could not have been dreamt of, by successfully applying co-operation to research. But in committee work it is always easier to reach agreement on factual aspects of research, whereas the more practical aspects—particularly when the matter is controversial—are kept out of vision or left open.

[2] In this light one also understands better the high emotions contained in such denunciations of 'pulpit orators', 'well-meaning theorists', 'arm-chair philosophers', 'ardent evangelists', 'artists', 'social reformers', 'religionists', 'journalists', 'promoters', 'advertisers', 'advocates', 'flag-wavers', 'day-dreamers' and 'idealists', as are frequently used by social scientists when they assert that they are going to be strictly factual and avoid practical conclusions.

The strong anti-practical inclination to which such denunciations testify is also to be understood as a reaction against the particularly 'practical' and moralistic culture in which the social scientists are living—the reaction itself thereby becoming moralistic.

author writing on, let us say, Negro education, politics, business, or labour, attempts to give us only the data he has collected and the analysis he has made, he can rarely refrain from value judgments on them.

These practical judgments are usually relatively simple. They are not presented as inferences from explicit value premises plus the data, but rather, in the age-old fashion, as being evident from the nature of things: *actually as part of the objective data.* They are not marked off properly from theoretical knowledge of truth, but are most often introduced by loading part of the terminology with valuations which are kept vague and undefined. Sometimes the reader is told what is right or what is wrong, desirable or undesirable, only by implication. It should be stressed that this criticism often applies even to the most ostentatiously 'pure' fact-finding research. Man is, as Aristotle told us, a political animal, and social science is a political science, in this sense. Valuations are present in our problems even if we pretend to expel them. The attempt to eradicate biases by trying to keep out the valuations themselves is a hopeless and misdirected venture.

Attaching importance to the presence or absence of practical conclusions also fosters a dangerously superficial view of what biases really are. I have often observed that social scientists who are responsible for the publications of other authors' works or who utilize them in their own writings, when they apprehend biases, believe that these can be 'edited away', by modifying certain expressions used or cutting out or revising certain practical conclusions drawn. Similarly, a general tendency toward understatement is observable in most social science literature. When an author has set down something which he feels to be unfavourable about a social class or a region, he looks for something favourable to say in order to 'balance the picture'. A 'balanced view', a colourless drawing, is considered to be more 'scientific'. Particularly in governmental investigations great care is usually taken to spare the readers. The deliberate attempt that is made in such reports not to offend anyone will often make them difficult to use for scientific purposes. This tendency is, of course, not only ineffective in mitigating biases, but, even worse, it is itself one of the main types of bias in research.

Biases in research are much deeper-seated than in the formulation of avowedly practical conclusions. They are not valuations *attached* to research but rather they *permeate* research. They are the unfortunate results of *concealed* valuations that insinuate themselves into research at all stages, from its planning to its final presentation.

The valuations will, when driven underground, hinder observation and inference from becoming truly objective. This can be avoided only by making the valuations explicit. *There is no other device for excluding biases in the social sciences than to face the valuations and to introduce them as explicitly stated, specific, and sufficiently concretized, value premises.* If this is done, it will be possible to determine in a rational way, and openly to account for, the direction of theoretical research. It will further be possible to cleanse the scientific workshop from concealed, but ever resurgent, distorting valuations. Practical conclusions may thus be reached by rational inferences from the data and the value premises. Only in this way does social engineering, as an advanced branch of social research, become a rational discipline under full scientific control.

The method of working with explicit value premises has a very evident advantage in this last respect of laying a rational foundation for practical research. There are only two means by which social scientists to-day avoid practical and political conclusions: (1) neglecting to state the value premises which, nevertheless, are implied in the conclusions reached; (2) avoiding any rational and penetrating analysis of the practical problems in terms of social engineering (which would too visibly distract from the announced principles of being only factual). By the first restraint the doors are left wide open for hidden biases. The second inhibition prevents the social scientist from rendering to practical and political life the services of which he is capable.

Regarding the last point, social scientists have become accustomed to answer that ' very much more detailed factual research is necessary before wise action can be planned upon the basis of scientific knowledge'. This statement, which, with few verbal variations, will be found so often in our literature, is an expression of scientific modesty. But it also expresses escape.

From the point of view of the practical man and of society, the rejoinder must be made: first, that practical action or inaction must be decided from day to day and cannot wait until eventually a lagging social science has collected enough detailed data for shouldering its part of the responsibility for social action; second, that, even with much more money and exertion spent on research, social science will, in this complicated and rapidly changing world, probably always be able to present this same excuse; and, third, that the scientist—even if his knowledge is only conjectural in certain respects—is in a position to assist in achieving a much wiser judgment than the one which is actually allowed to guide public policy.

The third point is the decisive one. Without doubt we know quite enough in most social problems to avoid a great number of wasteful mistakes in practical life and, consequently, to contribute to a better world. Even in science, although we may strive toward the absolute, we must always be prepared to deliver the incomplete knowledge we have on hand. We cannot plead that we must wait 'until all the facts are in', because we know full well that *all* the facts will never be in. Nor can we argue that 'the facts speak for themselves' and leave it 'to the politician and the citizen to draw the practical conclusions'. We know even better than the politician and the ordinary citizen that the facts are much too complicated to speak an intelligible language by themselves. They must be organized for practical purposes, that is, under relevant value premises. And no one can do this more adequately than we ourselves.

There is a common belief that the type of practical research which involves rational planning—what we have ventured to call 'social engineering'—is likely to be emotional. This is a mistake. If the value premises are sufficiently, fully, and rationally introduced, the planning of induced social change is no more emotional by itself than the planning of a bridge or the taking of a census. Even prior to the stage of social engineering proper, the research technique of accounting openly for one's value premises actually de-emotionalizes research Emotion and irrationality in science, on the contrary, acquire their high potency precisely when valuations are kept suppressed or remain concealed in the so-called 'facts'.

133

The primary task in the present inquiry on the Negro problem has been to ascertain relevant facts and to establish the causal relations between facts. The viewpoints and, consequently, the principle of selection in regard to both direction and intensity of analysis, however, have been determined by certain value premises. In the practical sphere it has been our main task to ascertain how situations and trends, institutions and policies, have to be judged when a given set of value premises is applied.

The question of the selection of value premises remains to be settled. Values do not emerge automatically from the attempt to establish and collect the facts. Neither can we allow the individual investigator to choose his value premises arbitrarily. *The value premises should be selected by the criterion of relevance and significance to the culture under study.* Alternative sets of value premises would be most appropriate. If for reasons of practicability only one set of value premises is utilized, it is the more important that the reservation is always kept in mind: *that the practical conclusions—and the direction of research—have only hypothetical validity* and that the selection of another set of value premises might change both.

The formulation of specific valuations to be utilized as instrumental norms in a scientific investigation is likely to emphasize the tremendous moral responsibility placed upon social scientists. A number of points already made should, however, be borne in mind. First, the same responsibility is actually carried by every student, whether he chooses to make his value premises explicit or not. Second, if he makes his value premises explicit, his responsibility is, in fact, smaller, as he then fixes his readers' attention on the matter and thus aids them to criticize his value premises and conclusions. Third, the research part of the work is mainly dependent on the value premises as to viewpoints and direction. Fourth, his method means that he has taken precautions to avoid hidden valuations, that is, biases.

3. THE HISTORY AND LOGIC OF HIDDEN VALUATIONS

In the preceding section we have given our main reasons why social science is essentially a 'political' science; why practical conclusions should not be avoided, but rather be considered as a main task in social research; why explicit value premises should be found and stated; and how, by this technique, we can expect both to mitigate biases and to lay a rational basis for the statement of the theoretical problems and the practical conclusions. The remainder of this note brings together under one head what is virtually a series of footnotes to the previous section. It contains arguments which are in the nature of digressions from the main argument in the text as technical qualifications.

Probably everyone with mastery of the writings in any large field of social science will agree with the description we have given of the present situation. We emphatically denounce valuations in social science, but they are constantly creeping into our work. Most of us declare just as emphatically that we want to abstain from any practical conclusions and to direct our effort wholly to the discovery of the truth of the matter, but in spite of this intention we make value judgments in a general, vague, hidden and unwitting manner. We have briefly mentioned certain facts in the social situation of science and scientists in America which make this situation more understandable.[1] In various degrees this tendency has characterized social research in all Western countries since its beginning in the eighteenth century. Leaving the question open for a moment as to how to cure this methodological confusion, we might point to some of its major historical determinants. In this short note we shall have to be inconclusive.[2] The problems of doctrinal history and the sociology and psychology of science involved are, in addition, so complex that we prefer to have our remarks considered as suggestions.

Basic to the eagerness in trying to drive valuations underground is the rationalism of our Western culture. Even the man

[1] Professor Robert S. Lynd has discussed the other-worldliness of social science in a suggestive manner from a somewhat different viewpoint in his challenging book, *Knowledge for What ?* (1939).

[2] For a fuller treatment of some of the problems dealt with in this section, we refer to the author's *The Political Element in the Development of Economic Theory* (1932, English translation 1953), and 'Das Zweck-Mitteldenken in der Nationalökonomie' in *Zeitschrift for Nationalökonomie* (1932), reprinted as Chapter X in this volume.

in the street, when he wants to appear enlightened, will attempt to avoid expressing primary and personal valuations. He wants to be 'objective' and to avoid arbitrariness. He will, therefore, give 'reasons' for his desires, and he tries to make the reasons appear purely 'factual' so that they will be acceptable to any 'rational' man.[1] He wants, in other words, to suppress his valuations *as valuations* and to present them as systems of rational beliefs concerning reality. The same tendency has for centuries driven the philosophers in their scholarly exertions to base systems of morals and politics upon 'the nature of things' and, later, upon the 'sensations', that is, in this context, upon empirical observations and rational inferences. The difference between the various moral philosophies which fought and superseded each other is—on this central point—not great. The philosophies of the seventeenth, eighteenth, and early nineteenth centuries—and, in particular, the then perfected systems of Natural Law and Utilitarianism—became the foundations, not only of our later moral and political thinking as it has developed in America among other countries, but also of the modern social sciences. The latter have, indeed, been a chief expression for the rationalistic desire in our culture to eradicate valuations and lay the basis for a factual and objective view of social problems.

The social sciences thus developed as branches of the philosophies of Enlightenment. New philosophical ideas have later been inserted; for instance, the ideas of social development attached to the names of Darwin, Hegel, Marx and Spencer. But certain central normative and teleological ideas of the philosophies of Natural Law and Utilitarianism have been preserved. One such idea is the thought that there is a *commune bonum*, a 'general' or 'common welfare', and that it can be ascertained by scientific investigation. Another one is the thought that, basically, human interests are in harmony.

The idea that there is such a thing as a 'common welfare', an 'interest of society', which can be known, has followed us up to present times. It is seldom discussed but rather taken for granted. When during the 'twenties the criticism of classical economics in America asserted itself, and the so-called

[1] See Chapter V.

institutionalists apparently followed a tendency to find as many faults as possible with the old school of economists, the most central concept of classical economics, the 'general welfare', was practically never challenged. Most work done in economics even to-day assumes tacitly the existence of such an entity. The availability of this concept makes it easy and natural for the economist, and also for other social scientists, to apply a concealed valuation, covered only by this vague phrase, directly to his material or factual data. Statements that something is, or is not, desirable from the viewpoint of 'society' will surprisingly often appear even in statistical work without any conclusive argument about how such a value judgment has been reached and what precisely it means.

From the beginning of social science the idea of a 'harmony of interests' was closely associated with the idea of 'common welfare'. 'Social value' was originally conceived of as a value common to all participants in a society. The harmony doctrine, obviously, made the calculation of the social value out of individual interests so much easier, and this fact, undoubtedly, has been an advantage in its use which has given it much of its survival strength.[1] We want to believe that what we hold to be desirable for society is desirable for all its members.

The harmony doctrine is essential to 'liberalism' as it has historically developed out of the philosophies of Enlightenment (the term 'liberalism' is here used in its most inclusive sense). From the very beginning liberalism was split into two wings, one radical, the other conservative. The radical wing upheld the opinion that a harmony of interests would exist only in a society where the institutions—and primarily the distribution of property—were changed so as to accord with the precepts of these philosophies. The 'natural order' studied by the radical liberals was, therefore, a hypothetical society where the 'natural laws' functioned undisturbed by 'corrupted institutions': where, thus, for example, all 'natural' titles to property—with Locke the 'fruits of labour'—were retained, but society was purified of all monopolies and privileges and, consequently, of 'exploitation'. The conservative wing, on the other hand, proceeded to apply the harmony doctrine

[1] Myrdal, *The Political Element in the Development of Economic Theory.*

directly to the unreformed society (which, incidentally, was a corruption of thought, as they all usually adhered to a philosophy which reserved the concepts 'natural order' and 'social harmony' for a society purged as severely as the radicals wanted it). The radical wing became the reformers, the visionaries, and the utopians: it gave birth to various schools of communism, socialism, syndicalism and anarchism. The conservative wing profited from its 'realism'. In its practical work it abstained from speculating about a 'natural order' other than the one that existed; it studied society *as it was* and actually came to lay the foundations for modern social science. For this we have to be grateful to conservative liberals. But they perpetuated in modern social science, also, their static and fatalistic political bias, a do-nothing liberalism. The harmony doctrine in this setting was, of course, even less well founded than the radical liberals' idea that only in a very different 'natural order' would human interests be mutually compatible.

Economics—or 'political economy', to use the old-fashioned but much more adequate term (the attribute 'political' has been dropped for convenience and as a tribute to the purity of science)—is the oldest branch of social science in the sense that it was the earliest to develop into a system of observations and inferences organized under the principle of social laws.[1] In economics we can most conveniently study the influence of the static and fatalistic general bias upon the development of a social science. From natural science it early borrowed the concept of 'equilibrium'. This concept, as well as the derived concepts of 'balance', 'stability', 'normal', are all often heavily loaded with the static and fatalistic valuations. To an extent these concepts have taken over the role of the conservative variant of the old harmony doctrine. It is, of course, possible to use them in a purely instrumental manner and the success of generations of economists in gradually perfecting our knowledge of economic relations is due to such a use of the various notions of social equilibrium and disequilibrium. The 'assumptions' of economic theory have been useful. But their load of inherited static and fatalistic valuations is heavy, and

---

[1] History and political science are, of course, older, but they never reached agreement upon a system of causation.

they will often turn into convenient covers for biases in this direction.

The direction is loose and general, however. Like 'welfare' and 'harmony of interest', those concepts can be bent considerably. Their role for the underhand presentation of practical conclusions is rather the formal one of providing objective-sounding, technical terms for the subjective valuations which are seeking expression. They thus permit entrance of the biases of a time, a social setting or a personality. These biases may be conservative or radical. The relation between, on the one hand, the specific biases in research and, on the other hand, these value-metaphysical thought-structures forming the frame for economic theory and research, is primarily this: that the arbitrariness inherent in the structures allows the specific biases room for play which, under the rules of scientific strictness, they should not have. But it is equally important to remember that they do not give absolutely free leeway. They are headed in one definite direction. As long as economics keeps its valuations implicit and hidden, the utilization of those concepts will tend to insert into scientific work a do-nothing bias.

The younger social sciences have followed much the same track. A few remarks, mainly by way of illustration, will be made concerning American sociology, particularly as it has influenced the study of the Negro problem.

Few have had more influence on contemporary American social science thinking than William Graham Sumner. He was a political economist of strong *laissez-faire* leanings before he became a sociologist, and he continued to indoctrinate generations of Yale undergraduates with the economic doctrines of Manchester liberalism.[1] Sumner is usually believed to have had two sides: on the political side he advocated Social Darwinism[2] and was a conservative; on the scientific side he was the great observer of 'folkways and mores'. These two sides were closer than is commonly thought. His observations

---

[1] Charles A. and Mary R. Beard, *The Rise of American Civilization*, Vol. II, (1927), pp. 236-237, 429 and 430.

[2] Social Darwinism refers to the continuation of the *laissez-faire* movement after it took on the Darwinian terminology of 'struggle for existence' and 'survival of the fittest'. The ideological father of Sumner was the founder of Social Darwinism—namely, Herbert Spencer.

that there were folkways and mores which gave societies a static stability buttressed his belief that social change was difficult to achieve. His desire to maintain the *status quo* led him to conclude that there should be no attempt to change the folkways and mores. The unification of the two streams in Sumner's thinking gives us an example of the fallacious attempt to draw practical conclusions from purely factual premises:

> The great stream of time and earthly things will sweep on just the same in spite of us . . . Everyone of us is a child of his age and cannot get out of it. He is in the stream and is swept along with it. All his science and philosophy come to him out of it. Therefore the tide will not be changed by us. It will swallow up both us and our experiments . . . That is why it is the greatest folly of which a man can be capable, to sit down with a slate and pencil to plan out a new social world.[1]

Sumner could not fail to have a particularly strong influence on social science thinking about the problems of the South and, specifically, about the Negro problem. The theory of folkways and mores was spread by the scientists and has in the educated classes of the South become a sort of regional political *credo*. The characterization of something as 'folkways' or ' mores' or the stereotype that 'stateways cannot change folkways'— which under no circumstances can be more than a relative truth—is used in the literature on the South and on the Negro as a general formula of mystical significance. It is expressed whenever one wants to state one's opinion that 'what is, must be' without caring to give full factual reasons. To a large extent the formula has also been taken over by the Negro writers. We may note a recent example of the same sort of reasoning on the part of a writer, who, if he had not been influenced by Sumner, is in perfect agreement with him. The example is the more striking because it is taken from the pages of the radical Negro periodical, *The Crisis*, and is part of a

---

[1] William Graham Sumner, 'The Absurd Attempt to Make the World Over', *Essays of William Graham Sumner*. Edited by A. G. Keller and Maurice R. Davie (1934), Vol. I, pp. 105-106.

review of a book whose author is trying to improve the lot of the Negro—though perhaps in a naïve manner.

It is the belief, on the other hand, of our author, and a considerable group of educators, largely members of the 'social frontier group' at Teachers' College, that education can lead in social reform instead of following in the wake of social trends. This belief is a form of wish-fulfillment thinking based upon the assumption that social life can be rationalized and that the *processus socialis* can be rid of its irrational elements and brought under the control of a previously established plan. *Res est ridicula et nimis iocosa.* Such a belief is not a product of scientific observation, but of the educator's *faith*, and one as naïve as any ever inherited by man. If the researches of science have established anything, it is that man is at bottom a most irrational animal; a rationalizing rather than a reasoning creature.[1]

Much less conservative than Sumner but still bound by a similar fatalism have been Robert E. Park and some of his followers. Park's influence on the research on the Negro problem has been great and direct, as so many of the contemporary students of this problem are his pupils or recognize his guidance as their most important inspiration. Park is not, as was Sumner, moved by any deeply felt desire to maintain the *status quo*. But his keen observation of social conditions—and, perhaps, also some disillusions from his reform activities—have made him realize the tremendous force exerted by 'natural' influences.[2]

[1] James W. Ivy, review of *An Analysis of the Specific References to Negroes in Selected Curricula for the Education of Teachers* by Edna Meade Colson, in *The Crisis* (October, 1941), p. 331.

[2] Park, of course, recognizes the possibility of rapid and radical social change. His theory concerning such change is centred around the concept of 'crisis'. This theory was first developed by W. I. Thomas, *Source Book for Social Origins* (1909), pp. 17-22. The theory, simply stated, is that under certain circumstances habits, mores, and folkways are recognized by people to be no longer useful as ways of meeting situations and needs, and, after a brief period of amoral disorganization, people come together to build up a new type of 'socially acceptable' behaviour, or such a new folkway develops naturally 'without discussion and organization'. The whole period is called a 'crisis'. This theory is not very clearly presented in Park's published writings, but the nearest thing to a complete statement of it may be found in the article on 'Collective Behaviour' in the *Encyclopedia of the Social Sciences* (1935), Vol. 3, pp. 631-633.

Not observing much in the way of conscious and organized planning in his contemporary America except that which was bungling and ineffective because it did not take due account of the natural forces, he built up a sociological system in terms of 'natural' causation and sequence. Probably because he has no intentional conservative bias, it is difficult to find simple statements in Park's writing which exemplify the fallacy of drawing practical conclusions from factual premises alone. What we do find is a systematic tendency to ignore practically all possibilities of modifying—by conscious effort—the social effects of the natural forces.[1] Occasionally the do-nothing (*laissez-faire*) implications of Park's assumptions are revealed:

The races of high visibility, to speak in naval parlance, are the *natural* and *inevitable* objects of race prejudice.[2]

Accommodation, on the other hand, is the process by which the individuals and groups make the *necessary* internal *adjustments* to social situations which have been created by competition and conflict. . . . Eventually the new order gets itself fixed in habit and custom and is then transmitted as part of the established social order to succeeding generations. Neither the physical nor the social world is made to satisfy at once all the wishes of the natural man. The rights of property, vested interests of every sort, the family organization, slavery, caste and class, the whole social organization, in fact, represent accommodations, that is to say, limitations of the natural wishes of the individual. These socially inherited accommodations have presumably grown up in the pains and struggles of previous generations, but they have been transmitted to and accepted by succeeding generations as part of the natural, inevitable social order. All of these are forms of control in which competition is limited by status.[3]

. . . the political process can only proceed in a relatively orderly way in so far as it generates a political power and

---

[1] With the same qualifications for the 'crisis' theory of social change, it can be said that William I. Thomas, who has had a great influence on practically all contemporary American sociologists, shows the same lack of interest for problems of induced change.

[2] 'Behind Our Masks', *The Survey* (May 1, 1926), p. 136. (Italics ours.)

[3] Robert E. Park and Ernest W. Burgess, *Introduction to the Science of Sociology* (1921), pp. 510-511. (Italics ours.)

authority capable of enforcing a certain degree of order and discipline until a new equilibrium has been achieved and the changes which the new programs initiated have been assimilated, digested and incorporated with the folkways of the original and historic society.[1]

Race relations . . . might comprise . . . all those situations in which some relatively stable equilibrium between competing races has been achieved and in which the resulting social order has become fixed in custom and tradition.

Under such circumstances the intensity of the race consciousness which a struggle for status inevitably arouses, where it did not altogether disappear, would be greatly diminished. The biracial organizations of certain social institutions that have come into existence in Southern states since emancipation exhibit the form which such racial accommodations sometimes take.[2]

Park's naturalistic and, therefore, fatalistic philosophy has been transmitted to most of his students who have been working on the Negro problem. Throughout the writings of Edward B. Reuter, for example, we find statements similar to the following taken from a recent consideration of race relations:

It is in the nature of a competitive order, and every natural and social order is competitive, to place groups and individuals in the position where they can survive, and it is in the nature of individuals and groups to develop the characters essential or conducive to survival in the natural and cultural area in which they are placed and in which they struggle to exist. Whether we consider plants, animals, or human beings we find that, in the large, they are in those areas where each is best fitted to thrive and prosper, and that each is somewhat nicely adapted in its structures and in its habit system to the special conditions of existence in the habitat. . . . Adaptation is the price of survival.[3]

[1] Robert E. Park, 'Social Planning and Human Nature', *Publications of the American Sociological Society* (August, 1935), p. 28.
[2] Robert E. Park, 'The Nature of Race Relations', in Edgar T. Thompson (editor), *Race Relations and the Race Problem* (1939), pp. 4–5.
[3] E. B. Reuter, 'Competition and the Racial Division of Labour', in Thompson, *Race Relations and the Race Problem*, pp. 46-47.

What has been said of Park could be said also of William F. Ogburn. The tremendous social influence of inventions and changes in economic organization and the march of social trends have convinced him that man's intentional efforts to do something about the world are futile.[1]

> ... much of our difficulty is due to the fact that the different parts of our highly inter-related civilization are changing at unequal rates of speed, bringing maladjustments and social problems that would not occur in a stationary society or in one where the different parts moved along simultaneously. When one part of our culture, as for instance, the technological economic organization, changes rapidly while another part, as for instance, government, changes more slowly, there comes a time when the maladjustment is sufficiently serious to occasion a whole series of rapid changes in the lagging institutions. In such times and for such changes the word 'Revolution' is often used.
>
> For the future, there is no particular reason to think that the technological inventions and scientific discoveries will slow up. Indeed, they are likely to come faster. However, we may, perhaps, be able to speed up the changes in other institutions slightly more quickly, by greater use of the communication inventions. But on the other hand, the process of keeping up with the pace set by technology may be slowed up because of the increasing heterogeneity of society and the possible greater number of institutional lags to be caught up. Therefore, no prospective integration of state and

---

[1] It should be noted in passing that the Marxian teleology implied in the materialistic conception of history is, from our point of view (however catastrophic the trends are pictured) of the do-nothing (*laissez-faire*) variety; that is, it is biased in the static and fatalistic direction as we have used these terms in this note. In his principal writings Marx shows—contrary to what is often popularly assumed—no interest whatsoever in social planning. He expected 'the reign of freedom' in the classless communistic society to arise full-fledged by natural force out of a political revolution caused by trends in technology and production. The interest in social reforms which he showed particularly in later days was a result of an ideological compromise. Modern social engineering has had virtually no inspiration from Marx's 'scientific' socialism, certainly less than from the early French and English socialists whom Marx repudiated as dilettantes and utopians.

The liberalistic character of Marxism is easily understood when its ideological roots are scrutinized. It explains also why elements of Marxian teleology have had such an easy access into modern American sociology and history.

industry is expected to deliver us in the future from grave social disturbances.[1]

The materials of social planning may, in general, be summed up in the phrase 'social forces'. They are what social planners have to deal with. What social forces may consist of does not concern us at the moment, but the effect of social forces is to produce motion. In the case of the above illustration the motion is in population growth. In fact, motion is the principal characteristic of our age, for we call it the 'age of change'. Social planning deals with changes, either with changes already started, or in planning new changes. It is difficult to name a single phase of our contemporary civilization that is not undergoing change. Some parts are changing more rapidly than others. It is this fact that we are living in a changing world which is the justification for asking the question: What is likely to happen? . . .

Technology enters the analysis at this point because these changes which are taking place are in large part instigated by invention. Thus many of the changes in international relations are affected by the airplane, just as in an earlier generation changes taking place in the relations of warring peoples were affected by gunpowder. Hence the knowledge of inventions supplies us partly with the answer to the question of what is going to happen. The wishes of human beings are relatively stable from age to age insofar as heredity or the physiological foundations are concerned. They take different expressions, however, because of the different social conditions in which men live. New inventions start changes in the behavior of mankind. They are new stimuli to which human beings respond.[2]

The social scientists we have cited could not have reached their negative views on planned and induced social change unless guided by a set of general assumptions in their selection and interpretation of the empirical data. This implies that they have introduced valuations along with facts in deriving

---

[1] William F. Ogburn, 'Man and His Institutions', *Publications of the American Sociological Society* (August, 1935), pp. 39-40.

[2] William F. Ogburn, 'Technology and Planning', in George B. Galloway and Associates, *Planning for America* (1941), pp. 179-180.

conclusions as to what can be and should be the nature of man's practical efforts. We all claim that our factual or theoretical studies alone cannot logically lead to a practical recommendation. A practical or valuational conclusion can be derived only when there is at least one valuation among the premises. When our premises consist exclusively of facts, only a factual conclusion can result.[1] If we proceed otherwise, and if we, further, denounce valuations, we are thus constantly attempting the logically impossible: From certain observations concerning the causation of a social phenomenon we jump to the valuational conclusion that we ought to do nothing to change this phenomenon because it has such and such a causation. To illustrate this common fallacy we have chosen examples from the writings of only a few leading sociologists. The specific error that is common to these three men—Sumner, Park, and Ogburn—has been with social science from the beginning and is still quite general in contemporary social science. This specific error is not that of observing a deep-rooted and all-pervasive social causation. The observations of such causation made by the particular authors chosen for exemplification are monumental contributions to knowledge of a most significant nature. The specific logical error is that of inferring from the facts that men should make no effort to change the 'natural' outcome of the specific forces observed. This is the old do-nothing (*laissez-faire*) bias of 'realistic' social science.

To bring out the nature of this bias and demonstrate the arbitrariness thereby inserted into research, we may consider the same facts that have been observed by Sumner, Park, and Ogburn and add to them an explicit and dynamic value premise (instead of the implicit, fatalistic and static one) and from these deduce a quite different practical conclusion. Recognizing the folkways and mores,[2] for example, and having a desire to *change some of them* in one direction or another, we

---

[1] The factual conclusion can, of course, be that certain practical efforts are bound to be useless. See below p. 158 (h).

[2] We stand in critical opposition to these concepts on theoretical grounds, as they tend to give an impression of a homogeneous and unproblematic valuational background for behaviour, which we think is mistaken (see Chapter V, Section 3), but this does not directly concern our present argument.

should be interested in studying the range and degree of inertia; all the exceptions to the folkways; the specialization of groups; the conflicts (between persons and within persons); the changes, the flexibilities, and the manageability of some factors in the social system; instead of, as Sumner usually[1] does, stressing and exemplifying the great over-all inertia. On the practical plane we should make not only the negative inference that a plan for social change should expect to be time-consuming and to meet strong resistance, but also the positive inference that it has to direct its attack on certain points where the mores are weakest and where people are already beginning to question them (or have a divided conscience with respect to them). We should also infer that it should not attack them directly but should create situations where the people themselves will strain the mores. Similarly, if we recognize the tremendous force of certain processes and sequences we might, with a dynamic value premise, deduce that strategy demands a re-direction or stoppage of processes which contain within themselves a motive power in a certain direction, and an effort *against* individuals coming to 'adjust' themselves to the processes. Finally, a recognition of the sweep of social trends and of the basic role of invention and economic organization in social causation, coupled with a dynamic instead of static valuation, would lead one to facilitate the perfection and adoption of those inventions which have the greatest promise of moving the society in a desired direction and to seek *social* inventions which would modify economic organization and the effects of mechanical inventions. Social scientists are so habituated to using static and fatalistic value premises with such facts as the mores, social processes, and social trends, and they are so prone to associate radical valuation premises with a complete disregard of the facts, that they often do not realize that it is quite possible to couple dynamic value premises with factual knowledge of mores, social processes or social trends. The static and fatalistic value premises have actually imbedded themselves into the data.[2] It should not surprise us that the great development

[1] See Chapter V, Section 2.
[2] The fact of static and fatalistic valuations in social science research may be accepted even though the analysis of its historical causation, presented on previous pages, may be questioned by some.

of the social sciences in recent decades in America has not been accompanied by a correspondingly important development of social engineering.

In the theory of folkways and mores the heavy load of do-nothing (*laissez-faire*) valuation becomes particularly apparent when Sumner and his many followers[1] set out with the purpose of proving the inefficacy of legislation. With reference to race relations in the South after the Civil War, Sumner said:

> The two races have not yet made new mores. Vain attempts have been made to control the new order by legislation. The only result is the proof that legislation cannot make mores. . . . It is only just now that the new society seems to be taking shape. There is a trend in the mores now as they begin to form under the new state of things. It is not at all what the humanitarians hoped and expected. . . . Some are anxious to interfere and try to control. They take their stand on ethical views of what is going on. It is evidently impossible for any one to inteɪfere. We are like spectators at a great natural convulsion. The results will be such as the facts and forces call for. We cannot foresee them. They do not

---

[1] Many other sociologists outside the Sumner tradition considered man-made legislation ineffectual and dangerous. Franklin H. Giddings, the leader of the Columbia School, for example, had this to say about 'stateways':

'Because the folkway is adaptive it is variable, and folkways, therefore, become various, not only because new ways from time to time arise out of new circumstances and demands, but also through differentiation. One has only to call to mind the fluctuations of fashion, the changing forms of address and ceremony, the rise and fall of recreations, the fleeting fads in games and sports, to realize the enormous flexibility of folkways. Stateways tend towards uniformity. Governments attempt to standardize not only rights at law but also legal procedure, administrative rules, and the conduct of citizens. Legislators are intolerant of exceptions, bureaucrats abominate them, and courts, while finding precedents for them when moral justice or the rule of reason requires, do not otherwise make them. Trial by jury, however, which mediates between folkways and stateways, is a venerable if not always a venerated defence against the governmentalists, who would dictate and ration our food and drink, write our medical prescriptions, cut our clothes, tell us what we may read and look at, and send us to bed at curfew.

'Stateways are instituted by command, backed up by physical force. They are formal, as machine-like as they can be made, and relentless. Folkways exert pressure which may be resistless, but it is indefinite, elastic, and automatically variable'. (*Studies in the Theory of Human Society* [1922], p. 193.)

depend on ethical views any more than the volcanic eruption on Martinique contained an ethical element.[1]

It should be noted that—in spite of its psychologism, its ethical relativism, its modernized terminology, and the abundant anthropological illustrations—this theory is nothing else than a reformulation and slight modification of the old *laissez-faire* doctrine of the 'natural order' as it was more naïvely set forth in the Enlightenment period: human relations are governed by 'natural laws'; 'natural laws' are not only the right laws but are also, in the main, and in spite of all the interferences of foolish governments, actually governing real life; they do not need to be legalized—if legislation adheres to the 'natural laws', it is not exactly damaging but useless; if legislation conflicts with the 'natural laws' it will be inefficacious though slightly damaging as it will disturb somewhat the smooth operation of the 'natural laws'. This is, for instance, the doctrine behind Adam Smith's well-known dictum that trade barriers, though, of course, irrational and cumbersome, will, by and large, not amount to much, as the smugglers will pierce them, acting here as the agents of the 'natural laws' with the same immutability as water seeking its level. The 'invisible hand' will inevitably guide human activity. On this central point, which apparently is largely the political purpose of the whole theory of folkways and mores, Sumner simply expresses a common American prejudice against legislation which we have discussed. (Cf. Chapter VI, Section 5.)

[1] William Graham Sumner, *Folkways* (1906), pp. 77-78. Other statements by Sumner, in his least opinionated book, revealing his attitude toward legislation, are the following:

'Acts of legislation come out of the mores. . . . Legislation, however, has to seek standing ground on the existing mores, and it soon becomes apparent that legislation, to be strong, must be consistent with the mores. Things which have been in the mores are put under police regulation and later under positive law. It is sometimes said that "public opinion" must ratify and approve police regulations, but this statement rests on an imperfect analysis. The regulations must conform to the mores, so that the public will not think them too lax or too strict.' (*Ibid.*, p. 55.)

'[The mores] never contain any provision for their own amendment.' (*Ibid.*, p. 79.)

'The combination in the mores of persistency and variability determines the extent to which it is possible to modify them by arbitrary action. It is not possible to change them, by any artifice or device, to a great extent, or suddenly, or in any essential element; it is possible to modify them by slow and long-continued effort if the ritual is changed by minute variations.' (*Ibid.*, p. 87.)

The presence of this same static and fatalistic valuation in the hidden *ethos* of contemporary social science is suggested by some of the terminology found throughout the writings of many sociologists, such as 'balance', 'harmony', 'equilibrium', 'adjustment', 'maladjustment', 'organization', 'disorganization', 'accommodation', 'function', 'social process' and 'cultural lag'. While they all—like the corresponding concepts in economics mentioned above—have been used advantageously to *describe* empirically observable situations, they carry within them the tendency to give a do-nothing (*laissez-faire*) valuation of those situations. How the slip occurs is easily understandable: When we speak of a social situation being in harmony, or having equilibrium, or of its forces being organized, accommodated, or adjusted to each other, there is the almost inevitable implication that some sort of ideal has been attained, whether in terms of 'individual happiness' or the 'common welfare'. Such a situation is, therefore, evaluated as 'good' and a movement in the direction is 'desirable'.[1] The negative terms

[1] There is practically no discussion in the literature on the value connotation in the terms exemplified in the text. When raising the question with representative social scientists, I have often met the following reaction: first, an acknowledgment that many authors in speaking of adjustment, accommodation, disorganization, and so forth, imply valuations of 'good' or 'bad' and that this is unscientific, but, second, that sometimes—even when a valuation is implied—this is so general that it is self-evident. 'Accommodation, for example,' it is said, 'is a process whereby people are able to co-operate and thereby maintain some social order; accommodation grows out of a conflict of interest and is only established after each party to the conflict has accepted a place in the social order and developed appropriate or reciprocal attitudes; but there always remains a latent conflict. The only "goodness" implied in accommodation is that thereby co-operation under social order is maintained.' Against this argument several criticisms can be raised: (1) the value given to co-operation and social order should be given explicitly rather than implicitly in the connotation of a term; (2) this valuation is certainly not under *all* conditions self-evident from the viewpoint of every party involved (to one party a continued conflict can in some conditions be preferable, if only for reaching another and more favourable status of accommodation); (3) this valuation is not, just because it is so general, precise enough to serve a scientific purpose even if it were made explicit (the status to which conflicting parties are actually brought to 'accommodate' is not given *a priori* but is the outcome of a social process, the actual result of which becomes condoned because 'accommodation' in general is condoned; this result could have been different not only because of a prolonged conflict but also because of a different type of accommodating behaviour by one person or the other). In the Negro problem almost every situation, except where a race riot is on, can be, and is often in the literature, described as an 'accommodation', and the *status quo* in every aspect can thus be, and is, implicitly justified because it preserves co-operation and the social order.

—disharmony, disequilibrium, maladjustment, disorganization—correspondingly describe an undesirable situation, as indicated by the etymological connection of their prefixes with the word 'bad'. A great arbitrariness—allowing for the more specific biases of a personality and a cultural setting—is present in deciding upon just *what* shall be considered as equilibrium and *what* as disequilibrium in a process of social change. The following quotation has been chosen to illustrate the working of a political bias through the vehicle of such terms, not only because the bias—directed against the Negro as his interests are commonly conceived—is expressed in a particularly blunt form, but also because it happens to be from the pen of a Negro sociologist:

> In the face of these opposing views, then, conclusions concerning the effect of education upon Negroes during this period may be reserved. If education brought disorganization among the former slaves, it may be counted as a liability. If, on the other hand, it served as an outlet for feelings that might otherwise have been directed into politics, where discord might have resulted, it may be counted on as an asset. The situation doubtless varied in different places at different times—assisting or retarding adjustment in areas where the one effect or the other, already mentioned, preponderated.[1]

Similarly, if a thing has a 'function' it is good or at least essential.[2] The term 'function' can have a meaning only in terms of a presumed purpose; if that purpose is left undefined or implied to be the 'interest of society' which is no further defined, a considerable leeway for arbitrariness in practical implication is allowed but the main direction is given: a description of social institutions in terms of their functions must lead to a conservative teleology. If there is a 'cultural lag', there is likewise a presumption that the elimination of the lag is desirable. While social processes and mores may not be good

[1] Bertram W. Doyle, *The Etiquette of Race Relations in the South* (1937), p. 127.
[2] How easily even a radical social scientist can slip into the expression of approval of something that he says has a function is illustrated by Durkheim's discussion of crime and punishment: Emile Durkheim, *The Rules of Sociological Method* (1938; first edition, 1895), translated by Sarah A. Solovay and John H. Mueller, pp. 66-70.

in terms of certain arbitrary standards, they are believed to exist or develop with an inevitability that defies all efforts directed toward their modification.

These and similar static terms constitute much of the basic descriptive and theoretical terminology in all the social sciences. It is certainly an important task of self-scrutiny for social science to determine why such terms and not more dynamic ones have been given such a strategic position in its thinking. The present author has suggested above that the origin of social science out of the philosophies of Enlightenment and the greater 'realism' of the *laissez-faire* wing of early liberalism is of central importance. The very fact that the evaluative nature of these terms has gone almost unnoticed suggests that the explanation of their choice must go deep into the roots of Western culture. Whatever the reason for their predominance, the fact that such terms—without much care to preserve for them a strictly theoretical meaning—are widely used to describe much of social life and serve as keystones in theoretical explanations of social structure and change, inserts into social science an implicit static and fatalistic value premise. The use of such terms makes it appear that a given situation is desirable or inevitable without the explicit specification by the social scientist of what he considers desirable or of the possibilities of the modification of 'inevitability'.

There is nothing to be criticized when a scientist explicitly states that he hopes a certain situation will develop, that such a situation is a good one according to certain standards which he sets up, or that a certain situation or development is inevitable beyond all possibility of modification by any contingency or directed effort whatsoever. What is to be criticized is the use of terms to hide the fact that there is a value premise in a value judgment. The observation of the facts of a given existing situation alone will never permit the conclusion that such a situation is good or desirable or even that this situation is inevitable in the future. In other words, we are making a plea for explicit value premises. We are also making a plea for unbiased research. The relation between these two *desiderata* is this, that it is the hidden valuations which give entrance to biases in social science.

The author is well aware that some of his criticisms and suggestions in the preceding pages on the history and logic of the hidden valuations in social science are controversial and would ask the reader to note that the following remarks on a positive methodology for social science as well as Sections 1 and 2 of this Chapter do not depend on the correctness of Section 3.

It should also be reiterated as a concluding remark that when we have illustrated our thesis by citing prominent American sociologists, this is only because American sociology has provided the main scientific frame for the study of the Negro problem which is our particular concern here. The tendencies criticized are, however, common to all social sciences in the entire Western world. Not all American sociologists have a do-nothing (*laissez-faire*) bias. In earlier generations Lester F. Ward, Simon Patten, and many others were reformers, and Ward thought of social science as social engineering. Their methodological principles were not clear, however. In the present generation Louis Wirth, to mention only one prominent representative of a growing group holding a dissenting view, has expressed opinions in fundamental agreement with ours.[1]

4. THE POINTS OF VIEW ADOPTED

Scientific facts do not exist *per se*, waiting to be discovered by scientists. A scientific fact is a construction abstracted from a complex and interwoven reality by means of arbitrary definitions and classifications. The processes of selecting a problem and a basic hypothesis, of limiting the scope of study, and of defining and classifying data relevant to such a setting of the problem, involve a choice on the part of the investigator. The choice is made from an indefinite number of possibilities. The

---

[1] Louis Wirth, 'Preface' in Karl Mannheim, *Ideology and Utopia* (1936), pp. xiii-xxxi and his article 'Ideological Aspects of Social Disorganization', *American Sociological Review* (August, 1940), pp. 472-482. John Dollard's *Criteria for the Life History* (1935) and *Caste and Class in a Southern Town* (1937) also exemplify a conscious interest in making biases explicit even if they do not reach a methodology centred on explicit value premises. Robert MacIver's *Social Causation* (1942) and Robert Lynd's *Knowledge for What?* (1939) are other sociological books which are free of implicit value premises.

same is true when inferences are drawn from organized data. Everything in the world is connected with everything else: when shall one stop, and in what direction shall one proceed when establishing causal relations? Scientific conventions usually give guidance. But, first, convention itself is a valuation, usually a biased one, and it is the more dangerous as it is usually hidden in tacit preconceptions which are not discussed or even known; second, progress in science is made by those who are most capable of freeing themselves from the convention in their science and of seeking guidance from other sciences and nonscientific endeavours.

Prior to research, therefore, are complicated theories. The architecture of these theories is arbitrary except when they are intentionally founded upon a definition of relevant interests. This is true no matter how much effort is invested in selecting terms of low valuational content and no matter how remote from public interest the causal analysis is. When one is out to determine such a simple thing as the level of 'real wages' in a community, for example, one has to rack one's soul to decide whether to base one's calculations on hourly rates or on annual wages: whether to consider articles outside of the staple commodities as necessities of consumption, whether to consider certain items, the consumption of which is not 'customary', as necessities because all dieticians think so, and generally speaking, how to decide the weights in the consumption budgets used for constructing a cost of living index. In a world of change and variation there can be no such thing as an 'ideal index'; in the final analysis, the weights have always to be *chosen* upon the basis of what one's interest in a study is. In comparing Negroes and whites, decisions must be taken in such problems as: is it more proper to make the comparison directly or to take into account the fact that Negroes are concentrated in the lower occupational brackets, in poorer and more backward regions of the country, and that they have been discriminated against in education and in other respects?[1]

These considerations sound trite to any scientist who is at all aware of his methodology. What we wish to point out, however,

[1] See Richard Sterner and Associates, *The Negro's Share* (1943), prepared for this study, pp. 3-9.

is that every choice involves valuations. One does not escape valuations by restricting research to the discovery of 'facts'. The very attempt, so prevalent in recent years, to avoid valuations by doing research that is simply factual and without use for practical or political efforts involves in itself a valuation. We hasten to explain that we are not criticizing pure fact-finding. Fact-finding is indispensable for the solution of most of the problems—both practical and theoretical—that we encounter. The criticism is directed against fact-seeking that is done without a problem. The full statement of a problem, including the decision of scope, direction, hypothesis, principles of classification, and the definition of all terms used, renders explicit the valuations necessary in fact-finding research. The author can, of course, explicitly disavow any practical interest and declare that he personally finds that the topic and the hypothesis appeal to him æsthetically—or that he has made all his choices at random. If, however, practical usefulness is an aim in science, even the direction of research becomes dependent upon much wider valuations concerning society.

It should be stressed that this complication of a science which is not mere 'art for art's sake' does *not* in the least decrease the demands upon objectivity in research. On the contrary, specification of valuations aids in reaching objectivity since it makes explicit what otherwise would be only implicit. Facts may be scientifically recorded and analysed with explicit value premises as well as without them, and this can actually be accomplished the better in the former case since the explicit value premises focus the investigator's attention upon the valuations which, if hidden, are the roots of biases, since they generally set a standard of relevance and significance. This is true also when the analysis proceeds to draw practical conclusions. The conclusions must simply be remembered to be only as valid as the premises, which is true in all science. In fact, only when the premises are stated explicitly is it possible to determine how valid the conclusions are.

1. *Theoretical and Practical Research.* Our entire discussion is based upon a distinction between two aspects, or stages, of social research: the 'theoretical' and the 'practical'. By 'theoretical' research we mean here all the research which is

directed purely and exclusively toward ascertaining facts and causal relations between facts. By 'practical' research we mean the logical procedure of relating value judgments to factual situations and to actual trends of change and, from this combination, deriving scientific plans for policies aimed at inducing alterations of the anticipated social trends ('social engineering').

The relations established in theoretical research are simply *causal*. In practical research the causal relations are transposed into *purposeful* relations. The sequence in theoretical research—from cause to effect—is in social engineering turned into the reverse order from ends to means. In practical research the causal relations established by theoretical research are taken as facts.

Theoretical research is primarily concerned with the *present* situation and the *past* development. It attempts to establish, out of systematized experience of the present and the past, a rational knowledge, in as general terms as possible, of the causal relations between elementary factors in the social process. Its final goal is to be able to forecast on this basis the *future* by rational prognoses.

Practical research is exclusively concerned with the *future*. Its principal viewpoint is that the future represents a set of alternatively possible trends of development. What future development will actually occur is, from the practical point of view, a matter of choice, in so far as decisions and actions on the part of the citizen and society can determine this development. Its final goal, therefore, is the scientific planning of 'induced changes'.

Between the two aspects, or stages, of social research there exist the following main relations:

(a) The direction of theoretical research is determined by the practical purposes held in view. In a study of the American Negro problem which is as predominantly practical in its intentions as ours, the frame for all our theoretical research thus consists of certain practical questions concerning the future status of the Negro and the future of race relations in America.

(b) Practical problems can, on the other hand, be approached only on the basis of the theoretical analysis of facts and their causal interrelations.

(c) On theoretical grounds some practical goals can be shown to be futile—that is, impossible of execution. Theoretical research thus sets the scope of practical research by determining what is feasible.

(d) Knowledge of facts is never enough for posing the practical problems concerning what is right, just, desirable and advisable. Practical conclusions are, by logical necessity, inferences from value premises as well as from factual premises.

In our study it is our ambition to keep this distinction between theoretical and practical research clear throughout the various specific problems dealt with; to treat the practical problems as problems of scientific research. We shall, therefore, have to devote the closest attention to value premises, in order to make them central in our work.

2. *Value Premises.* Value premises in research have to satisfy the following criteria :

(a) They must be *explicitly stated* and not hidden as tacit assumptions.

(b) They must be as *specific* and *concrete* as the valuation of reality in terms of factual knowledge requires.

(c) They cannot be derived directly from factual research but they will have to be *purposively selected*.

(d) They cannot be *a priori*, self-evident, or generally valid; they can have only an *hypothetical* character.

(e) Since incompatible valuations are held in society, the value premises should ideally be given as a number of sets of *alternative* hypotheses. The value judgments reached as conclusions from factual data and from these value hypotheses consist of a corresponding number of alternative plans for practical policy.

(f) In a scientific treatment of the practical aspects of social problems, the alternative sets of hypothetical value premises should not be chosen arbitrarily. The principle of selection should be their *relevance*. Relevance is determined by the interests and ideals of actual persons and groups of persons. There is thus no need of introducing value premises which are not actually held by anybody.[1]

[1] This is a rule of economy. There are, of course, no logical reasons why we might not anticipate combinations, syntheses, mutual modifications of existing value premises or even conjure up new ones and thus enlarge still more our perspective. Certainly we could go outside the culture and epoch under study and use the value premises operating there and see what would happen if they were in the culture and epoch.

(g) Within the circle of relevance so determined a still more narrow circle of *significance* may be taken to denote valuations which are held by substantial groups of people or by small groups with substantial social power. Realistic research on practical problems will have to concentrate its attention upon value premises corresponding to valuations which have high social significance or are likely to gain in social significance. On the other hand, it is certainly not necessary to adopt only those value premises which are held by a majority of the population or by a politically dominant group.

(h) The goals set by the value premises must also be *feasible*. Some courses of future development might be proved—by theoretical investigation of relevant data—to be impossible or highly improbable. Valuations bent upon the impossible should, of course, not be chosen as value premises but be theoretically criticized as infeasible. This theoretical criticism in terms of feasibility of people's actual valuations is, indeed, one of the most important tasks of social science.

(i) The set of value premises selected must not include mutually incompatible ones but must be *consistent*. In this context we must observe that sometimes a balance or a compromise in the set of value premises must be worked out and defined (to take an over-simplified example, progress may mean a sacrifice of stability and order). Some value premises are more inclusive than others and subsume others under them. Some value premises stand in a proximate relationship to others (as means to ends).

If these rules could be observed, the analysis of social problems in theoretical terms would become released from arbitrariness in the setting of problems and protected from the unconscious effect of biases. The analysis in practical terms would be elevated to the rational plane and made specific and realistic. *The aim of practical research*—starting out from the data revealed by theoretical research and from sets of explicitly stated, concretely specified, alternatively assumed, hypothetical value premises which are relevant, significant, and attainable—*is*, in general terms, *to show precisely what should be the practical and political opinions and plans for action from the point of view of the various valuations if their holders also had the more correct and comprehensive factual knowledge which science provides.*

3. *Prognoses and Programmes.* A study of valuations as they, in the form of interests and ideals, are actually held in various racial, regional, economic, and social groups of American society is, naturally, an important task in itself in the theoretical exploration of social reality. As the future social development will, in part, depend upon the reactions of the various groups and upon their relative power, the *prognoses* of future trends— which represent the ultimate goal for theoretical research— must include an investigation of the valuation and of the power behind valuations.

Prognoses and programmes are in this scheme of thinking naturally interdependent : (a) the prognoses will partly depend on the actually conceived programmes of various individuals and groups with diverse valuations and with various amounts of power; (b) rational programmes must, on the other hand, be built upon the prognoses of trends which these various groups and individuals intend to bend in one way or the other; (c) even the existing programmes of individuals and groups are, of course, founded upon ideas about future trends; (d) practical research tries to rationalize the existing programmes by connecting the valuations basic to those programmes with available scientific knowledge; (e) to the degree that practical research is successful in this, and to the extent that the educational agencies in society are effective in disseminating knowledge, it will influence trends and, consequently, be a cause of change of programmes to be considered in theoretical prognoses.

Existing programmes are multiple and conflicting, at least in a democratic society where no one group has all the power.[1] Practical research cannot, therefore, proceed on the old liberalistic doctrine that there is a 'harmony of interest' and that there is only one programme which is directed toward all

---

[1] The more 'normal' conditions are, the greater is the number of conflicting programmes. In a crisis—economic, social, or political—there really is an approximation to 'interest harmony' in society because interests have, for the time being, been taken away from long-range objectives and concentrated upon one, mutually shared, short-range objective. In a depression both employers and employees can be shown to have a common interest in economic expansion, raising volume of credit, demand, prices, production, employment and wage-earnings. In war the common interest rising above all other goals is to win victory. In a crisis the methodological problem for practical research is, therefore, relatively simple.

the good in the world. Theoretical analysis reveals that there is actual struggle and competition between individuals and between groups, and that social trends take their form as an outcome of this struggle and competition. For practical analysis, therefore, there must be alternative programmes.

4. *The Selection of Value Premises.* The scheme of principles for selecting value premises and introducing them into scientific research, presented in the last two sections, represents an ideal for social science. The possibilities of approaching it, however, are severely restricted by a number of circumstances:

(a) The scientific basis for constructing our 'field of valuations' is poor. Public opinion with respect to the Negro problem has not been studied much, and the studies made do not meet our requirements.[1] For the most part we have been forced to base our generalization on impressionistic observations of the values held by different groups and individuals.

(b) Many of the valuations held with respect to the Negro problem have much broader application than this problem, and consequently cannot be completely restricted to a uni-linear pro- and anti-Negro scale of valuations. They branch out into the whole complex of economic, social, and political problems where the Negro has a stake in contemporary American civilization. Valuations which can be observed in behaviour and opinions are not formed with respect to the Negro in abstraction, but to the Negro in specific social relations. This difficulty is, however, somewhat relieved, as there apparently is a high degree of correlation between the valuations along various scales.

(c) Valuations concern not only goals or 'ends' in the treatment of the Negro, but also the 'means' of achieving these goals and the 'by-effects' of the achievement.

(d) We cannot assume that the conflicts of valuation are raging only *between* individuals and *between* groups. It is too significant to overlook that these conflicts are also housed *within* single individuals.[2] This makes both the observation of valuations and the imputation of power to various valuations a most delicate problem.

---

[1] See Chapter V.
[2] See Chapters III and V.

(e) Partly because a single individual may hold several logically imcompatible valuations, a set of valuations is seldom systematized and made self-consistent.

(f) Another difficulty in extracting value premises arises out of the fact that they are bound up with beliefs.[1] People's opinions represent not only their volitional attitudes to social problems but also their incomplete and incorrect views as to the facts of social reality. Beliefs may influence valuations, just as valuations influence beliefs. Because we can get at only expressed opinions, which are themselves a modified form of complexes of beliefs and valuations, it is a complicated task to detect valuations. From behaviour and expressed opinions we must infer back to those complexes. From them we must infer back to basic valuations. This latter step includes the speculation as to what people's valuations would be if they were juxtaposed with correct knowledge instead of incorrect knowledge. The tracing out of a set of existing valuations, and a determination of their relevance and significance, is—for this reason alone—a difficult undertaking.

(g) Aside from all this, the very multiplicity of relevant and significant sets of valuations will, of course, raise great operational difficulties in research. The number of sets of value premises applied will have to be reduced by way of abstraction. As there is a high correlation between valuations along different scales, some main composite axes can be defined. On each axis not every point need be represented but only a few, so that one can see what difference it makes in scientific approach and practical conclusions when one moves to the one extreme or the other. But even after a reduction of the sets of value premises to a few, the analysis will tend to be complicated.

5. *The 'Instrumental Norm'*. With these complications and difficulties in view, it becomes evident that to try to consider all the existing, relevant, and significant sets of valuations with respect to the Negro problem, to relate them to relevant facts, and to draw up various sets of practical programmes is a task which cannot be accomplished within the confines of present research resources. The ideal should, however, be held clearly and uncompromisingly before our eyes as the goal for research.

---

[1] See Chapter V, Section 1.

In this situation we have seen fit to adopt the following solution: *that one single set of relevant and significant value premises be selected for utilization in a preliminary analysis* and *that other significant sets of value premises be introduced at a later stage of the investigation to make possible judgments in terms of alternative valuations and policies.*

The purely *technical and instrumental character* of the preliminary set of value premises must be borne in mind constantly. The valuations of situations and trends, institutions and policies reached in terms of the instrumental value premises also are only preliminary.

But we must not deceive ourselves on this point: the selection of the instrumental norm *has* material significance. The whole direction of our theoretical research actually becomes determined by this norm. We have given one particular set of valuations a *strategically favourable position* in the study. This is not a characteristic of our study in particular but of all research working within the same limits of research resources. It is not a bias, as the direction of research has been determined under conscious control and with the aid of explicit valuations. But measured by the standards of our ideal for research and keeping in mind all other possible sets of value premises, it is a one-sided approach, and we should be fully aware of it. In the present volume time and space have, further, prevented the subsequent complementation of our results by applying alternative sets of value premises, except at a few points.[1]

Under these circumstances the utmost importance must be attached to the choice of the instrumental norm. In Chapter IV, Section 2, we have given the reasons why we have organized this book around a set of valuations which we have called the 'American Creed'.

6. *The Value-Loaded Terms.* This very set of dynamic valuations contained in the American Creed has actually, to a great extent and despite compromises with the inherited static valuations of social science, determined the object and direction of previous research on the Negro problem. We are thus keeping to the tradition, only attempting to clarify what we are doing. The scientific work on the Negro in politics has been

[1] See, for example, Chapter VIII, Section 10.

centred upon disfranchisement. This means that the interest has been defined out of the notion that the extraordinary thing to be studied is the fact that often in America the Negro is not given the right to suffrage as other citizens. In the same vein the work on the Negro's legal status has been focused upon the specific disabilities of the Negro under the law. Negro education has likewise been studied under the main viewpoint of discrimination. The same is true of the research on the Negro as a breadwinner. Negro standards of living have been compared with those of the whites. The Negro's share in social welfare policy has been measured by the standards of equality. *Discrimination* has been the key word for most studies on the Negro problem. This very term—and all its synonyms and specifications—and the theoretical approach which it signifies are derived out of the precepts of the American Creed.

It has often been observed that these terms, and a great many other terms of more general import for social research, as, for instance, class and caste, are all value-loaded. Many scientists attempt to avoid what they rightly (as they are not specifying the value premises involved) conceive of as biases by choosing new terms for the same things which do not carry such apparent connotations of valuation. This attempt is in our view misdirected. Biases are not so easily eradicated. And in this case they signify—though in a concealed and therefore uncontrollable way—valuations necessary for the setting of scientific problems. 'Without valuations', Professor Louis Wirth writes, 'we have no interest, or sense of relevance or of significance, and, consequently, no object'.[1]

The value-loaded terms have a meaning and represent a theoretical approach, because the theoretical approach itself is determined by the valuations inherent in the governing *ethos* of a society. When this is seen clearly, and when those valuations are made explicit, and consequently, *the terms are defined in relation to the valuations*, then, and only then, are we in the position to use the terms freely without constantly endangering the theoretical analysis by permitting biases to slip in. There is thus no sense in inventing new scientific terms for the purpose. New terms for old things can give only a false sense of security

[1] In a letter to the author, September 29, 1939.

to ourselves and bewilder the general public. If the new terms covered the facts that we discussed in the old familiar terms— the facts which we *want* to discuss, because we *are interested* in them—they would soon become equally value-loaded in a society permeated by the same ideals and interests. Scientific terms become value-loaded because society is made up of human beings following purposes. A 'disinterested social science' is, from this viewpoint, pure nonsense. It never existed, and never will exist. We can make our thinking strictly rational in spite of this, but only by facing the valuations, not by evading them.

CHAPTER EIGHT

FACETS OF THE NEGRO PROBLEM[1]

1. AMERICAN MINORITIES[2]

SEVERAL attempts have been made to see the American Negro problem as part of the wider problem of minorities in America. The aspirations of minorities in the United States of America are different from those of minorities in Europe, particularly in Central and Eastern Europe. In America, minority groups are fighting for status in the larger society; in Europe they claim independence from it, and self-determination. Immigrants into America were eager to give up their language and other cultural heritages, and to adopt the ways of their new mother country. The American Creed denounces suppression and discrimination, affirms human equality, and, until recently, welcomed the immigrant minority groups.

In addition to cultural differences, there were also class differences of immigrants. They tended to be poorer than those already settled. Yet, their children and grandchildren were assimilated with astonishing success. The American educational system contributed to these adjustments. But perhaps even more important is the influence on the immigrant of the great national *ethos*, in which optimism and carelessness, generosity and callousness, are blended to give him hope and endurance.

The social scientist is also interested in the failures of the process of assimilation, and the tensions it creates. Class stratification still corresponds closely to national groups. The split of the nation into a dominant 'American' group, and a

---

[1] The following Chapter is a combination of summaries of sections of Chapter 3 of *An American Dilemma* and direct quotations from the same chapter. It also incorporates summaries of some discussions from other parts of the book.

[2] Summary of *An American Dilemma*, Chapter 3, pp. 50-53.

large number of minority groups means animosities and prejudices attached to ethnic origin, popularly called 'race'. Yet, these frictions run against the American Creed, which denounces discrimination for reasons of 'race, creed or colour'.

In trying to reconcile these conflicting valuations, the American believes that the minority groups (with some important exceptions) will, in time, be assimilated. This long-run view of ultimate assimilation can be found side by side with any amount of race prejudice. In spite of race prejudice, few Americans seem to doubt that it is the ultimate fate of their nation to incorporate without distinction not only all the Northern European stocks, but also the peoples from Eastern and Southern Europe, the Near East and Mexico. They see obstacles; they emphasize the religious and 'racial' differences; they believe it will take time. But they assume that it is going to happen, and do not have, on the whole, strong objections to it—provided it is all in the distant future.

2. The Anti-Amalgamation Doctrine[1]

The Negroes, on the other hand, are assumed to be unassimilable. Therefore the Negro problem cannot be treated simply as just another minority problem. The Negroes, together with other coloured peoples like the Chinese and the Japanese, are set apart. But unlike the Chinese and Japanese, they do not have a nation and an accepted culture of their own outside America. They cannot seek comfort in their own history or past achievements, and are thus more helplessly imprisoned as a subordinate caste in America.

The caste line is based upon, and defended by, the anti-amalgamation doctrine. Following a general methodological principle, we start from the ordinary white man's notion of what constitutes the heart of the Negro problem. When he objects to Negro assimilation, he believes that Negro stock is inferior and inter-marriage therefore undesirable. Miscegenation is considered a threat to 'racial purity', 'contrary to nature' and 'detestable'. 'Would you like to have your sister or

[1] Summary of *An American Dilemma*, Chapter 3, pp. 53-60.

daughter marry a Negro?' This stereotyped and hypothetical question is regularly raised without any intermediary reasoning as to its relevance to the problem discussed. It is an unargued appeal to 'racial solidarity' as a primary valuation. It follows from this attitude that the offspring of miscegenation is relegated to the Negro race.

Considering the biological emphasis of the anti-amalgamation doctrine, and the strong social sanctions against intermarriage tied to this doctrine, the astonishing fact is the indifference of most white Americans towards illicit miscegenation. Cohabitation with a Negro woman is, in some regions, considered a less serious breach of sexual morals than illicit intercourse with a white woman. But the tolerated illicit relations are restricted to those between white men and Negro women. A white woman's relation with a Negro meets with the full fury of anti-amalgamation sanctions.

It is true that the American Negroes too object to amalgamation. But it is our impression that their reluctance to amalgamate is merely a reaction to the white doctrine. The large number of Negroes of mixed blood makes it difficult for them to espouse the doctrine of pure blood. Yet, Negro race pride exists, but is probably a defence reaction. Exploitative sexual intercourse between white men and Negro women, the disgrace of their women who are not accepted into matrimony by the white men, and the inferior status of the mixed offspring, are practical reasons for the Negroes' race pride in his own group. But it is almost certainly not based on the condemnation of miscegenation on racial or biological grounds. The attitudes of the whites are primary and decisive; the Negroes' in the nature of accommodation or protest.

This attitude of refusing to consider amalgamation—felt and expressed in the entire country down to the non-coloured minority groups and the poor and socially insecure whites— constitutes the centre in the complex of attitudes which can be described as the 'common denominator' in the problem. In what way does this anti-amalgamation doctrine determine race relations? There is an almost unanimously held 'white man's theory of colour caste'. It is made up of the following components :

(a) The primary concern is to preserve 'race purity'. The whites are prepared to use every means to this end.

(b) Rejection of social equality is a precaution to prevent miscegenation and particularly intermarriage.

(c) The danger of miscegenation is so great that segregation and discrimination must be extended to almost every sphere: recreation, religious services, education, the law, politics, housing, shops, employment.

This popular theory is in principle open to two types of criticism: First, the end (preventing miscegenation) may be rejected; or it can be considered not worth the sacrifices which it involves: lower living standards, misery, etc. Second, one may accept the end but argue that it could be achieved without the costly caste apparatus. To undermine the popular theory of the caste mechanism, based on the anti-amalgamation maxim, one would have to prove that other motives are really at work. Some people have tried to show that competitive economic interests are at the root.

Even although the popular theory may be a rationalization it may still be a powerful force. There can be no doubt that other than economic interests are at work. (Were these the only ones the popular theory would be utterly destroyed). There are also sexual urges, inhibitions, jealousies, social fears and cravings for prestige and security. A clarification of these would explain, e.g., why the presumably biological doctrine applies only to marriage and only to relations between Negro men and white women, but not to extra-marital relations between white men and Negro women.

An analysis of the sexual and social complexes would reveal the psychological basis of the anti-amalgamation doctrine. Sex and social status are the danger points where security is most precarious. They are particularly charged in America, as a result of the Puritan tradition on the one hand, and great social mobility on the other. Both emotional complexes (sex and social status) have become connected with the Negro problem. Although they are normally concealed, and only occasionally out in the open, they determine interracial behaviour on the white side.

Facets of the Negro Problem

3. THE 'RANK ORDER OF DISCRIMINATIONS'[1]

The anti-amalgamation doctrine represents a strategic con-stellation of forces in race relations. Their charting will allow us a first general view of the discrimination patterns and will have the advantage that white Americans themselves will recognize their own paths on the map we draw. When white Southerners are asked to rank, in order of importance, various types of discrimination,[2] they consistently present a list in which these types of discrimination are ranked according to the degree of closeness of their relation to the anti-amalgamation doctrine. This rank order—which will be referred to as '*the white man's rank order of discriminations*'—will serve as an organiz-ing principle in this book. It appears, actually, only as an elaboration of the popular theory of colour caste sketched above. Like that theory, it is most clearly and distinctly per-ceived in the South; in the North ideas are more vague but, on the whole, not greatly divergent. Neither the popular theory of caste nor the rank order of discriminations has been noted much in scientific literature on the Negro problem.

The rank order held nearly unanimously is the following :

Rank 1. Highest in this order stands the bar against inter-marriage and sexual intercourse involving white women.

Rank 2. Next come the several etiquettes and discrimina-tions, which specifically concern behaviour in personal relations. (These are the barriers against dancing, bathing, eating, drinking together, and social intercourse generally; peculiar rules as to handshaking, hat lifting, use of titles, house entrance to be used, social forms when meeting on streets and in work, and so forth. These patterns

---

[1] From *An American Dilemma*, pp. 60–67.

[2] In this introductory sketch the distinction between 'segregation' and 'dis-crimination' is entirely disregarded. This distinction, signified by the popular theory and legal construct 'separate but equal', is mainly to be regarded as an equalitarian rationalization on the part of the white Americans, indicating the fundamental conflict of valuations involved in the matter. 'Segregation' means only separation and does not, in principle, imply 'discrimination'. In practice it almost always does.

are sometimes referred to as the denial of 'social equality' in the narrow meaning of the term.)

Rank 3. Thereafter follow the segregations and discriminations in use of public facilities such as schools, churches and means of conveyance.

Rank 4. Next comes political disfranchisement.

Rank 5. Thereafter come discriminations in law courts, by the police, and by other public servants.

Rank 6. Finally come the discriminations in securing land, credit, jobs, or other means of earning a living, and discriminations in public relief and other social welfare activities.

It is unfortunate that this cornerstone in our edifice of basic hypotheses, like many of our other generalizations, has to be constructed upon the author's observations.[1] It is desirable that scientifically controlled quantitative knowledge be substituted for impressionistic judgments as soon as possible.[2] It should be noted that the rank order is very apparently determined by the factors of sex and social status, so that the closer the association of a type of interracial behaviour is to sexual and social intercourse on an equalitarian basis, the higher it ranks among the forbidden things.

Next in importance to the fact of the white man's rank order of discriminations is the fact that *the Negro's own rank order is just about parallel, but inverse, to that of the white man.* The Negro resists least the discrimination on the ranks placed highest in

---

[1] There are some studies, however, which provide evidence for the hypothesis of the 'rank order of discriminations', even if they are not comprehensive enough to serve as conclusive proof. There are a host of attitude studies showing how whites have different attitudes towards Negroes in different spheres of life. Probably the earliest of these studies was that of Emory S. Bogardus, 'Race Friendliness and Social Distance,' *Journal of Applied Sociology* (1927), pp. 272-287. As an example of such studies which apply solely to Negro issues, we may cite the study by Euri Relle Bolton, 'Measuring Specific Attitudes towards the Social Rights of the Negro', *The Journal of Abnormal and Social Psychology* (January-March, 1937), pp. 384-397. For a summary of other such studies see Eugene L. Horowitz, "Race Attitudes" in Klineberg (editor), *Characteristics of the American Negro*, pp. 123-148.

[2] Such studies should not only break the rank order into finer distinctions, but also develop a measure of the distance between the ranks in the order. It would, further, be desirable to ascertain individual differences in the apprehension of this rank order, and to relate these differences to age, sex, social class, educational level and region.

the white man's evaluation and resents most any discrimination on the lowest level. This is in accord with the Negro's immediate interests. Negroes are in desperate need of jobs and bread, even more so than of justice in the courts, and of the vote. These latter needs are, in their turn, more urgent even than better schools and playgrounds, or, rather, they are primary means of reaching equality in the use of community facilities. Such facilities are, in turn, more important than civil courtesies. The marriage matter, finally, is of rather distant and doubtful interest.

Such reflections are obvious; and most Negroes have them in their minds. It is another matter, however, whether the white man is prepared to stick honestly to the rank order which he is so explicit and emphatic in announcing. The question is whether he is really prepared to give the Negro a good job, or even the vote, rather than to allow him entrance to his front door or to ride beside him in the street car.

Upon the assumption that this question is given an affirmative answer, that the white man is prepared to carry out in practice the implications of his theories, this inverse relationship between the Negro's and the white man's rank orders becomes of strategical importance in the practical and political sphere of the Negro problem. Although not formulated in this way, such a relationship, or such a minimum moral demand on the ordinary white man, has always been the basis of all attempts to compromise and come to a better understanding between leaders of the two groups. It has been the basis for all interracial policy and also for most of the practical work actually carried out by Negro betterment organizations. Followed to its logical end, it should fundamentally change the race situation in America.

It has thus always been a primary demand upon every Negro leader—who aspires to get any hearing at all from the white majority group, and who does not want to appear dangerously radical to the Negro group and at the same time hurt the 'race pride' it has built up as a defence—that he shall explicitly condone the anti-amalgamation maxim, which is the keystone in the white man's structure of race prejudice, and forbear to express any desire on the part of the Negro people to aspire to intermarriage with the whites. The request for intermarriage is easy for the Negro leader to give up. Intermarriage cannot possibly be a practical object of Negro public policy. Independent of the Negroes' wishes, the opportunity for intermarriage is not favourable as long as the great majority of the white population dislike the very idea. As a defence reaction a strong attitude against intermarriage has developed in the Negro people itself.[1] And the Negro people have no interest in defending the exploitative illicit relations between white men and Negro women. This race mingling is, on the contrary, commonly felt among Negroes to be disgraceful. And it often arouses the jealousy of Negro men.

The required soothing gesture toward the anti-amalgamation doctrine is, therefore, readily delivered. It is iterated at every convenient opportunity and belongs to the established routine of Negro leadership. For example, Robert R. Moton writes:

> As for amalgamation, very few expect it; still fewer want it; no one advocates it; and only a constantly diminishing minority practise it, and that surreptitiously. It is generally accepted on both sides of the colour line that it is best for the two races to remain ethnologically distinct.[2]

There seems thus to be unanimity among Negro leaders on the point deemed crucial by white Americans. If we attend carefully, we shall, however, detect some important differences in formulation. The Negro spokesman will never, to begin with, accept the common white premise of racial inferiority of the Negro stock. To quote Moton again:

. . . even in the matter of the mingling of racial strains,

---

[1] This goes far back. Frederick Douglass nearly endangered his position among Negroes by marrying a white woman. About Douglass, Kelly Miller observed: '. . . he has a hold upon the affection of his race, not on account of his second marriage but in spite of it. He seriously affected his standing with his people by that marriage.' (Kelly Miller, *Race Adjustment—Essays on the Negro in America* (1908), p. 50.) And W. E. B. Du Bois tells us in his autobiography: 'I resented the assumption that we desired it (racial amalgamation). I frankly refused the possibility while in Germany and even in America gave up courtship with one 'coloured' girl because she looked quite white, and I should resent the inference on the street that I had married outside my race'. (*Dusk of Dawn* (1940), p. 101.) See also Chapter 30, Section 2, *An American Dilemma*.

[2] *What the Negro Thinks* (1929), p. 241.

however undesirable it might seem to be from a social point of view, he [the Negro] would never admit that his blood carries any taint of physiological, mental, or spiritual inferiority.[1]

A doctrine of equal · natural endowments—a doctrine contrary to the white man's assumption of Negro inferiority, which is at the basis of the anti-amalgamation theory—has been consistently upheld. If a Negro leader publicly even hinted at the possibility of inherent racial inferiority, he would immediately lose his following. The entire Negro press watches the Negro leaders on this point.

Even Booker T. Washington, the supreme diplomat of the Negro people through a generation filled with severe trials, who was able by studied unobtrusiveness to wring so many favours from the white majority, never dared to allude to such a possibility, though he sometimes criticized most severely his own people for lack of thrift, skill, perseverance and general culture. In fact, there is no reason to think that he did not firmly believe in the fundamental equality of inherent capacities. Privately, local Negro leaders might find it advisable to admit Negro inferiority and, particularly earlier, many individual Negroes might have shared the white man's view. But it will not be expressed by national leaders and, in fact, never when they are under public scrutiny.[2] An emphatic assertion of equal endowments is article number one in the growing Negro 'race pride'.

Another deviation of the Negro faith in the anti-amalgamation doctrine is the stress that they, for natural reasons, lay on condemning exploitative illicit amalgamation. They turn the tables and accuse white men of debasing Negro womanhood, and the entire white culture for not rising up against this practice as their expressed antagonism against miscegena-

---

[1] *Ibid*, p. 239.

[2] An exception, which by its uniqueness, and by the angry reception it received from the Negroes, rather proves our thesis, is the remarkable book by William H. Thomas, *The American Negro* (1901). The fact that Negroes privately often enjoy indulging in derogatory statements about Negroes in general is not overlooked. It is, however, a suppression phenomenon of quite another order. See Chapter 36, Section 2, *An American Dilemma*.

tion should demand. Here they have a strong point, and they know how to press it.[1]

A third qualification in the Negro's acceptance of the anti-amalgamation doctrine, expressed not only by the more 'radical' and outspoken Negro leaders, is the assertion that intermarriage should not be barred by law. The respect for individual liberty is invoked as an argument. But, in addition, it is pointed out that this barrier, by releasing the white man from the consequences of intimacy with a Negro woman, actually has the effect of inducing such intimacy and thus tends to increase miscegenation. Moton makes this point:

> The Negro woman suffers not only from the handicap of economic and social discriminations imposed upon the race as a whole, but is in addition the victim of unfavourable legislation incorporated in the marriage laws of twenty-nine states, which forbid the intermarriage of black and white. The disadvantage of these statutes lies, not as is generally represented, in the legal obstacle they present to social equality, but rather in the fact that such laws specifically deny to the Negro woman and her offspring that safeguard from abuse and exploitation with which the women of the white race are abundantly surrounded. On the other side, the effect of such legislation leaves the white man, who is so inclined, free of any responsibility attending his amatory excursions across the colour line and leaves the coloured woman without redress for any of the consequences of her defencelessness; whereas white women have every protection, from fine and imprisonment under the law to enforced marriage and lynching outside the law.[2]

But even with all these qualifications, the anti-amalgamation doctrine, the necessity of assenting to which is understood by nearly everybody, obviously encounters some difficulties in the minds of intellectual Negroes. They can hardly be expected to accept it as a just rule of conduct. They tend to accept it

---

[1] 'The rape which your gentlemen have done against helpless black women in defiance of your own laws is written on the foreheads of two millions of mulattoes, and written in ineffaceable blood'. (W. E. B. Du Bois, *The Souls of Black Folk* (1924; first edition, 1903), p. 106.)

[2] *Op. cit.*, pp. 208-209.

merely as a temporary expedient necessitated by human weakness. Kelly Miller thus wrote:

> . . . you would hardly expect the Negro, in derogation of his common human qualities, to proclaim that he is so diverse from God's other human creatures as to make the blending of the races contrary to the law of nature. The Negro refuses to become excited or share in your frenzy on this subject. The amalgamation of the races is an ultimate possibility, though not an immediate probability. But what have you and I to do with ultimate questions, anyway ?[1]

And a few years later, he said:

> It must be taken for granted in the final outcome of things that the colour line will be wholly obliterated. While blood may be thicker than water, it does not possess the spissitude or inherency of everlasting principle. The brotherhood of man is more fundamental than the fellowship of race. A physical and spiritual identity of all peoples occupying common territory is a logical necessity of thought. The clear seeing mind refuses to yield to give its assent to any other ultimate conclusion. This consummation, however, is far too removed from the sphere of present probability to have decisive influence upon practical procedure.[2]

This problem is, of course, tied up with the freedom of the individual. 'Theoretically Negroes would all subscribe to the right of freedom of choice in marriage even between the two races ',[3] wrote Moton. And Du Bois formulates it in stronger terms:

> . . . a woman may say, I do not want to marry this black man, or this red man, or this white man. . . . But the impudent and vicious demand that all coloured folk shall write themselves down as brutes by a general assertion of their unfitness to marry other decent folk is a nightmare.[4]

Negroes have always pointed out that the white man must not be very certain of his woman's lack of interest when he rises

---

[1] *Race Adjustment*, p. 48.   [2] *Out of the House of Bondage* (1914), p. 45.
[3] *Op. cit.*, p. 241.   [4] Editorial, *The Crisis* (January, 1920), p. 106.

to such frenzy on behalf of the danger to her and feels compelled to build up such formidable fences to prevent her from
marrying a Negro.

With these reservations both Negro leadership and the Negro
masses acquiesce in the white anti-amalgamation doctrine.
This attitude is noted with satisfaction in the white camp.
The writer has observed, however, that the average white man,
particularly in the South, does not feel quite convinced of the
Negro's acquiescence. In several conversations, the same white
person, in the same breath, has assured me, on the one hand,
that the Negroes are perfectly satisfied in their position and
would not like to be treated as equals, and on the other hand,
that the only thing these Negroes long for is to be like white
people and to marry their daughters.

Whereas the Negro spokesman finds it possible to assent to
the first rank of discrimination, namely, that involving miscegenation, it is more difficult for him to give his approval to
the second rank of discrimination, namely, that involving
'etiquette' and consisting in the white man's refusal to extend
the ordinary courtesies to Negroes in daily life and his
expectation of receiving certain symbolic signs of submissive-
ness from the Negro. The Negro leader could not do so without
serious risk of censorship by his own people and rebuke by the
Negro press. In all articulate groups of Negroes there is a demand to have white men call them by their titles of Mr., Mrs.,
and Miss; to have white men take off their hats on entering a
Negro's house; to be able to enter a white man's house through
the front door rather than the back door, and so on. But on the
whole, and in spite of the rule that they stand up for 'social
equality' in this sense, most Negroes in the South obey the
white man's rules.

Booker T. Washington went a long way, it is true, in his
Atlanta speech in 1895 where he explained that: 'In all things
that are purely social we [the two races] can be as separate as
the fingers, yet one as the hand in all things essential to mutual
progress.'[1] He there seemed to condone not only these rules of
'etiquette' but also the denial of 'social equality' in a broader
sense, including some of the further categories in the white

[1] *Up from Slavery* (1915; first edition, 1900), pp. 221-222.

man's rank order of discrimination. He himself was always most eager to observe the rules. But Washington was bitterly rebuked for this capitulation, particularly by Negroes in the North. And a long time has passed since then; the whole spirit in the Negro world has changed considerably in three decades.

The modern Negro leader will try to solve this dilemma by iterating that no Negroes want to intrude upon white people's private lives. But this is not what Southern white opinion asks for. It is not satisfied with the natural rules of polite conduct that no individual, of whatever race, shall push his presence on a society where he is not wanted. It asks for a general order according to which *all* Negroes are placed under *all* white people and excluded from not only the white man's society but also from the ordinary symbols of respect. No Negro shall ever aspire to them, and no white shall be allowed to offer them.

Thus, on this second rank of discrimination there is a wide gap between the ideologies of the two groups. As we then continue downward in our rank order and arrive at the ordinary Jim Crow practices, the segregation in schools, the disfranchisement, and the discrimination in employment, we find, on the one hand, that increasingly larger groups of white people are prepared to take a stand against these discriminations. Many a liberal white professor in the South who, for his own welfare, would not dare to entertain a Negro in his home and perhaps not even speak to him in a friendly manner on the street, will be found prepared publicly to condemn disfranchisement, lynching, and the forcing of the Negro out of employment. Also, on the other hand, Negro spokesmen are becoming increasingly firm in their opposition to discrimination on these lower levels. It is principally on these lower levels of the white man's rank order of discriminations that the race struggle goes on. The struggle will widen to embrace all the thousand problems of education, politics, economic standards, and so forth, and the frontier will shift from day to day according to varying events.

Even a superficial view of discrimination in America will reveal to the observer: first, that there are great differences, not only between larger regions, but between neighbouring communities; and, second, that even in the same community changes occur from one time to another. There is also, contrary to the rule that all Negroes are to be treated alike, a certain amount of discretion depending upon the class and social status of the Negro in question. A white person, especially if he has high status in the community, is, furthermore, supposed to be free, within limits, to overstep the rules. The rules are primarily to govern the Negro's behaviour.

Some of these differences and changes can be explained. But the need for their interpretation is perhaps less than has sometimes been assumed. The variations in discrimination between local communities or from one time to another are often not of primary consequence. All of these thousand and one precepts, etiquettes, taboos, and disabilities inflicted upon the Negro have a common purpose: to express the subordinate status of the Negro people and the exalted position of the whites. They have their meaning and chief function as symbols. As symbols they are, however, interchangeable to an extent: one can serve in place of another without causing material difference in the essential social relations in the community.

The differences in patterns of discrimination between the larger regions of the country and the temporal changes of patterns within one region, which reveal a definite trend, have on the contrary, more material import. These differences and changes imply, in fact, a considerable margin of variation within the very notion of American caste, which is not true of all the other minor differences between the changes in localities within a single region—hence the reason for a clear distinction. For exemplification it may suffice here to refer only to the differentials in space. As one moves from the Deep South through the Upper South and the Border states to the North, the manifestations of discrimination decrease in extent and intensity; at the same time the rules become more uncertain and capricious. The 'colour line' becomes a broad ribbon of arbitrariness. The old New England states stand, on the whole, as the antipode to the Deep South. This generalization requires important qualifications, and the relations are in process of change.

The decreasing discrimination as we go from South to North

in the United States is apparently related to a weaker **basic** prejudice. In the North the Negroes have fair justice and are not disfranchised; they are not Jim-Crowed in public means of conveyance; educational institutions are less segregated. The interesting thing is that the decrease of discrimination does *not* regularly follow the white man's rank order. Thus inter-marriage, placed on the top of the rank order, is legally permitted in all but one of the Northern states east of the Missis-sippi. The racial etiquette, being the most conspicuous element in the second rank, is, practically speaking, absent from the North. On the other hand, employment discriminations, placed at the bottom of the rank order, are at times equally severe, or more so, in some Northern communities, even if it is true that Negroes have been able to press themselves into many more new avenues of employment during the last generation in the North than in the South.

There is plenty of discrimination in the North. But it is—or rather its rationalization is—kept hidden. We can, in the North, witness the legislators' obedience to the American Creed when they solemnly pass laws and regulations to condemn and punish such acts of discrimination which, as a matter of routine, are committed daily by the great majority of the white citizens and by the legislators themselves. In the North, as indeed often in the South, public speakers frequently pronounce principles of human and civic equality. We see here revealed in relief the Negro problem as an American Dilemma.

4. RELATIONSHIPS BETWEEN LOWER CLASS GROUPS[1]

A comparison of the Negro problem with American minority problems in general yields useful perspectives, both in the similarities and dissimilarities. America is not merely a 'white man's country', but it belongs more specifically to the elderly, male, upper-class, Protestant Northerner. In this wider context, the Negro problem is but a local and temporary feature of the eternal problem of regulating fairly and justly the conflicting interests of different groups.

[1] Summary of *An American Dilemma*, pp. 67-73.

There is a general structure of relations between groups with different powers and advantages. Our hypothesis is that in a society where there are broad social classes and more minute distinctions and splits in the lower strata, the lower class groups will, to a large extent, keep each other subdued, thus relieving, to that extent, the higher classes of this otherwise painful task of monopolizing their own power and advantages. This hypothesis contradicts the Marxian theory that there is solidarity between the lower class groups. The Marxian view derives partly from a value judgment that such solidarity is desirable, but it has also been put forward as a description of actual trends. The solidarity between poor whites and Negroes has been said to be 'natural', and the conflicts due to 'illusions'.

Psychological evidence is against the Marxian view. Human frustration and aggression, and the displacement of aggression, exaggerate any split within the lower class groups, preventing the identification necessary for solidarity and thus strengthening spite and resentment.

Caste consigns the majority of Negroes to the lower class. At the same time it accentuates the desire for prestige and social distance within the Negro caste. It sometimes causes a more minute class division than exists outside. Social distinctions within a minority group are often an index of the social isolation of that group from the larger society. At the same time, there is a strong feeling of fellowship within the caste as a whole.

The Negroes' friends are often found amongst the upper class of whites, amongst people with economic security and social confidence, who are not competing with the Negroes. A liberal outlook is more likely to emerge from a position of security and education. The poor, generally, are not liberal or radical, although such opinions would often be in their interests. But reforms in the South may cause an upheaval in opinions that would also affect the Negro problem.

5. CASTE AND CLASS[1]

Several terms have been used to describe the inferior status of the Negroes. The term 'caste', already in use before the

[1] Summaries of Chapter 31 and Appendix 8, *An American Dilemma.*

Civil War, has been widely employed in the literature. Alternatives to be found are 'race' and 'class'. 'Race' is inappropriate, because it has biological and genetic connotations which are both false and dangerous. The term 'class' is confusing because it is used to refer to a non-rigid status group from which individual members can rise or fall. There is a class stratification *within* each of the two groups. But applied to the difference *between* Negroes and whites the term 'class' blurs a significant distinction. 'Minority group' and 'minority status' are also not appropriate because they fail to distinguish between the *temporary* special disabilities of recent white immigrants and the *permanent* disabilities of Negroes and other coloured people. We have adopted throughout this book the term 'caste'.

In attempting to define our value premise for the discussion of social stratification, we must first note that Americans in all castes and classes strongly disapprove of distinctions in social status. Class differences are denounced with patriotic pride. This egalitarian philosophy is often contrasted favourably with the philosophy of the Old World. Indeed, the amount of class discrimination in Europe is frequently exaggerated in the attempt to compare the free competition and boundless opportunities in the New World with the supposedly rigid system of class privilege in England and Continental Europe.

There is a paradox in the tremendous differences in wealth and social position, and the condemnation of class differences. But this is partly explained by the nature of the American Creed: it does not demand equality of economic and social rewards independent of an individual's luck, ability and push. It demands equality of opportunity. Hence the class differences denounced are those that are rigid. The Creed demands free competition. In the sphere of social stratification this means the combination of 'equality' and 'liberty'. Inequality, in so far as it is the outcome of competition, is accepted. Our value premise will be the American ideal of free competition and equal opportunity.

Classes and class differences in America are in fact the results of the restriction of free competition and thus of the absence of full social integration. The upper classes enjoy their privileges because the lower classes are restricted in their 'pursuit of happiness' by various types of relative or absolute social monopolies.

Caste consists of much more drastic restrictions of free competition. The member of a lower caste cannot change his status, except by secret and illegitimate 'passing', which is open to only a few. Caste may thus be viewed as the extreme case of absolute rigid class. Such a harsh deviation from the normal American social structure and the American Creed cannot occur without internal conflict and without a system of false beliefs and ignorance, aided by certain mechanical controls in the law and in institutions. To the extent, however, that false beliefs in Negro inferiority are removed by education and to the extent that white people are made to see the degradations they inflict upon Negroes, the American Creed will be able to make its assault on caste.

A discussion of caste and class structures tends to acquire a static bias, and most studies of the Negro class structure have contributed little to our knowledge of the social dynamics. Caste and class structures are changing all the time, and an important aspect of the problem is the way in which the relations change.

Another weakness of the studies has been that the correlation between the factors giving status—occupation, income and wealth, education, family background, complexion, etc. —have not been quantified. In order to forecast trends in social mobility, and to make practical proposals, the weighting of these factors is essential.

The ideal community study should start from a statistical analysis of vital, social, and economic data. The less measurable data on attitudes, cultural traits, behaviour patterns in which social stratification is expressed, and the 'feeling' of social status or towards social status, should then be observed and the results integrated into the statistical knowledge. All the time, we should be aware that the Negro class structure is rapidly changing. The dynamics consist not merely in the tensions and frictions within the class structure, but, more important, in the movement of the whole class structure.

Furthermore, we must observe the differences in social stratification between the South and the North, between rural and urban districts, between city communities of different sizes, etc. A picture of the cross section of any particular community inevitably involves distortions that can be corrected only by contrasting it with knowledge derived from other sources.

With respect to most characteristics, human beings do not fall into 'natural' groups. Such divisions involve abstractions and arbitrary decisions. When we choose 'class' and 'caste' as tools to organize our observations, we must be on our guard lest we unduly limit our view of other distinctions. Such traits as age, sex, 'personality', 'race philosophy', rural or urban background, and perhaps others are important to the study of any Negro community.

For the purposes of illustration, we may indicate briefly how 'age' is an important concept for the study of such a community. The continuous advance of education and related factors of change make the younger Negroes different from the older ones. Age differentials are a basis of solidarity and create tension within the class structure. As time passes, the young become the old and move the entire class structure. Taking a cross-sectional view, the constellation of caste, class and age may give a configuration like the one which Hortense Powdermaker compresses in the following statement:

> The White aristocrats are the least, and the Poor Whites are the most, hostile towards the other race. Among the Negroes the upper class is the most, and the lower class the least, antagonistic toward the Whites. Again, the older generation of Whites are the ones in whom most affect is aroused by the inter-racial situation, while the younger generation is inclined to view the problem more casually. The reverse is true for the Negroes: the older generation shows the tolerance and calmness traditionally associated with age, while the young people are the ones who feel most intensely on racial issues.[1]

Such a situation is, of course, fraught with impending changes for the fundamental class and caste relations. Taking a long-range view, the Negro class structure of to-day is only the passing arrangement of a society in transition.

[1] *After Freedom* (1939), p. 334.

6. A Parallel to the Negro Problem[1]

There are at least two groups of people, besides the Negroes, who stand out by their appearance, dress, and behaviour, and whose status in some ways resembles that of the Negroes: women and children. In order to gain perspective to the Negro problem, and avoid falling, as a result of concentrated study, into the trap of considering it unique, a consideration of the women's problem may be useful.

Historically, there are interesting similarities. In early common law, women and children were placed under paternal jurisdiction. When a legal status had to be found for the imported Negro servants in the seventeenth century, the most natural analogy was the status of women and children. Bible passages could also be invoked to link women, servants, mules and other property. Thus slaves were originally placed under the power of the *pater familias*.

There were, of course, from the beginning important differences: Women were elevated as ornaments and displayed with pride, while the Negro slaves became chattels. But the paternalistic construction was useful as a moral defence of slavery. The literature before the Civil War is full of such apologies.

The parallel, however, goes deeper than providing a mere defence ideology. Women then lacked many rights which all free white citizens of age enjoyed. They were subjected to political, legal, educational, social and economic restrictions. Although the status of women everywhere was similar, there was a particularly close relation in the South between the subordination of women and that of Negroes. It is well expressed in a comment attributed to Dolly Madison, that the Southern wife was the 'chief slave of the harem'.

From the beginning, the fight of the Negro slaves for liberation was, therefore, closely linked with the fight for women's emancipation. In the beginning of the political emancipation of women during the first decades of the nineteenth century, the Southern States led the way in granting civil rights to women. The South was then still the stronghold of liberal

1 Postscript, pp. 237–262.

thinking. Abolitionist societies flourished while the North was uninterested. Afterwards, the two movements developed in close relation and were both gradually driven from the South.

Women suffragists received their political education from the Abolitionist movement. Many began their public careers by speaking for Negro emancipation and only later came to fight for women's rights. The women's movement recruited much of its support as a result of its affiliation with the Abolitionists. They were convinced that victory in the Civil War would bring the suffrage to them as well as to the Negroes.

But the Union's victory brought disappointment. Even their abolitionist friends turned against them, and the Republican party shied away from their demands. The women leaders were charged with being democrats and traitors. Even a few Negroes, invited to the women's convention in January, 1869, denounced the women for jeopardizing the black man's chances for the vote. There had been earlier signs of antipathy between the Abolitionists and the women's suffrage movement. As early as 1833, when Oberlin College opened its doors to women—the first College to do so—the Negro men students joined other men students in protest. The Anti-Slavery Convention held in London in 1840 refused to seat the women delegates from America, and it was on this instigation that the first women's rights convention was called. The Civil War and Reconstruction sharply divided the women's problem from the Negro problem, aggravating the rift. After the passage of the 13th, 14th and 15th Amendments, which gave legal rights to Negroes but not to women, the women's movement split off completely from the Negroes' movement, except for such support of both movements as that by rare old liberals like Frederick Douglass. In 1903, Anna Howard Shaw, one of the leaders of the women's movement at that time, said at a convention in New Orleans: 'Never before in the history of the world have men made former slaves the political masters of their former mistresses!'

The ideological and economic forces behind the two movements had much in common. Both women and Negroes broke away, with the progress of the Industrial Revolution, from the

185

pre-industrial paternalistic system. Most men, until recently, accepted the doctrine that women, like Negroes, had inferior endowments of many of those qualities that carry prestige and power. The study of women's intelligence and personality has broadly the same history as that of Negroes'. Women, like Negroes, have often been brought to believe themselves in their inferiority. As the Negro was awarded his 'place' in society, so there was a woman's 'place'. In both cases men believed that, in confining them to their place, they acted in the true interests of the subordinate groups. The myth of the 'contented women', who did not want suffrage or other civil rights, had the same social function as the myth of the 'contented Negro'. In both cases there was probably—in a static sense—some truth behind it.

Political franchise was not granted to women until recently. Even now it is in all countries difficult for a woman to attain public office. As with Negroes, there are certain 'women's jobs'. They carry usually low salaries and few opportunities of promotion. Trade unions prevent women from competing. Women's competition, like Negroes', has been particularly dreaded by men because of the low wages for which women are prepared to work, just because they have so few alternative opportunities. Women often object to working under women, just as Negroes often prefer white bosses.

In personal relations with both women and Negroes white men generally are less professional and more human, more paternalistic and protective. As in Germany every gentile was said to have had his pet Jew, so in the South every white has his 'pet nigger', or—in the upper strata—several. We sometimes marry the pet woman. We tend to be kinder to women, treating them as wards, not as competitors and equals.

The parallel between the position of Negroes and women remains, even though the paternalistic order of society, in which the historical origin of the parallel can be found, is disappearing. Women are handicapped in the competitive race by the function of procreation; Negroes are labouring under the doctrine of unassimilability, which has survived slavery. To-day the latter barrier is stronger in America than the former. But the former is more inexorable in the long run.

7. THE MANIFOLDNESS AND THE UNITY OF THE NEGRO PROBLEM[1]

The Negro problem has the manifoldness of human life: it touches every other social issue: race, culture, population, bread-winning, economic and social policy, law, crime, class, family, recreation, school, church, press, organizations, politics, attitudes.

These links with other aspects of American life have been multiplied, first, by the migration of Negroes and by the industrialization of the South, and, second, by the policies of the New Deal, the War and post-war government activities. Before these recent upheavals, the practical Negro problem involved civil rights, education, charity, and little more. Now it has widened, in step with welfare policies, and it involves housing, nutrition, medicine, education, relief and social security, wages and hours, working conditions, child and women labour, and the armed forces and war industries. The Negroes have thus acquired a broader and more diversified front from which to push on. The great importance of the New Deal for the Negroes is that almost for the first time has the government carried out substantial social policies without excluding them.

Some, also amongst the Negroes themselves, have concluded that the Negro problem has disappeared and given place to a 'class problem'. They have argued that the Negro sharecropper is poor, not because of his colour, but because of his class—like some equally poor whites. Although from a practical angle there is some truth in this argument, theoretially it is another form of escapism. It draws heavily on the idealistic Marxist doctrine of the 'class struggle'. It obscures the whole system of special deprivations imposed on the Negro only because he is not white. There is, behind the manifold manifestations of the Negro problem, a unity. It clusters round the complex of valuations of American caste. This fundamental complex derives its emotional charge from race prejudice, from its manifestations in discrimination, and, indeed, from its inconsistency with the American Creed.

[1] Summary of Chapter 3, pp. 73-75, *An American Dilemma.*

8. THE THEORY OF THE VICIOUS CIRCLE[1]

A deeper reason for the unity of the Negro problem will be apparent when we try to formulate our hypothesis concerning its dynamic causation. The mechanism that operates here is the 'principle of cumulation', also commonly called the 'vicious circle'.[2] This principle has a much wider application in social relations. It is, or should be, developed into a main theoretical tool in studying social change.

Throughout this inquiry, we shall assume a general inter-dependence between all the factors in the Negro problem. White prejudice and discrimination keep the Negro low in standards of living, health, education, manners and morals. This, in its turn, gives support to white prejudice. White prejudice and Negro standards thus mutually 'cause' each other. If things remain as they are and have been, this means that the two forces balance each other. Such a static 'accommodation' is, however, entirely accidental. If either of the factors changes, this will cause a change in the other factor, too, and start a process of interaction where the change in one will continually be supported by the reaction of the other factor. The whole system will be moving in the direction of the primary change, but much further. This is what we mean by cumulative causation.

If, for example, we assume that for some reason white prejudice could be decreased and discrimination mitigated, this is likely to cause a rise in Negro standards, which may decrease white prejudice still a little more, which would again allow Negro standards to rise, and so on through mutual interaction. If, instead, discrimination should become in-tensified, we should see the vicious circle spiralling downward. The original change might equally well be a change of Negro standards upward or downward. The effects would, in a similar manner, run back and forth in the interlocking system of interdependent causation. In any case, the initial change would be supported by consecutive waves of repercussions from the reactions of the other factor.

---

[1] *An American Dilemma*, pp. 75-78.
[2] See Chapter IX in this volume. We call it the 'principle of cumulation' rather than 'vicious circle' because it can work in an 'upward' desirable as well as in a 'downward' undesirable direction.

The same principle holds if we split one of our two variables into component factors. A rise in Negro employment, for instance, will raise family incomes, standards of nutrition, housing, and health, the possibilities of giving Negro youth more education, and so forth, and all these effects of the initial change will, in their turn, improve the Negroes' chances of getting employment and earning a living. The original push could have been on some other factor than employment, say, an improvement of health or educational facilities for Negroes. Through action and interaction the whole system of the Negro's 'status' would have been set in motion in the direction indicated by the first push. Much the same thing is true of the development of white prejudice. Even assuming no changes in Negro standards, white prejudice can change, for example, as a result of an increased general knowledge about biology, eradicating some of the false beliefs among whites concerning Negro racial inferiority. If this is accomplished, it will in some degree censor the hostile and derogatory valuations which fortify the false beliefs, and education will then be able to fight racial beliefs with more success.

By this we want only to indicate an explanatory scheme of dynamic causation which we are going to use throughout this inquiry. As pointed out in Appendix 3,[1] and as we shall find in later chapters, the interrelations are in reality much more complicated than in our abstract illustrations, and there are all sorts of irregularities in the reaction of various factors. But the complications should not force us to give up our main hypothesis that a cumulative principle is at work in social change. It is this hypothesis which gives a theoretical meaning to the Negro problem as a special phase of all other social problems in America. Behind the barrier of common discrimination, there is unity and close interrelation between the Negro's political power; his civil rights; his employment opportunities; his standards of housing, nutrition, and clothing; his health, manners, and law observance; his ideals and ideologies. The unity is largely the result of cumulative causation binding them all together in a system and tying them to white discrimination. It is useful, therefore, to interpret

[1] Chapter IX in this volume.

all the separate factors from a central vantage point—the point of view of the Negro problem.

Another corollary from our hypothesis is practical. In the field of Negro politics any push upward directed on any one of those factors—if our main hypothesis is correct—moves all other factors in the same direction and has, through them, a cumulative effect upon general Negro status. An upward trend of Negro status in general can be effected by any number of measures, independent of where the initial push is localized. By the process of cumulation it will be transferred through the whole system.

But, as in the field of economic anti-depression policy, it matters a lot how the measures are proportioned and applied. The directing and proportioning of the measures is the task of social engineering. This engineering should be based on a knowledge of how all the factors are interrelated: what effect a primary change upon each factor will have on all other factors. It can be generally stated, however, that it is likely that a rational policy will never work by changing only one factor, least of all suddenly and with great force. In most cases that would either throw the system entirely out of gear or else prove to be a wasteful expenditure of effort which could reach much further by being spread strategically over various factors in the system and over a period of time.

This—and the impracticability of getting political support for a great and sudden change of just one factor—is the rational refutation of so-called panaceas. Panaceas are now generally repudiated in the literature on the Negro problem, though usually without much rational motivation. There still exists, however, another theoretical idea which is similar to the idea of panacea: the idea that there is *one* predominant factor, a 'basic factor'. Usually the so-called 'economic factor' is assumed to be this basic factor. A vague conception of economic determinism has, in fact, come to colour most of the modern writings on the Negro problem far outside the Marxist school. Such a view has unwarrantedly acquired the prestige of being a particularly 'hard-boiled' scientific approach.

As we look upon the problem of dynamic social causation,

this approach is unrealistic and narrow. We do not, of course, deny that the conditions under which Negroes are allowed to earn a living are tremendously important for their welfare. But these conditions are closely interrelated to all other conditions of Negro life. When studying the variegated causes of discrimination in the labour market, it is, indeed, difficult to perceive what precisely is meant by 'the economic factor'. The Negro's legal and political status and all the causes behind this, considerations by whites of social prestige, and everything else in the Negro problem belong to the causation of discrimination in the labour market, in exactly the same way as the Negro's low economic status is influential in keeping down his health, his educational level, his political power, and his status in other respects. Neither from a theoretical point of view —in seeking to explain the Negro's caste status in American society—nor from a practical point of view—in attempting to assign the strategic points which can most effectively be attacked in order to raise his status—is there any reason, or, indeed, any possibility of singling out 'the economic factor' as basic. In an interdependent system of dynamic causation there is no 'primary cause' but everything is cause to everything else.

If this theoretical approach is bound to do away in the practical sphere with all panaceas, it is, on the other hand, equally bound to encourage the reformer. The principle of cumulation—in so far as it is true—promises final effects of greater magnitude than the efforts and costs of the reforms themselves. The low status of the Negro is tremendously wasteful all around—the low educational standard causes low earnings and health deficiencies, for example. The cumulatively magnified effect of a push upward on any one of the relevant factors is in one sense a demonstration and a measure of the earlier existing waste. In the end, the cost of raising the status of the Negro may not involve any 'real costs' at all for society, but instead may result in great 'social gains' and actual savings for society. A movement downward will, for the same reason, increase 'social waste' out of proportion to the original saving involved in the push downward of one factor or another.

These dynamic concepts of 'social waste', 'social gain', and 'real costs' are mental tools originated in the practical man's workshop. To give them a clearer meaning—which implies expressing also the underlying social value premises—and to measure them in quantitative terms represents from a practical viewpoint a main task of social science. Fulfilling that task in a truly comprehensive way is a stage of dynamic social theory still to be reached but definitely within sight.

9. A THEORY OF DEMOCRACY[1]

The factors working on the white side in our system of dynamic causation were brought together under the heading 'race prejudice'. For our present purpose, it is defined as discrimination by whites against Negroes. One viewpoint on race prejudice needs to be presented at this point, chiefly because of its close relation to our hypothesis of cumulative causation.

The chemists talk about 'irreversible processes', meaning a chemical process that moves in one direction but, for practical purposes, cannot be moved back to its original state (as when a house burns down). When we observe race prejudice as it appears in American daily life, it is difficult to avoid the reflection that it seems so much easier to increase than to decrease it. One is reminded of the old saying that nineteen fresh apples do not make a single rotten apple fresh, but that one rotten apple rapidly turns the fresh ones rotten. When we come to consider the various causative factors underlying race prejudice—economic competition; urges and fears for social status; and sexual drives, fears, jealousies, and inhibitions— this view will become understandable. It is a common observation that the white Northerner who settles in the South will rapidly take on the stronger race prejudice of his new surroundings; while the Southerner going North is likely to keep his race prejudice unchanged and perhaps even to communicate it to those he meets. The Northerner in the South will find the whole community intent upon his conforming to local patterns. The Southerner in the North will not meet such concerted action, but will feel, rather, that others are adjusting towards

[1] *An American Dilemma*, pp. 78-80.

him wherever he goes. If the local hotel in a New England town has accommodated a few Negro guests without much worry one way or the other, the appearance one evening of a single white guest who makes an angry protest against it might permanently change the policy of the hotel.

If we assume that a decrease in race prejudice is desirable—on grounds of the value premise of the American Creed and of the mechanism of cumulative wastage just discussed—such a general tendency, inherent in the psychology of race prejudice, would be likely to force us to a pessimistic outlook. One would expect a constant tendency towards increased race prejudice, and the interlocking causation with the several factors on the Negro side would be expected to reinforce the movement. Aside from all valuations, the question must be raised: Why is race prejudice, in spite of this tendency to continued intensification which we have observed, nevertheless on the whole not increasing but decreasing?

This question is, in fact, only a special variant of the enigma of philosophers for several thousands of years: the problem of Good and Evil in the world. One is reminded of that cynical but wise old man, Thomas Hobbes, who proved conclusively that, while any person's actual possibilities to improve the lot of his fellow creatures amounted to almost nothing, everyone's opportunity to do damage was always immense. The wisest and most virtuous man will hardly leave a print in the sand behind him, thought Hobbes, but an imbecile crank can set fire to a whole town. Why is the world, then, not steadily and rapidly deteriorating, but rather, at least over long periods, progressing? Hobbes raised this question. His answer was, as we know: the State, *Leviathan.* Our own tentative answer to the more specific but still overwhelmingly general question we have raised above will have something in common with that of the post-Elizabethan materialist and hedonist, but it will have its stress placed differently, as we shall see subsequently.

Two principal points will be made by way of a preliminary and hypothetical answer, as they influence greatly our general approach to the Negro problem. The first point is the American Creed, the relation of which to the Negro problem will become apparent as our inquiry proceeds. The Creed of progress, liberty, equality, and humanitarianism is not so uninfluential on everyday life as might sometimes appear.

The second point is the existence in society of huge institutional structures like the church, the school, the university, the foundation, the trade union, the association generally, and, of course, the state. It is true, as we shall find, that these institutional structures in their operation show an accommodation to local and temporary interests and prejudices—they could not be expected to do otherwise as they are made up of individuals with all their local and temporary characteristics. As institutions they are, however, devoted to certain broad ideals. It is in these institutions that the American Creed has its instruments: it plays upon them as on mighty organs. In adhering to these ideals, the institutions show a pertinacity, matched only by their great flexibility in local and temporary accommodation.

The school, in every community, is likely to be somewhat more broadminded than local opinion. So is the sermon in church. The national labour assembly is prone to decide slightly above the prejudice of the median member. Legislation will, on the whole, be more equitable than the legislators are themselves as private individuals. When the man in the street acts through his orderly collective bodies, he acts more as an American, as a Christian, and as a humanitarian than if he were acting independently. He thus shapes social controls which are going to condition even himself.

Through these huge institutional structures, a constant pressure is brought to bear on race prejudice, counteracting the natural tendency for it to spread and become more intense. The same people are acting in the institutions as those who manifest personal prejudice. But they obey different moral valuations on different planes of life. In their institutions they have invested more than their everyday ideas which parallel their actual behaviour. They have placed in them their ideals of how the world ought to be. The ideals thereby gain fortifications of power and influence in society. This is a theory of social self-healing that applies to the type of society we call democracy.

10. PRACTICAL CONCLUSIONS FROM ALTERNATIVE VALUE PREMISES[1]

In the South, the whole unique political system, particularly the poll tax, is becoming increasingly shaky. And this is realized by Southerners with any insight into politics, even if they do not admit it publicly. More specifically, the disfranchisement of Negroes is losing its entire legal foundation and now depends mainly on illegal measures. From a conservative point of view, this is the more dangerous as respect for law is undoubtedly gaining ground in the South. Not only the legal but also the political security of the white primary will crumble, and this is well known to conservative whites. They always stress in discussion that its only basis, and, therefore, the only basis of the one-party system and the 'Solid South', is the strict adherence to the 'gentleman's agreement' between the defeated and the victorious candidates in the primary. If there are going to be more serious splits on real political issues in the South—and many changes tend to build up liberal counterforces in the South—it is not only possible but, as I have often heard Southerners stress, probable that such agreements will not be upheld. As during the period of Popularism in the 1890's, the Negroes are then going to be allowed to register and vote. And more Negroes will then have lawful rights to suffrage.

Our conclusion is, thus, that the Southern franchise situation, which on the surface looks so quiet, is highly unstable and that, indeed, *the Southern conservative position on Negro franchise is politically untenable for any length of time*. If this analysis is accepted, and if the value premise is agreed upon, that *changes should, if possible, be made not by sudden upheavals but in gradual steps*, we reach the further practical conclusion that it is an urgent and truly conservative interest for the South *to start enfranchising its Negro citizens as soon as possible*. This is seen by a small group of Southern liberals.[2]

[1] *An American Dilemma*, Chapter 23, pp. 518–520.

[2] 'For the dominant political party in a third of the United States to rule that in 1942 only qualified "white voters" shall be allowed to participate in the selection of the officials of our democratic government would be an anachronism too dangerous to democratic principles and Christian ideals to be preserved for the sake of old days and old ways'. Statement by Association of Southern Women for the Prevention of Lynching, in Jessie Daniel Ames, *The Changing Character of Lynching*, published by Commission on Interracial Cooperation (July, 1942), p. 70. See also Virginius Dabney, *Liberalism in the South* (1932), pp. 253–254.

It is true, as Woofter reminds us in discussing this point, that the situation is complicated. In many areas of the South where the Negro population is most densely concentrated, 'this group is less intelligent, less familiar with American institutions, farther down in the economic scale, and most likely to constitute the corrupt mass-voting element.''[1] So are also large sectors of the poor white masses in the South. As we have seen, Southern conservative politics is not without guilt in this situation. But for this very reason—the foreseeable changes being what they are—the more urgent is it from a conservative point of view *to begin allowing the higher strata of the Negro population to participate in the political process as soon as possible, and to push the movement down to the lowest groups gradually*. The more urgent is it also *to speed up the civic education of these masses who are bound to have votes in the future*. It would, in this late stage of the development, be wise also to go the full way and gradually open the white primary to Negroes. This, actually, would be a means of decreasing the temptation for defeated primary candidates to break the 'gentleman's agreement' and, consequently, to preserve the one-party system for a longer time than would be possible otherwise.[2]

In their own history of the past century, the Southern conservatives can see abundantly the negative proofs, and from the history of democratic politics all over the world the positive proofs, for this thesis, that political conservatives, who have been successful for any length of time, have always foreseen impending changes and have put through the needed reforms themselves in time. By following this tactic they have been able to guard fundamental conservative interests even in the

[1] T. J. Woofter, Jr., *The Basis of Racial Adjustment* (1925), p. 151.

[2] I am here looking on the problem from a conservative point of view and assuming that to preserve the one-party system would be desirable. The liberals want, on the contrary, to get away from the white primary and from the one-party system altogether, but they do not anticipate radical changes in the future. They further want to do away with political discrimination and, therefore, come to the same conclusion:

'For the white South, what is needed above all is fairness, a determination to enforce suffrage tests equitably on white and black alike, and resolve to break away from the one-party system and to regain pre-eminence in the national forums of political action by building a political system around the live national issues and forgetting the more or less dead issue of Negro domination.' (T. J. Woofter, Jr., *The Basis of Racial Adjustment* (1925), p. 167.)

framing of the reforms. They have thereby also succeeded in slowing them up; changes have not overwhelmed them as avalanches. They have kept control and preserved a basis for the retention of their political power. Southern conservatism should further learn from history that, over a period of time, the conservative forces in a society cannot afford to abstain from the tremendous strategic advantage of forming the party of 'law and order'. This is such an immense interest for conservatism that if—for constitutional and other reasons—the law does not come to the conservatives even when they are in power, the conservatives had better come to the law.

But the great majority of Southern conservative white people do not see the writing on the wall. They do not study the impending changes; they live again in the pathetic illusion that the matter is settled. They do not care to have any constructive policies to meet the trends. They think no adjustments are called for. The chances that the future development will be *planned* and *led* intelligently—and that, consequently, it will take the form of cautious, foresighted reforms instead of unexpected, tumultuous, haphazard breaks, with mounting discords and anxieties in its wake—are indeed small. But we want to keep this last question open. Man is a free agent, and there are no inevitabilities. All will depend upon the thinking done and the action taken in the region during the next decade or so. History can be made. It is not necessary to receive it as mere destiny.

CHAPTER NINE

THE PRINCIPLE OF CUMULATION[1]

IN social science we have been drawing heavily on the notions and theories of the much farther developed natural sciences, particularly physics. The notion of equilibrium, for instance, has been embedded in our reasoning for centuries. It is present in most research of the present day, even when it is not formally introduced. In most social research we have restricted our use of the equilibrium notion to that simple and static variant of it, the *stable equilibrium*. It is this equilibrium notion which is implicit in the sociological constructions of 'maladjustment' and 'adjustment' and all their several synonyms or near-synonyms, where equilibrium is thought of as having a virtual reality in determining the direction os change.[2] We propose the use of *other equilibrium notions* besides this simplest one. For dynamic analysis of the process of change in social relations, it is highly desirable that we disengage our minds from the stable equilibrium scheme of thinking. The other types of equilibrium notions are often better descriptions of social reality than the stable one.

If we succeed in placing a pencil upright on its end, it is also in equilibrium, but an unstable one, a *'labile status'* of balancing forces, as we discover when we touch it. No 'adjustment', 'adaptation', or 'accommodation' toward the original position will follow the application of a push, but only an accelerated movement away from the original state of balance. A third type of equilibrium is present when a pencil is rolling on a plane

---

[1] *An American Dilemma*, Appendix 3, pp. 1065–1070.

[2] These equilibrium concepts have been used also as vehicles for introducing hidden valuations—i.e., bias—into research; see Chapter VII. Our interest in this chapter is directed only upon their usefulness as theoretical tools. To explain these other notions it is convenient to think in terms of analogies. The stable equilibrium is like a hanging pendulum, unmoving, and with no tendency to move unless jolted.

surface: it may come to rest anywhere. A fourth type is what we might call 'created equilibrium', that is, arranging a disordered pile of pencils so that they fit into a box by intelligent 'engineering'.

The most important need is to give place in our hypothetical explanatory scheme to a rational recognition of the cumulation of forces. In one branch of social science, economics, these various types of equilibrium notions have lately been used to great advantage. The principle of cumulation has given us, for the first time, something which approaches a theory of economic dynamics.[1] In a previous chapter[2] we referred to the theory of the 'vicious circle' as a main explanatory scheme for this inquiry into the Negro problem; the scheme reappears in every part of our book. The following brief notes are intended to give an abstract clarification of the theory and a perspective on some of its future potentialities as a method of social research.

In considering the Negro problem in its most abstract aspect, let us construct a much simplified mental model of dynamic social causation. We assume in this model society of our imagination a white majority and a Negro minority. We assume, further, that the interrelation between the two groups is in part determined by a specific degree of 'race prejudice' on the side of the whites, directed against the Negroes. We assume the 'plane of living' of the Negroes to be considerably lower than that of the whites. We take, as given, a mutual relationship between our two variables, and we assume this relationship to be of such a type that, on the one hand, the Negroes' plane of living is kept down by discrimination from the side of the whites while, on the other hand, the whites' reason for discrimination is partly dependent upon the Negroes' plane of living. The Negroes' poverty, ignorance, superstition, slum dwellings, health deficiencies, dirty appearance, disorderly conduct, bad odour and criminality stimulate and feed the antipathy of the whites for them. We assume, for the sake of simplicity, that society, in our abstract model, is in 'balance' initially. By this we mean that conditions are static, that our two

[1] For a simplified model of cumulative economic causation, see Gunnar Myrdal, *Monetary Equilibrium* (1939), pp. 24 ff.
[2] Chapter VIII, Section 8 in this volume.

variables exactly check each other: there is—under these static conditions—just enough prejudice on the part of the whites to keep down the Negro plane of living to that level which maintains the specific degree of prejudice, or the other way round.

If now, in this hypothetically balanced state, for some reason or other, the Negro plane of living is lowered, this will —other things being equal—in its turn increase white prejudice. Such an increase in white prejudice has the effect of pressing down still further the Negro plane of living, which again will increase prejudice, and so on, by way of mutual interaction between the two variables, *ad infinitum*. A cumulative process is thus set in motion which can have final effects quite out of proportion to the magnitude of the original push. The push might even be withdrawn after a time, and a permanent change will still remain or the process of change will even continue without a new balance in sight. If, instead, the initial change had been, say, a gift from a philanthropist to raise the Negro plane of living, a cumulative movement would have started in the other direction, having exactly the same causal mechanism. The 'vicious' circle works both ways.

The Negroes' 'plane of living' is, however, a composite entity. Let us, while retaining our major assumptions, approach a more realistic conception by splitting up this quantity into components, assuming that the cumulative principle works also in their causative interrelations. Besides 'relative absence of race prejudice on the side of whites', we introduce a number of variables: levels of 'Negro employment', 'wages', 'housing', 'nutrition', 'clothing', 'health', 'education', 'stability in family relations', 'manners', 'cleanliness', 'orderliness', 'trustworthiness', 'law observance', 'loyalty to society at large', 'absence of criminality' and so on. All these variables—according to our hypotheses—cumulate. In other words, we assume that a movement in any of the Negro variables in the direction toward the corresponding white level will tend to decrease white prejudice. At the same time white prejudice is assumed to be, directly or indirectly, one of the causative factors effective in keeping the levels low for the several Negro variables. It is also our hypothesis that, on the whole, a rise in any single one of the Negro variables will tend to raise all the other Negro variables and thus, indirectly as well as directly, result in a cumulatively enforced effect upon white prejudice. A rise in employment will tend to increase earnings; raise standards of living; and improve health, education, manners, and law observance: and *vice versa*; a better education is assumed to raise the chances of a higher salaried job, and *vice versa*; and so all the way through our whole system of variables. Each of the secondary changes has its effect on white prejudice.

If, in actual social life, the dynamics of the causal relations between the various factors in the Negro problem correspond to our hypotheses, then—assuming again, for the sake of simplicity, an initially static state of balanced forces—*any change in any one of these factors, independent of the way in which it is brought about, will, by the aggregate weight of the cumulative effects running back and forth between them all, start the whole system moving* in one direction or the other as the case may be, with a speed depending upon the original push and the functions of causal interrelation within the system.

Our point is not simply that many forces are 'working in the same direction'. Originally we assumed that there was a balance between these forces, and that the system was static, until we introduced one push coming in at one point or the other. When the system starts rolling, it is true that *the changes in the forces*—though not all the forces themselves—work in one direction; but this is because the variables are assumed to be interlocked in such a causal mechanism that a change of any one causes the others to change *in the same direction*, with a secondary effect upon the first variable, and so on.

We may further notice that the 'balance' assumed as initial status was not a stable equilibrium at all—of the type which is tacitly assumed in the notions of 'maladjustment', 'adjustment', 'accommodation', 'social lag'—and, further, that on our hypotheses there is not necessarily assumed to exist any new 'balance', or 'equilibrium', or 'harmony' toward which the factors of the system 'adjust' or 'accommodate'. In the use of this theoretical model for problems of social reality, the initial state of labile balance, which we assumed for simplicity in our demonstration, will, of course, never be found. What we shall have to study are *processes of systems actually rolling* in the one direction or other, systems which are constantly subjected to all sorts of pushes from outside through all the variables, and which are mov'ng because of the cumulative effect of all these pushes and the interaction between the variables.

The individual factors into which we split the Negroes' plane of living can, of course, be split again, and it is the purpose of scientific analysis to do so. The causal relations between the sub-factors, and between them and all other factors, will be assumed to be ruled by the same cumulative principle. White race prejudice, here assumed as the 'cause' of discrimination, is not a solid and static factor. To begin with, it depends upon discrimination itself. If, for some reason—for example, the demand of the employer during a war emergency, or the ruling of a trade union—white workers actually come to work with Negroes as fellow workers, it has been experienced that prejudice often adjusts to the changed amount of discrimination. White prejudice itself can be split into a great number of beliefs and valuations; to a degree, both of these two types of factors are dependent upon each other as we have seen[1] and, consequently, are under the rule of the cumulative principle.

Throughout this treatise on the Negro problem the model of dynamic causation—and the implied scepticism toward the idea of stable equilibrium—is kept steadily at the back of our mind. A main viewpoint in our study of every single factor in the Negro problem is thus its interrelation with all other factors and their cumulative effect upon the status of the Negro. The principle of cumulation allows us to see that there is sense in the general notion of the 'status of the Negro'. We should, indeed, have liked to present in our study a general index, year by year or at least decade by decade, as a quantitative expression of the movement of the entire system we are studying: the status of the Negro in America. Such an index would have about the same significance as the general indices of production or prices or any other complex systems of interdependent variables. The index is an average. It would, for the same principal reasons, have to be broken down for regions, classes, and items, and this breaking down would have the same

[1] Chapter V in this volume.

scientific function in an analysis. It would give quantitative precision to the concept of the general status of the Negro —a concept which, because of the cumulative principle, we cannot escape. And it always clarifies our reasoning to be compelled to calculate a quantitative value for a notion we use. Materials for such an index of (relative and absolute) Negro status are, to a great extent, available, and the general theory of the index offers a methodological basis for its construction. But the work of constructing and analysing a general index of Negro status in America amounts to a major investigation in itself, and we must leave the matter as a proposal for further research.

Our chief task is to analyse the causal interrelation within the system itself as it works under the influence of outside pushes and the momentum of the processes within. The system is much more complicated than appears from our abstract presentation. To begin with, all factors must be broken down by region, social class, age, sex and so on. Since we are studying a race relation, the number of combinations increases by multiples for each classification applied. White prejudice, for instance, varies not only with the status of the white man, but also with the Negro's social class and the field of Negro behaviour in relation to which race prejudice is active. There are also Negro prejudices in the system.

Each factor has its peculiarities and irregularities. White prejudice, for instance, changes not only as a reaction to actual changes in the Negro plane of living, but also to expectations of such changes. The latter reaction may be totally different from the former: a higher plane of living among Negroes, when it is actually achieved, may be expected to effect a *decrease* of white prejudice, but the *expectation* of it in the future might *increase* prejudice, particularly in the South. It is possible, finally, that certain social classes of whites—say poor whites in the South—even in the fairly long-range perspective will react with increased prejudice against the Negro's approaching the white man's status.

The system thus becomes complicated, but the fundamental principle of cumulative causation remains. The scientific ideal is not only to define and analyse the factors, but to give for each one of them a measure of its quantitative strength in influencing the other factors, as well as a measure of ability to be influenced itself by outside forces. The time element becomes of paramount importance in these formulas. As we have exemplified for the factor of white prejudice, the effects might have different signs in the short and in the long run. Even when this is not the case, the effects will be spread differently along the time axis. A rise of employment, for instance, will almost immediately raise some standards of living, but a change in levels of education or health is slow to be achieved, its effect on the other factors is in turn delayed, which slows up the whole process of cumulation. The system regularly develops under a great multitude of different outside pushes, primarily directed against almost every single factor. The actual pushes go in both directions, thus often *turning the system around on its axis as it is rolling*. Ideally, the scientific solution of the Negro problem should thus be given in the form of an interconnected series of quantitative equations, describing the movement of the actual system under various influences. That this complete, quantitative and truly scientific solution is far beyond the horizon does not need to be pointed out. But in principle it is possible to execute, and it remains as the scientific ideal guiding our endeavours.

This conception of a great number of interdependent factors, mutually cumulative in their effects, disposes of the idea that there is *one* predominant factor, a 'basic factor'. This idea—mainly in the form of a vague conception of economic determinism—has been widely accepted in the writings on the Negro problem during the last decade. As we see the methodological problem, this one-factor hypothesis is not only theoretically unclear but is contradicted by easily ascertainable facts and factual relations. As a scientific approach it is narrow.[1]

[1] The usual economic one-factor theory is available in two extreme versions, depending upon the type of political teleology involved: (1) a radical Marxist version, where the expectation is an economic revolution which will change everything and even eradicate race prejudice; (2) a liberalistic version which does not expect an economic revolution and which—on the assumption that no significant change can be brought about except by tackling the 'basic factor', the economic system—is pessimistic about any type of induced change. There are all sorts of intermediary positions and also compromises toward recognizing that factors other than the economic one have some influence. But the one-factor theory always implies a fatalistic tendency and prevents a rational conception of interdependence and cumulative dynamic causation. See Chapter VII, Section 3.

The theoretical system of dynamic social causation we have selected corresponds more closely to the practical man's common-sense ideas than to the apprehension of reality met in scientific writings on the Negro problem. The social scientist tends to rely too much on static notions and to give *a priori* too dominant a role to a 'basic factor'. The professional philanthropist, the Negro educator, the Negro trade unionist, the leaders of Negro defence organizations like the N.A.A.C.P., the Urban League, or the Inter-racial Commission, and, indeed, the average well-meaning citizen of both colours, on the other hand, pragmatically applies our hypothesis.[1] To use once more our parallel from modern economic theory: when the economists during the last two decades abandoned the classical static equilibrium approach and went on to construct a dynamic theory of causal interrelations in a process of change, what they did was to apply the pragmatic notions of bankers, businessmen, and labour leaders and to systematize them. This revolutionized economic theory and had great importance for the scientific planning of economic policy. A rational strategy in the Negro problem also assumes a theory of dynamic causation.[2]

[1] The best formulation of our hypothesis available in the literature is, thus, to be found in a book by a practical man writing without scientific pretensions but out of lifelong experiences: 'There is a vicious circle in caste. At the outset, the despised group is usually inferior in certain of the accepted standards of the controlling class. Being inferior, members of the degraded caste are denied the privileges and opportunities of their fellows and so are pushed still further down and then are regarded with that much less respect, and therefore are more rigorously denied advantages, and so around and around the vicious circle. Even when the movement starts to reverse itself—as it most certainly has in the case of the Negro—there is a desperately long unwinding as a slight increase in good will gives a little greater chance and this leads to a little higher accomplishment and that to increased respect and so slowly upward toward equality of opportunity, of regard, and of status.' (Edwin R. Embree, *Brown America* (1931), p. 200.) To this it should only be added that even if the unwinding process is working with time lags so is the opposite movement. In spite of the time lags, the theory of the vicious circle is a cause for optimism rather than for pessimism. The cumulative principle works both ways.

[2] Some remarks on this problem are made in Chapter VIII, Section 8.

PART 3

CHAPTER TEN

ENDS AND MEANS IN POLITICAL
ECONOMY[1]

ECONOMISTS use the categories 'ends' and 'means' in order to systematize the material of knowledge, not simply causally, but teleologically.[2] They start from a situation which they take to have been analysed and explained; they then postulate that a certain situation is desirable and its attainment possible (the 'end' or 'purpose'), and they examine the various courses of action ('means') suitable for the attainment of the end. Normally, 'end' refers not to the total final situation but only to some part of it which is considered important. Thus a third category has to be introduced, in addition to 'means' and 'ends', viz., 'incidental effects' or 'by-effects'. These may be desired or not. Occasionally 'by-effects' embrace all components of the process which are not 'means' in a narrow sense; or again sometimes the whole process is looked upon as 'means'. By-effects then refer only to the final situation.

The use of the categories ends and means to order and arrange knowledge did not become important until political economy had outgrown the naïve philosophy of natural law. The essence of this philosophy was a direct identification of teleology and causality. The law of nature was also a norm. Hence the philosophy of natural law was, and was bound to be, fundamentally a theory of *laissez-faire*. It is, of course, true that the doctrine of liberty can assume either a revolutionary or a conservative content. But revolution is only a means for setting free the play of the natural forces through which the

[1] From *Zeitschrift für Nationalökonomie*, vol. IV, number 3, 1933, translated from the German by the editor.
[2] The German *final* is translated throughout as 'teleological'.

norm is fulfilled. The revolution is therefore final. Once carried out, it has only to be protected against reaction. Once freedom is won, a consideration in terms of ends and means becomes pointless, indeed meaningless, for the causal and the teleological aspects now coincide. The realization of natural laws is the end, and also the means.

If, on the other hand, we think of social life in terms of ends and means, we arrive, not at the *laissez-faire* inherent in the philosophy of natural law, but at some kind of 'economic planning'. This does not mean that non-intervention may not be looked upon as a more appropriate policy to promote a given end than any alternative. But it is never a foregone conclusion. It can be seen to be the case only after the consequences of all possible courses have been explored. Modern economic liberals attempt to prove the desirability of non-intervention in this manner. By acknowledging that this kind of proof is required, they accept the ends-means scheme, and the element of planning inherent in it. They implicitly reject, at any rate methodologically, the old a-prioristic theory of *laissez-faire*.

Neither the physiocrats nor the early classical writers had therefore any use for the dichotomy between ends and means as a central principle of organizing knowledge. Pre-physiocratic writers, on the other hand, whose interests were more directly 'practical', frequently did think in these terms. In concrete and practical matters the use of these concepts is, indeed, as old as the attempt to rationalize what we call 'the will'. They appeared frequently also in the economic literature of natural law. But they were not used as the basis of a system. Nor could they have been used as such until a clear distinction had been drawn between causal and teleological, between theoretical and 'practical' economics. J. S. Mill in his fifth essay (in *Essays on Some Unsettled Questions of Political Economy*, London, 1844) expresses this attempt clearly for the first time in economic theory.

It is significant that the later classics felt the need to draw this distinction. In the attempt to reorient themselves after the inconclusive controversy between the two old natural law doctrines of liberty—the revolutionary and the conservative—they sought a unifying solution, weighing the arguments on both sides against each other. As a result, they came to recognize the logical impossibility of rationalizing 'ought' directly in terms of 'is'. Eclectic liberalism thus turned into social policy and 'planning'.

In the course of this reorientation 'practical' economics was separated from theoretical, and analysis was pressed into the categories of ends and means. (Marxist theory represents another solution in which the original natural law identification is preserved but bolstered up with the notion of historical inevitability and deprived of its utopian optimism.) The significance of this distinction between 'practical' and 'theoretical' economics is not always clear, because it is confused with an entirely different meaning of these terms. 'Practical' is identified with 'concrete', and 'theoretical' with 'abstract'.

The above, only roughly sketched, line of thought is important for an understanding of why a split between the 'causal' and the 'teleological' occurred already at a time when doubts about the objectivity of ends and the truth of values had not yet arisen. It was then still believed that ends can be established scientifically, the only difference being that proof of those ends was required; proof was no longer seen to lie in 'the nature of things'. As before, ends were thought to be a proper subject of research, requiring, however, special methods for their discovery. These methods were believed to differ from those employed in other spheres of knowledge.

But this philosophical conception of the objectivity of ends is by no means the only possible basis for a teleological approach. Later writers became more relativistic with respect to values, without abandoning the ends-means scheme as an instrument of arranging and organizing knowledge. They hoped thereby to be able to answer practical questions of policy, believing that we can make only *hypothetical* value judgments as to what ought to be done. J. S. Mill already used to argue in this fashion, although he had economic 'theory' alone in mind ('theory' in the second sense of only schematic, incomplete knowledge; Mill's and Senior's authority established this meaning in economics). In Mill's view our practical judgments are hypothetical until, after a more complete scientific inquiry into the sphere of values, we can establish the ends. But his successors were even more sceptical, saying that this can never be done. To postulate ends for social activity is a moral choice for the individual. Yet, they continued, this does not prevent us from determining the proper means of attaining those ends, once we assume the ends to be given. The trend towards this more relativistic view of the relation between ends and means is gradual. It is a slow process, a groping towards a clear and thorough formulation, culminating in Max Weber's methodological essays.

Now all scientific activity consists of generalization and systematization. It may, perhaps, be argued that only *causal* explanations can be systematized and generalized in such a way that they could, ideally, contain all knowledge, but that the teleological approach can be applied only to a particular case: Take a concrete situation which is intended to be changed in a specified manner; given the political and institutional set-up, only a limited number of all theoretically possible means would be feasible. What would be the by-effects of the various courses? This would be the problem. It could arise only in a particular concrete situation. It could not be immediately generalized. On the other hand, it would be inconvenient to have to muster our whole knowledge of reality for each particular case. It would be useful to have a systematic organization of our data, yet with a practical orientation; to have a science of 'practical', yet systematic, economics that would bring order into the countless practical political problems with which we are daily faced.

But, on reflection, it appears that even in the concrete practical case, of which we have suggested that it could be handled without a general practical systematic framework (although less conveniently than with such a framework) this view can be shown to be untenable. For we must have systematized at least our theoretical knowledge of causal relations, even if we could forego the advantages of a systematized teleological practical economics. All science, at any rate all social science, is 'practical', even in its purely causal theory, because it must choose one from amongst an infinite number of possible ways of collecting and ordering its infinitely large mass of empirical data. This choice is dictated by the demands of practical economics. But we cannot read off the demands of practice on theory, which shaped decisively all causal explanation, from the concrete and particular political questions. The demands must be based upon a *generalizing* and *teleological* orientation towards the crude raw material of knowledge.

To what extent, and in what way, can such a thoroughly relativistic, yet systematic, practical political economy, which logically precedes any causal explanation, be built upon the categories, ends and means as principles of organization? This is the central methodological problem of practical political economy, a problem all the more crucial since there can hardly be any other principle on which to base it.

*　　　*　　　*

The basic idea of this principle is this: By splitting economic processes into (1) a given initial situation, (2) alternative means, and (3) the hypothetical end, it should be possible to concentrate all value judgments on the third link, viz., the purpose. This is particularly important for relativists. They can now discuss purely scientifically not only the initial situation but also the means. They can conduct a teleological argument objectively. Values are attached to the means only indirectly, via the values attached to the end which the means can serve. In themselves, means are supposed to be neutral, value-free.

This argument leads to the core of utilitarianism. According to the utilitarians the morality of an action should be judged solely by its probable consequences. No action is good or bad in itself. Thus the purpose of production is consumption. It is not an end, and therefore neither good nor bad in itself. Or, to take another illustration, the same idea underlies the notion of the so-called economic principle. Apart from particular connotations in certain connections, this principle expresses simply the idea that means are ethically 'neutral'. The notion of the neutrality of means has, incidentally, been the reason why moralists have always been irritated by what they decried as the 'dismal science'. We now see that this notion is implicit in the whole method of thinking that runs in terms of ends and means.

Now it is quite obvious that values are attached not only to 'ends' but also to 'means'. Means are not ethically neutral.

The value judgement must compare and choose between alternative courses. Value judgments thus refer always to whole sequences, not merely to the anticipated final outcome. This is too obvious not to have been vaguely felt to be true. But we begin to see why it has never been stated explicitly and why it has led only to muddles and contradictions.

For once it is admitted that means are not neutral, the whole construction collapses, or at any rate loses its simplicity. But its simplicity has been the main argument in its favour. For the denial of the simple dichotomy implies—unless we return to the belief in the objectivity of values—that reservations and hypotheses have to be introduced *at each stage* in the argument, not merely for postulating the end.

Moreover, as we have seen, by 'end' we do not normally mean the *total* final situation (nor by 'means' the total sequence), but only a relevant section of it. (Otherwise a discussion of alternative means would be impossible: only exceptionally do different means lead to precisely identical total results.) Therefore, even if it were possible to isolate means as neutral, we would still have to discuss the by-effects which may not be neutral.

Modern theorists are prone to stress the hypothetical character of their practical and political recommendations, emphasizing the distinction between their analysis and economic policy by pointing out that they are not competent to make value judgments on social goals. But the admission that values cannot be known objectively, or even the decision to eliminate value judgments from the discussion—which can be done irrespective of whether they are held to be objective or subjective—complicates greatly the ends-means construction. The political value judgment refers not only to the end but to every component in all possible alternative sequences which are to be compared.

If we could assume that the value judgment applies to the end only and that the means are neutral, and if we could ignore the by-effects, the analysis could normally be limited to a sufficiently small number of alternative sequences. By eliminating a large number of irrelevant cases the problem would be greatly simplified. The analysis could be strictly limited for the same reason for which the problem would become objectively soluble. All possible means could then be compared with each other directly and objectively. (This, indeed, is meant by saying that the means are 'neutral', i.e., that they are valuable only with respect to a purpose, assumed to be given.) But as soon as we admit that values can be attached to means independently, every single link in the chain of the argument is opened. It follows, first, that the problem can no longer be solved unequivocally even if the end is given. Second, we are no longer entitled to confine ourselves without an intensive examination to a limited selection of the infinite number of alternative sequences which may flow from the initial situation. Such a selection would have to follow some guiding principle of how to weigh objectively the various possible courses against each other. Just because it would make this selection possible would the ends-means scheme be such a convenient basis for a systematic arrangement of our data.

The question is simply how much can be done on a relatively high level of abstraction. All scientific analysis is bound to abstract a good deal. Suppose a definite end is given and that this end is the only value hypothesis. Only those courses which would bring about this end would then be relevant. This is the first elimination. The remaining alternatives (means) lead to a greater or lesser extent to the end. The differences between these alternatives are purely quantative. Now all those alternatives that lead to the end only less effectively are excluded. This is the second elimination. Now only a few alternatives remain which have to be examined thoroughly. We have thus been able to limit the field of inquiry by an objective but highly abstract analysis.

The initial choice of an end is, however, both logically and politically arbitrary. That it is logically arbitrary need not trouble us: it follows from the admission of relativism. But we can overcome the political arbitrariness, at least to some extent, by discussing more than one end. Every new choice of an end presents us with the same problem of elimination. Things are now more complicated, but since the comparison for any given single end is still purely quantitative, this whole preliminary analysis can still be conducted on a fairly high level of abstraction.

Now relativists can easily be forced to admit further that neither means, nor, of course, their by-effects are value-free. But it follows from this admission that we cannot simply subordinate means to ends objectively. Ends cease to be the sole value premises and can no longer be used as simple categories for classifying alternative courses of action. Every *combination* of end, means, and by-effects, i.e., every alternative sequence itself, thus becomes a value premise and a category of classification. But the simplification essential for analysis depends upon the possibility of eliminating the large majority of alternatives. If the elimination is not guided by objective principles the remaining choice between alternatives is arbitrary, and the practical results of the analysis of these alternatives have no claim to scientific objectivity.

*   *   *

None of these difficulties, however, stems from relativism. If values were knowable, we could indeed tie up all the links, and we could dispense with hypothetical ends, but only after a causal analysis of the possible sequences of events. Causal knowledge of *all* these sequences is a pre-condition for the establishment of the objective values, which can then be attached to the components of the sequences. Then, after having compared the now valued alternatives, we could discover objectively the right conduct in a particular situation. But, since the organization of causal knowledge in turn presupposes a practical organization (although now conducted in terms of objective values), we are faced with the same difficulty of finding a starting point.

For, if a particular means has an independent positive or negative value in an objective system of values, it has also instrumental value as a means. This instrumental value can be discovered only through a causal analysis of alternative courses and end situations, in relation to postulated ends and by-effects with independent values. It follows that objectivism is no better off than relativism: Unless we deny that means can have independent value, unless we abstract entirely from side-effects, and unless we assume that particular ends have independent value only, and never instrumental value in relation to some other end—and none of these assumptions is justified—we are not entitled to use the ends-means construction for an abstract but objective limitation of our field of inquiry. Even if we could somehow limit the field of inquiry by some kind of (objective) intuition, any further analysis of sequences within the ends-means scheme would require knowledge of the objective values of all components of the sequences under examination; but this knowledge can be gained only through a theoretical analysis of infinitely more sequences than those which were especially selected for analysis by the initial intuition. Indeed, this intuition already would have to embrace all sequences relating the particular ends-means problem to the whole social problem, of which it is an integral part.

This is the crucial point. Since the difficulty concerns the establishment of values themselves, the inquiry would have to go into the general theory of objective value, and thus beyond the particular methodological problem with which I am concerned here. Valuations can be integrated only as valuations of whole sequences. Valuations can be understood only through an analysis which embraces, amongst other things, all possible causal knowledge. Social scientists, irrespective of their value positions, often seem to agree that objectivism with respect to values, were it only tenable, would substantially simplify their work. We have argued that this is a mistake. All the difficulties would still be there.

One could not even conceive that somebody should have direct access to a catalogue of objective values, or to infallible revelations, so that he only has to read them off when required. This is obviously impossible and the idea would appear nonsensical even to an objectivist. But the reason for this can be found in what we have said above. Any factual change, such as a change of climate, population, or technology, would alter the whole value catalogue. Such a catalogue can therefore never be given *a priori*. An infallible intuition into objective values, say through our conscience, would have to encompass, complete and error-free, not only the sphere of values, but also the whole of reality, in all its particulars.

The notion of objective values implies, of course, that valuations can be not mutually inconsistent and yet correct.

Even then there would have to be interdependence between the objective values, which would mean that values have instrumental value in relation to others. If causal connections are correctly understood in every detail, the instrumentality of values can be judged correctly. Then valuations are mutually consistent. If not, particular valuations are false since a more accurate observation of causal connections reveals contradictions.

In the doctrine of objective values it is also often assumed that all values form part of a single hierarchy, that they can all be derived from a single supreme norm. This is neither self-evident nor does it follow from the thesis of consistency. For there are inherent values, and all values contain an element of inherent value, besides their instrumental value.

Such an assumption appeals, however, to our sense of order. It proved also convenient when people attempted what we have shown to be the impossible task of compiling a catalogue of specific values. The following well-known recipe was adopted: Postulate a supreme value, but make it as vacuous as you can, so that nobody can cast doubt on it. At the same time, try to choose one with sufficiently numerous loose associations with general moral ideas, so that this supreme value appears to have moral content. (The most important example in the history of economic doctrines is the maxim of utility.) Next, try to arrange sets of sub-values underneath the supreme value and proceed to increasingly specific valuations. Particularly specialists, who are less plagued by philosophical doubts, have gone far in the direction of specific valuations. The deduction follows a rather loose, conveniently simplified and adjusted causal analysis. This is true, particularly of utilitarian arguments, which tend to reject the inherent value of means by saying that nothing is good or bad in itself, but only in relation to the anticipated result. But perhaps we ought not to be too critical. It is truly a hard task to have to fill the empty supreme principles with content.

I have mentioned these tendencies amongst objectivists only in order to throw light upon certain corresponding tendencies of relativists, especially among economists. One such tendency can be found in the following argument: Let us admit that there are no objective values, only subjective valuations. But let us imagine that these valuations of social phenomena—viewed from the individual's standpoint—be such that the judgments to which they give rise are logically consistent (or at least that they *ought to* be, if the person were only to think correctly): The value judgments do not contradict each other and they are also logically co-ordinated in such a manner that they follow, more or less directly, from the supreme postulate of value. The latter, of course, is not an objective value but a valuation by a particular individual, implicit in all his valuations of a lower order. We thus preserve the whole scheme of thought of an objective political theory—from which the notion of a conceptual hierarchy of values is a heritage—with the only small difference that we have to introduce somewhere, and perhaps best in the supreme valuation, a subjective, yet general, premise. Max Weber also occasionally belongs to this group of writers.

This notion of a logical hierarchy of values is scientifically untenable. Perhaps the most important result of modern psychology of major philosophical interest is the clarification of the untenability of this dogma. The fallacy can be shown without recourse to the now plentiful psychological evidence. It is sufficient to point out that the connection between the different value *attitudes* of an individual or a social group is itself psychological, and thus, from the here relevant point of view, subjective. It is true that the value *notions*, which have to be distinguished from the *attitudes*, contain certain, not always correct, logical and theoretical attempts at co-ordination. But these notions are only rationalizations of deeper-seated attitudes. The rationalizations in turn are psychologically determined by, amongst other things, traditional objectivist habits. These habits are not, of course, real valuations of an individual. Behind his rationalizations are his attitudes. These neither are, nor could they be, logically coherent. Although it is the task of rationalization to attempt such a co-ordination, it must inevitably remain logically unsound. But there is a psychological repercussion from the rationalizations on the attitudes. This repercussion is one of the main problems of the sociological inquiry into ideologies and opinions, and, to a lesser extent, of the psychological study of personality and character. But it is only an integrating component. Rationalization can never transform valuations into a logically closed system. One can show this also by studying the value ideas of an individual or a social group.

The proposition that values *ought* to form such a hierarchy, and would, *if* only individuals were to deduce correctly from their deepest value premises, is entirely unfounded. It is based upon not only an unjustified, but a demonstrable false intellectualistic conception of the manner in which ideas of value are actually, and can only be, formed. If, furthermore, one postulates that they *ought to be* made in such a way as to justify the proposition, one merely announces a valuation without, from the point of view of relativism, any foundation. In real life, moreover, such a postulate cannot be endowed with any concrete content, which alone could make it useful in the discussion of values.

Let us now disregard all these objections. For the present purpose it is sufficient to point out that the notion of a subjective hierarchy of values, even if justified, would not remove the previously discussed weakness inherent in the ends-means schema as a principle of systematization in practical political economy. There is no need to expand on this. Not even a wholly objectivist value theory could overcome this difficulty. It arises from the fact that not only ends, but also means and by-effects, i.e., whole sequences with all their components, must be valued *before* they can be compared. But an elimination of sequences at an abstract level presupposes in turn such a comparison, which again is possible only after all possible sequences have been classified. But this classification cannot be made in any other way than through valuations. The mere affirmation—whether justified or not—of a logical connection between valuations does not help at all. For this connection, which is supposed to determine the valuations, can itself be determined only by a detailed study of *all* alternative sequences, whose components are subject to valuation. The fact that the thesis of a hierarchy of ends does not by itself render the ends-means schema more effective explains why this thesis has not penetrated practical political economy more thoroughly. It has played more the role of an indeterminate general principle,

217

which, just as in moral philosophy, is intended to provide a reason for arguing so much over valuations, without any deeper preliminary sociological and psychological study as to what valuation is.

The other tendency amongst relativist economists is more interesting, because it seems to lead somewhere. They admit frankly the subjective nature of valuations and perhaps also, if tackled on this point, the absence of a hierarchy amongst them. Instead, they draw a distinction: They split the practical problem—and with it all alternatives to be compared with respect to their values—into two parts. One part, they admit, is political, and with the aid of certain abstract assumptions it is best kept outside the bounds of the discussion. They then concentrate their attention on the second, which is supposed to comprise a 'purely economic' or 'purely financial' sphere, and therefore to be value-free. The division usually runs along the old classical line drawn between income distribution and production. They say, for example, that they disregard the effects on income distribution, or that they pre-suppose a just distribution, etc. Such a separation of a political problem into a political and a purely economic section is, however, impossible. In examining the purely economic problem there are two possibilities—in so far as any general conclusions are drawn, however guarded and qualified.

Either we disregard all inherent value components. This would be the most obvious course. But it is an inescapable fact that value assumptions have been dressed up in economic terms. Such an attempt inevitably leads to fallacies. Any attempted proof must traverse value gaps which are bridged only by stylistic tricks. It is therefore vulnerable, particularly to value criticism. The doctrine of free trade may serve as an illustration. It maintains that, if trade is 'free', the social product is maximized, without indicating according to which principles quantities of goods are to be added to yield the social product. If we are to introduce such a theorem into a political argument as an objective element—and this is the whole point of the doctrine; for an *analysis* of international price formation it is superfluous—we must have a principle of weighting. With its aid the social product should be defined in such a manner that from the standpoint of any political valuation it is measured 'correctly'. For the 'social product' is, besides other quantities, contained in every valuation as a factual premise. If even first-class economists are content with pseudo-solutions of the problem of weighting such as 'current prices' or 'production costs' etc., this superficial treatment follows from their adherence to an untenable way of posing the problem.

Or—this is the second possibility—we are forced to render more precise the assumption of the neutrality of pure economic inquiry by making the value hypotheses more explicit. The logic of the problem and particularly the attempt to give the inquiry a quasi-objective character, force the economist to build upon a general value premise which—since it is general and above all independent of changes inside the theoretical connections which are studied by an analysis of these changes— cannot conceivably correspond to real valuations. An example is the 'pure' doctrine of public finance. It explicitly presupposes a 'just distribution of income and property', without taking into account that taxes and other public interventions necessarily alter the distribution. I have discussed these arguments in detail elsewhere, and it may suffice here to refer to my *Political Element in the Development of Economic Theory*.

* * *

It would, nevertheless, be superficial to believe that to point simply to the difficulties inherent in the ends-means scheme and to criticize the traditional attempts to overcome them, could spare us the task of developing a teleologically oriented, 'practical' political economy. Indeed, the necessity of this task is thus brought out more clearly. We can certainly not do without the ends-means scheme. It is difficult to conceive of any other way of systematizing practical inquiry. Something, though not perhaps very much, is already gained when the critique gets rid of several pseudo-objectivist theorems, liberating concrete discussions somewhat from their domination. Particularly concrete practical discussions have been ruled by such normative concepts and *a priori* principles, even although they were suppressed and introduced only implicitly in the choice of assumptions, thus leading to erroneous conclusions.

Yet, these general normative theorems fulfil, up to a point, a certain 'function' in the practical inquiry into social problems. The treatment of the concrete political problems of the day requires a general foundation. The 'purely economic' value theorems serve this purpose. Beneath an innocent surface, they contain all that is needed. Psychologically, they are a peculiar rationalization both of the legitimate need of the scholar for a conceptual framework, and of his political intentions. Industrious systematizers, and, following them, textbook writers, attempt to classify these theorems systematically, pushing into them all they know, or believe they know. Intelligent practitioners prefer to ignore these theorems, if they can. But this does not prevent them from using the theorems with a conscience all the clearer for not having given them explicit attention. As theories, they are, of course, failures. Serious logical analysis destroys them.

If this is the situation, we need a substitute. Otherwise, the same theorems will be served up again, in a new and possibly more innocent formulation, in spite of all criticism. No comfort can be derived from these more innocent formulations. On the contrary, they are precisely the vehicle for smuggling in the theorems. It is therefore justified to ask the critic what he intends to put into their place.

If a substitute is necessary, and if it meets with difficulties, there is always one way open: to retain the normative doctrines. I am half serious about this. Even an economist who sees through their deficient theoretical foundation, recognizing all their theoretical imperfections, which follow from the attempt to give them the guise of a theory, might want to tolerate them. They fulfil in his research a 'function', just because they contain political attitudes, even though in theoretical disguise. With a more or less coherent system of political doctrines the data acquire a conceptual order, and theoretical research a certain direction, which correspond at least partly to the practical questions that are considered important in the particular political ideology that is rationalized in the normative theorems. We thus gain a general point of view and a directing principle for the treatment of specific practical questions. We can then modify and apply this principle conveniently to various practical situations. Specific problems can thus be treated in a manner which creates the illusion of coherence and consistency, and this is always particularly pleasing to a scholar.

If, moreover, these inherent political ideologies correspond to some degree to widespread political attitudes, this method becomes also of practical importance. The ends-means schema, which provides the framework for the arguments of political theory, thus apparently works quite satisfactorily. This is so because the overwhelming majority of possible sequences have already been eliminated at a highly abstract level as *a priori* without interest from the viewpoint of the ideology in question. It is now clear that this is not due to an analysis *within* this schema. Rather, it is the result of certain intuitive and, with respect to scientific analysis *a priori, total judgments*, contained in the political attitude which is the nucleus of the doctrinal system. Because of the attempt to suppress explicit value judgments the ends-means schema, developed in the framework of this *a priori* selection of sequences, is only an incomplete rationalization and lacks logical cogency. But what, from a deeper point of view, is logic for? Could it be an end-in-itself? It should be added that the purely causal analysis, conducted on the basis of the normative concepts, no doubt enlarges our knowledge. In the long run this must affect the basic ideology itself. In the course of this analysis our understanding of reality becomes more correct and more complete. This in turn makes both the general and the more specific practical postulates continually more rational in the sense that they express the political attitudes underlying the system with a more complete and more correct comprehension of reality. Now *if* these political attitudes corresponded to the actual political convictions of large social groups, the thing would work, as we have seen, relatively well. Why not play a little trick on the demands of logic and strictly scientific method? Should one want to conceal it, one could add a pinch of German 'As If' or '*Wesensschau*' or, even more conveniently, a little American 'pragmatism' or 'functionalism'. One need not even go as far as that. One can simply say that it is, as always, a matter of being 'sensible'. What this means is that one should not think too clearly.

But this is about all that can be said in favour of the theoretically disguised political doctrines. On the other side of the balance sheet there is a formidable array of counter-arguments, of which I shall stress only the most important. First, one cannot higgle with scientific method. The scholar has not yet been born who could experience a hysterical conflict in the foundations of his research, without being seriously disturbed in his work: the conflict between clearly recognizing the unscientific character of his political theorems, and yet of using them in a manner suitable to his purpose. Such conscious Machiavellianism is exceedingly improbable amongst those scholars, utterly devoted to the search for truth, who have always formed the cream of the world of science. As a result, we probably get a grouping into two camps, with a division of responsibilities: The members of one specialize in the critique of doctrine. In so far as they cannot solve the problem how a practical economic science can be constructed, their attitude remains negative and they refrain from positive collaboration in the practical sphere. The others cultivate their methodological naïveté and are, if they are good at it, called upon to do the required practical work. It is difficult to maintain that this situation is very desirable.

But I do not want to go into this more personal aspect. There is, however, another, related, point. The normative scholar who is concerned with appearing scientifically objective must always be ready to change quickly the level of his discourse. In order to remain objective and ward off criticism, he must empty his normative concepts of all meaning, making them, as the saying is, entirely formal, only in order to fill them in the next instant, without allowing himself or others to notice it, with political content. Yet, he must be ready at any moment to take off again for a flight into the purely formal stratosphere. This manœuvre takes nerve and skill.

There are also other difficulties in this. Our whole scientific discourse rests upon an acknowledgment of the need for strict scientific method. We criticize our own conclusions and those of others by asking whether they are sufficiently well-founded, and whether the arguments supporting them hold together logically. This method has become second nature to us, it is

part of our personalities. If we attempted to preserve such pseudo-scientific political doctrines, it would mean that we tolerated *a certain* absence of foundation and of logical rigour; yet, not *all* absence, for how could then any argument continue? How and where are we then to draw the line between legitimate scientific criticism and that which is to be ignored? The question becomes acute as soon as two scholars with different political attitudes and differently shaded doctrines enter into a discussion. Boundless confusion often prevails, and the intelligent layman is dumbfounded with astonishment over the fact that the two disagree not only over details but also over matters of principle, frequently without even being able to make clear what it is over which they disagree.

Let us now turn to the political ideology that underlies the doctrinal system. I have already admitted that the purely theoretical analysis conducted inside the framework of the system no doubt helps to strengthen this ideology through a more reliable understanding of reality. This also makes the ideology more consistent in its practical orientation. But this is only one side. At the same time the original political attitude must become petrified, stereotyped, and externalized. This is not the result of a better understanding of reality, which would, if anything, have the opposite effect. It happens in the process of theorizing the political attitudes. This has nothing to do with enlarging our knowledge but becomes necessary only because we attempt to lend these attitudes the appearance of pure theory.

This mutilation and sterilization of the ideologies cannot be easily dismissed. I have already indicated that the very nature of the doctrinal system as an expression of political attitudes makes it possible to 'solve' the fundamental problem of political economy, at least up to a point. The system contains certain general principles in the field of action, and a conceptual framework, and it gives theoretical analysis a certain direction. I have also stressed that the practical importance of this approach for theoretical research depends upon how far the underlying political ideology enables us to compare immediately and intuitively whole possible sequences at a high level of abstraction, and how far it provides a framework in which further teleological arguments lead to practical conclusions.

These conclusions are significant only in so far as the political ideology from which they spring corresponds to the attitudes of large social groups. From these two points of view the emaciation of the attitudes through theoretical rationalization is a serious drawback. It casts doubt upon the value of the whole approach, a value which I do not deny, in spite of all the objections raised.

Another point should be noted. *All* items on the credit side of the traditional method rest upon the fact that the doctrines in question contain a political ideology. *All* debit items stem from the desire to dress up this political ideology in the barbs of pure theory. Would it not be simpler to start with actually prevailing political attitudes, without rationalizing or theorizing them? Should this be possible, the solution would, in principle, be at hand.

In other words, let the value premises in economics stand as value premises. Recent decades have, indeed, witnessed attempts to move in this direction, but they have not been carried out satisfactorily. Usually, one stops short at a more or less seriously intended question on a general level. The question apparently is asked only in order to be affirmed, thus giving weight to the rest of the argument. Thus one may say: 'It can, of course, be questioned whether people really seek to maximize national income, even if we disregard the problem of distribution', and then continue 'but if they do . . .' etc. (The implied assumption is, of course, that such an objective is not in doubt, and one can therefore allow it to be questioned in principle.) Or one may ask with Professor Hans Larsson: 'This objective (general welfare) might seem to be valuable without need for any further comment. But we must remember that, according to Weber's theory, this objective too, or rather especially this objective, rests ultimately upon an emotive or conative decision. A sceptic can rightly ask: Why should I pay attention to the general welfare? Why should I heed my neighbour?' *If*, however, we can assume welfare to be a generally accepted objective . . . etc. Behind the cover of this admission, which no decent person can refuse, the whole ideology is then developed. This manœuvre having, moreover, been embellished with the idea of a necessary hierarchy of ends, is simply a farce whose sole function is to send the critical faculty to sleep. The whole ideology thus developed is, as it were, absorbed in the concept 'general welfare' or 'national income', and acquires through this innocent, purely formal, value postulate a kind of blanket confirmation. Apart from all the weaknesses already mentioned, this method is vulnerable to the objection that human valuations never refer, nor ever could refer, to such abstract alternatives as 'general welfare' or 'not general welfare'— even if their meaning were clear; and it is not. Human valuations relate to *concrete* total situations, either real or imagined.

If we want to introduce value premises, to make them determinate, and to relate them to actual human valuations, we are forced to use those methods, gradually developed by social psychology and sociology, which concern themselves with the actual valuations of people. In other words, a systematic study of the political attitudes of various large groups must precede the construction of a general practical science of political economy.

I have stressed elsewhere that we must not stop short at the programmes of the political parties, or similar general declarations. These are only superficial rationalizations of more deepseated attitudes, very much like the 'value premises' whose use in political economy I have indicated above. They, too, are often available in the form of 'welfare' propositions. Moreover, programmes are to some extent always determined by entirely accidental conditions. They avoid on purpose going into concrete questions, lest these split the electorate.

Above all is this true when politics is in the hands of machines, and when the boundaries of political parties cut across homogeneous social groups. In the U.S.A., for example, one could often listen to hundreds of speeches during an important election campaign, without discovering a trace of the questions which really divide the nation. These are systematically suppressed, although they are taken carefully into account by the party bosses, and although they influence the nomination of candidates and the election results. Such declarations therefore do not reflect directly the probable behaviour dispositions of different social groups, which alone from our point of view are relevant.

Nor is it sufficient to study the behaviour of these groups in actual situations, in order to discover these dispositions.

Although such behaviour is, of course, an important source of knowledge, it is not identical with it. What we seek to know relates to dispositions *in the future* and *in different conditions*. This is implied in the demand upon practical economic science to be systematic and general, or at least more general than it would be, were it to apply only to a particular time and situation. Nevertheless, practical economics cannot be entirely general in the classical sense. Its validity must be limited in time and space, in a manner similar to that which the German historical school demanded, if only because it must be based on a study of actual attitudes. For a practical economic science, built upon the attitudes of all large groups in history, and accounting for all conceivable formations of attitudes in all future time, is surely impossible and, moreover, only of dubious interest.

It should be added that a study of the political attitudes of the various social groups, and with it of their dispositions to act, is necessary not only because it yields the required value premises, but also for the purely theoretical study of the selected causal sequences which are compared with each other in the light of the value premises when we conduct the practical analysis. For these sequences are always partly determined by the political actions of the different social groups. This becomes increasingly important as the nineteenth century liberal order is penetrated by monopolies, market controls, and attempts at supervision through the formation of controlling groups and central state planning.

We are concerned here with a social psychology and not with a more or less relativistic, but logicistic ethics as hitherto, particularly in neo-classical economics, where it reached its peak in the eclectic English 'Welfare Economics'. The history of science provides sufficient evidence that we cannot rely upon the 'natural intuition' of the social scientist. On the relatively general plane, on which practical economics must proceed, the problems of social psychology mentioned above are difficult to master. Without a developed psychological technique and substantial empirical material the necessary systematic arrangement of the political premises must inevitably degenerate into amateurish ethical speculation of a metaphysical-logicistic nature.

Elements of social psychology are intricately woven into the problems of practical economics, not only because they, in their turn, determine the causal sequences under consideration, but also because they are of primary importance in posing the questions and in systematically organizing the material. The results of practical economic theory are reliable only in so far as this foundation in social psychology is laid by a thorough empirical study of how individuals and groups actually behave, not by inspired, often quite brilliant, armchair speculations, which throw more light upon the psychology of their author than on society. The results consist of norms that are objective, although only from specific concrete value premises, given in the form of particular political complexes of attitudes of different social groups. The results are important and interesting in so far as the groups in question are politically influential. We ought to direct ourselves towards such a relativistic, practical economic science, founded on social psychology. A systematic social policy, for example, which attempts to confine itself to 'economic' phenomena and to avoid the problems of social psychology, contains logical contradictions already in the manner in which it poses its questions.

* * *

On reflection, all this will surely be admitted. But have we not side-stepped the main difficulty of practical economics— the difficulty whose emphasis has been the *leitmotiv* of our inquiry? Granted that the value premises of political economy must be gleaned from a psychological study of attitudes, that several value premises which correspond to the attitudes of different social groups must be used together as starting points, that they must be kept in sight as value premises through all the links of the argument, without being theorized, and that it is concrete sequences which have to be evaluated, not abstruse concepts such as 'general welfare' or 'maximum national income'; we also take it for granted that we can hardly do without the ends-means scheme in our practical analysis. But the objection to its use is that not only the end but all components of the sequence must be evaluated in a comparison of alternative sequences, and that therefore an elimination of

227

the large majority of possible sequences *must precede*—at a highly abstract level and hence without intensive analysis—an examination in accordance with the ends-means schema. At closer inspection the boundaries of practical analysis are set by just these eliminations of 'uninteresting' sequences—an elimination which is *a priori* in relation to the proper analysis. Only thus does the purely theoretical analysis acquire its conceptual framework and its direction. Such an *a priori* limitation of the field of vision must take place. Chaos cannot be the object of scientific inquiry. The ascertainment of values or valuations does not by itself enable us to set this fine instrument of scientific analysis. On the contrary, awareness of the necessity to make valuations concrete underlines the difficulty: If valuations were to be of any use they would have to be rather general and confined to principles. But we have shown that such premises are untenable.

This, indeed, is the crux of all science: We can never get away from the *a priori*. The large, unordered, mass of crude facts does not fall into order by itself. Without a principle of organization scientific observation is impossible. Naïve empiricists, particularly common amongst American institutionalists, attempt the impossible: to gaze at reality without preconceptions, hoping that things will fall into place, and thus give rise to scientific laws. But they are, of course, the victims of an illusion to which they give the semblance of objectivity by carefully concealing from themselves their *a priori* ideas. Without such ideas they could not have reached any conclusions. The ideas are ultimately an expression of a valuation which lends 'interest' to certain hypotheses and certain relations between facts.[1]

[1] An interesting study, which has, as far as I know, never been attempted, would be to examine more thoroughly the political ideology that underlies American institutionalism. If Veblen can be taken to be its founder, it began with a radical critique of society, apparently influenced by Marx. But institutionalism has since become increasingly conservative. This shift is not surprising. The political ideology of institutionalism has been rationalized largely in terms of functions. It is always a question of what 'functions' the various social phenomena fulfil in economic life. It is a general experience that analysis in functional terms leads almost inevitably to an affirmation of 'society'—the ultimate norm for all functions. There is a parallel in the fact—which I have discussed elsewhere— that the technique of normative logic, particularly in its more primitive phase of natural law, lends itself more readily to a theoretical interpretation of conservative than of radical norms.

The *a priori* and interest-determined arrangement of concepts and the organization of evidence must always be an expression of a certain *total* ideological attitude. It is no longer a question of separating end, means, and by-effects, for the procedure lies beyond the rules of this method. For those who admit that the value premises must be clearly exposed, but must ultimately be related to the actual attitudes of the different social groups, the task consists in reaching a *synthetic* understanding of the whole *complex* of attitudes. One would have to get, as it were, inside the skin of the various groups, so that the different attitudes to various social phenomena of each group in turn express a unity. This unity cannot be presented as a theoretical or conceptual hierarchy of valuations. It cannot be crystallized into a 'principle'. The ideologies assume, indeed, a rationalized form, but we are interested in their true form as part of the social reality. Their structure is psychological and must be understood synthetically, like that of 'personality' or 'character' in individual psychology. Such 'empathy' always *de facto* determines the preliminary work that lies beyond the ends-means schema. Perhaps this is ultimately not science in the strict sense. It cannot be reduced precisely to true and false. But we must insist on one essential requirement: We must work with the complexes of attitudes of a sufficiently large number of social groups, so that our discussion does not exclude the demands of particular groups for their interests to be discussed.

This procedure beyond the ends-means schema would be largely intuitive and would call upon the artistic imagination. Our objective is to achieve, after careful psychological studies of as many groups as possible, certain total psychological co-ordinations, similar in nature to the co-ordinations that constitute personalities, and to use these intuitively to set the sights of scientific analysis—giving our vision boundaries and direction. The process resembles the empathy of the poet and his identification with a group. Although this way of putting it may sound somewhat pretentious, this is how in fact the economist proceeds in his discussion of the practical affairs of the day. His ability to identify himself with the various aspirations of his time determines to what extent he can recruit interest for his expositions. If the results of such identifications were not so often spoilt by the metaphysics of rationalization inherent in traditional objectivist thinking, we could start from the topical discussions of economists for the purpose of a general and systematically practical political economy. But they *are* spoilt, and the layman adheres to his belief that there is a difference between 'theory' and 'practice'—as he puts it in his unsophisticated way—and only smiles incredulously when the economist attempts to convince him that 'there is nothing so practical as good theory'.

Finally, two points should be stressed. One may think whatever one likes about this last question about the processes of thought that, lying beyond the ends-means schema, make the schema possible. One can hardly deny that scientific thought *within* the schema must bring out clearly the value premises at all stages of the argument. The valuation must apply to alternative sequences with all their concrete components. To be of practical interest, these value premises must be taken from real life. Practical discussions in economics must, as far as possible, be based upon modern sociological and psychological studies of attitudes, behaviour, opinions, and ideologies.

Moreover, should we ever succeed in achieving value relativism in economics, this would not mean a divorce of science and politics—of thought and will, as a Swedish economist once put it, or of 'theory and practice', as the layman has it. On the contrary, it would mean that science is incorporated in politics, the two forming a more intimate union than J. S. Mill and his disciples thought possible. The political attitudes would become alternative and simultaneous premises for science, without having previously been put through the workshop of objectivist theory. The classics would probably have found the new practical political economy—for which we hope —too 'political' rather than the opposite. The paradox lies in the fact that practical political economy can become objective only through ascertaining the political will without disguise, in all its important manifestations, and through fitting these directly into scientific analysis as its alternative, simultaneously present, value premises.

CHAPTER ELEVEN

THE LOGICAL CRUX OF ALL SCIENCE[1]

1. The Relation between the Moral and the Intellectual Discords

WHEN the facts of international economic inequalities and their tendency to increase are confronted with the public conscience in the richer nations and with the economic theory which has developed in the cultural setting of those countries, both moral and intellectual discords are brought into the open.

The moral discord is undoubtedly more fundamental. On the one hand, these nations adhere on the general plane of valuations to the ideal, deep-rooted in Western civilization, of the rights of all individuals to equality of opportunity, irrespective of race and colour, religion and creed, social status and nationality. On the other hand, the citizens of these nations are not in fact prepared to accept in their daily lives the full implications of this great moral principle.

Economic theory is only a segment of the total culture. It partly serves the needs of opportunistic rationalization. In order to live comfortably with the moral discord these nations need an economic theory that diverts attention from this discord.

This need enhances the strength of those old predilections of economic theory which serve as antidotes to that theory's basic doctrine of equality. It also prolongs the life of theoretical devices that 'prove' those predilections, such as stable equilibrium models and the abstraction from 'non-economic' factors. Equilibrium analysis, with the positive value connotations attached to equilibrium, tends to confirm a bias for *laissez-faire* in policy. The separation of 'economic factors', together

---

[1] From *Economic Theory and Under-developed Regions*, 1957, Chapter 12.

231

with *ceteris paribus* assumptions relating to 'non-economic' factors, support the fatalistic slant of the equilibrium model, because it is just in the sphere of the so-called non-economic factors that cumulative causation and interaction are most important, and the assumption of givenness therefore least warranted. An inclusion of the so-called non-economic factors, which are commonly disequilibrating, strengthens the presumption in favour of the alternative model of the cumulative process. Analysis of cumulative processes suggests in the sphere of policy (a) that without government action there is a deadlock or movement away from the desired state, e.g., growing international inequality, and (b) that partial government action may go a long way if the strategic points are chosen.

The combined effect of stable equilibrium analysis and abstraction from 'non-economic' factors in economic theory—both logically related to each other and to the philosophies of natural law and utilitarianism from which economic theory has branched off—has been to keep theory, as far as possible, aloof from those facts and causal relations which, if analysed, would focus attention on the economic inequalities between regions and countries and thus on the fundamental moral discord.

In this situation the untheoretical twist which we have observed in the rapidly growing literature on the problems of the under-developed countries would seem to be a sound reaction of the social scientists who are devoting their efforts to these problems. Attempting to do without a general theory would seem to be a safer course than using one that is biased and faulty.

2. The Logical Necessity of a Theory and the Need of Adjusting it to Facts

It must be said, however, that theory is indispensable for scientific work. Theory is necessary not only to organize the findings of research so that they make sense, but, more basically, to determine what questions are to be asked. Scientific knowledge never emerges by itself, so to speak, from empirical research in the raw, but only as solutions to problems raised ;

and such solutions presume a logically co-ordinated system of problems stated.

Theory, therefore, must always be *a priori* to the empirical observations of the facts. Facts come to mean something only as ascertained and organized in the frame of a theory. Indeed, facts as part of scientific knowledge have no existence outside such a frame. Questions must be asked before answers can be obtained and, in order to make sense, the questions must be part of a logically co-ordinated attempt to understand social reality as a whole. A non-theoretical approach is, in strict logic, unthinkable.

Underlying and steering every systematic attempt to find out the truth about society, there is therefore always a theory: a vision of what the essential facts and the causal relations between them are. This theory which determines the direction of research should be made explicit. The danger of keeping the theory implicit—as unstated reasons for asking the particular questions that are asked, and of organizing the findings in the way they are organized—is, of course, that it escapes criticism.

If theory is thus *a priori*, it is, on the other hand, a first principle of science that the facts are sovereign. Theory is, in other words, never more than a hypothesis. When the observations do not agree with a theory, i.e., when they do not make sense in the frame of the theory used in carrying out the research, the theory has to be discarded and replaced by another one which promises a better fit.

Theory and fact-finding research should thus be continually readjusted to each other, on the principle, however, that in the final analysis the facts are decisive. As the theory is merely a hypothesis, the criterion of its truth can never be anything other than the pragmatic one of its usefulness in bringing our observations of facts into a meaningful and non-contradictory system of knowledge. And so scientific progress can be expected to result from a process of trial and error.

In the moral sphere, the corresponding logical process is moral criticism, proceeding on the assumption that there should be consistency between our valuations, a demand raised by feelings which are real because of the rationalism which is also part of our culture. As the valuations refer to social reality, and as therefore their interrelations logically involve people's beliefs concerning this reality, the process of correcting their theories to fit the facts plays at the same time an important role in the attempts to give clarity, honesty and consistency to their moral ideas: to purify and strengthen the public conscience. For people want to be rational. Scientific truth-seeking, by rectifying their beliefs also influences their valuations. 'In a rationalistic civilization it is not only that the beliefs are shaped by the valuations, but also that the valuations depend upon the beliefs'.[1]

3. THE PROVENANCE OF TRUTHFUL THEORY

For realism and relevance scientific research thus depends on a major *a priori*: an insight into what the essential facts and causal relations really are. This *a priori* theory then is corrected in the course of research to fit more closely the reality studied. But from where, in the first place, is the *a priori* theory inferred? Where is its fountainhead?

To take it from one's own hunches is almost certain to be a choice of one of the innumerable roads to unreality and irrelevance. The theorist's individual hunches are not even random, which would at least preserve a slight possibility that occasionally he would by pure chance strike upon what is essential and thus be in a position to pose questions which truly reveal reality and draw relevant inferences. For he is mostly, *nolens volens*, under the impact of the inherited theory which tends to serve as a vehicle for the conservative predilections which are the heritage of economic theory.

The 'purer' a theorist is, the more he seems to be under the influence of the inherited predilections. The devotion of so much theoretical effort even in recent decades to 'welfare economics'—though long ago conclusively proved unrealistic and without logical basis—is a demonstration of this point.

There is no other rational way to gain insight into what is essential and indispensable for the choice of variables for a theory than the cumbersome and laborious one of comprehensive and intensive empirical research. Only on the basis of a

[1] See p. 60 and Chapter V in this volume.

close contact with social history and social knowledge generally can we hope to construct the 'model of the models' which can be used as the guide to realism and relevance for our abstract theory.

This basic empirical research would need to encompass social facts and relations in all fields. I have noted that our traditional division of knowledge into separate and delineated branches of social knowledge has no correspondence in reality: concrete problems are never simply economical, sociological, psychological, or political. A theory of under-development and development which works only with 'economic' variables is for logical reasons doomed to be unrealistic and thus irrelevant.

This comprehensive research prior to the construction of the abstract theory, needed for its realism and relevance, should be freed as far as possible from the powerful predilections I have referred to. The general method for accomplishing this is to work with explicit value premises, themselves tested both as to relevance and significance.

This comprehensive research, however, needs itself, from the start and continually as it proceeds, to formulate hypotheses in order to direct observations and ask pertinent questions. It needs theory. As I just stated, empirical knowledge cannot be assembled and systematized without organizing principles, i.e., an insight into what are the essential facts and relations. Empirical research needs in fact for its own pursuit a nucleus of the theory which I am insisting can only be constructed on itself as a basis.

4. THE CRUX OF ALL SCIENCE

This is the logical crux of all science: it assumes in all its endeavours an *a priori*, but its ambition must constantly be to find an empirical basis for this *a priori*. A worth-while theory of under-development and development, if it can ever be formulated, would have to be based on ideas distilled from the broadest empirical knowledge of social change in all its manifold aspects, acquired under the greatest freedom from tradition-bound predilections. Only thereby can the bold simplifications be safely founded which can serve as the theoretical direction of research. But the empirical knowledge itself cannot be acquired without principles of selection and organization, i.e., without a vision of a theory.

We are thus constantly attempting what in its perfection is impossible and we are never achieving more than makeshifts: these, however, can be better or worse. In our present situation the task is not, as is sometimes assumed, the relatively easy one of filling 'empty boxes' of theory with a content of empirical knowledge about reality. For our theoretical boxes are empty primarily because they are not built to hold reality. We need new theories which, however abstract, are more realistic in the sense that they are more adequate to the facts.

Meanwhile, I believe it to be a disciplining force in our dispersed efforts in the field of under-development and development, that a clear concept of the ideal is constantly kept in mind and given a directing role in all our research. To begin with, we need to free ourselves from the impediment of biased and inadequate predilections and unreal and irrelevant theoretical approaches which in our academic tradition we are carrying with us as a heavy ballast.

POSTSCRIPT

I

How is scientific knowledge of social facts and relations possible ? How can the biases of a scientist's own personality and of his time and his local and class milieu be prevented from influencing the direction of his search for the facts and his inferences from them ?

How can he liberate his thinking from the powerful tradition of the living and the dead masters of his science ? More specifically, how can he free himself from normative and teleological notions, inherited from previous generations and founded upon the metaphysical moral philosophies of natural law and utilitarianism from which all our social and economic theories have branched off ? Do not these doctrinal elements still set the stage for our inquiries, determine the direction of our research and prejudice the conclusions from it ? How can the social sciences overcome their irrational impact and become entirely relativist with respect to values, as a systematic search for truth should be ? These, as I recall, were the questions with which I found myself confronted in my earliest endeavours to prepare myself to become an economist.

When, as newly appointed *docent* at the University of Stockholm, I had to deliver a series of lectures, I chose for the Spring term of 1928 the topic : " The Concepts ' Value ' and ' Utility ' in Economic Theory." My main interest at that time was negative : to demonstrate that certain practices of reasoning common in economics were logically defective. In spite of general pronouncements by almost all leading economists, from N. Senior and J. S. Mill onwards, that the science of economics should be concerned only with what is and not what ought to be, economic theory had preserved elaborate structures of normative speculation built upon the

237

concepts of value, utility and welfare. Even when these doctrinal elements were concealed—as, for instance, in the writings by Cournot, Walras and Cassel—they were implicit in the selection of the problems raised, in the approach to them, and in the solutions offered. As objective valuations are unthinkable, the theories containing them could be exploded by immanent criticism.

Out of my further work along this line grew a book, originally published in Swedish in 1930 and early translated into German and some other languages ; it was finally in 1953 brought out in an English edition, *The Political Element in the Development of Economic Theory*, by the publishers who are also sponsoring the present volume.

By writing that book, however, I had not succeeded in working the value problem out of my system. It continued and, I am afraid, will continue to be one of my main preoccupations: a complex of fundamental problems in the methodology of the social sciences which raises its head in any field of social research into which I stray. As a result, my work has been spattered by methodological preludes and interludes to a greater extent than is usual. The present volume, which should be read as a companion to the *Political Element*, contains some of these excursions over the years.

The translation of the earlier book into English was ably made by a friend of much intellectual affinity both in the interest for the basic philosophical questions and in attitudes to them, Mr. Paul Streeten of Balliol College, Oxford, who also contributed an Appendix on " Recent Controversies ". When Paul Streeten, having made this earlier investment of effort to make my views on the value problem more easily accessible, has now also taken upon himself the trouble of selecting from my various later publications, and thereafter editing, the present collection of essays on methodological questions related to the value problem, I feel more deeply grateful than I can duly express.

He has suggested that I contribute a personal account of how I happened to develop this particular line of interest and how it interplayed with other experiences I had, as I came to work in different fields of social research and also, occasionally, in shaping policy. After some hesitation, I have in response produced the following pages which, I hope, will not be looked upon as pretentious. I am well aware that I have not reached the stage of life when an autobiographical exercise is easily forgiven. But the personal may, to some extent, be typical. My sketch will also give me an opportunity to give a few personal impressions of that remarkable group of economists who reigned in Sweden after the First World War, to whom my whole generation owes so much and to whom personally I was deeply attached in veneration and friendship. Finally, I shall try to explain and defend the logical short-cuts by which I and other social scientists, who have become aware of the overpowering complexity revealed by the rational decision to work with explicit value premises, nevertheless continue to do our work and to write our books.

II

PSYCHOLOGICALLY, my embarkation upon the attempt at immanent criticism of economic theory, out of which grew the *Political Element*, and from which a life-long preoccupation arose, represented undoubtedly an individual manifestation of a common urge among the younger generation of Swedish economists of the 'twenties to liberate our minds from the teaching of the older generation. The main inspiration was negative : the need to protest against the intellectual domination of the older generation. It led me to a critical scrutiny of the value problem, because I was aware that this was their weak spot. Professor Lawrits V. Birck, of Copenhagen University (1871–1933),[1] whom in his last years I came to know and who honoured me with his friendship, was well aware of this and used to call me jokingly parricide.

Now that they have all passed away it stands out as even less

---

[1] Birck had himself written an important and original exposition of the neo-classical value theory, *Vaerditeori* (The Theory of Value) (2 vols.), Copenhagen, 1902, and remained, with all his non-conformist adventures in social and economic criticism, which earned him the right to be called the political conscience of Denmark, a faithfully orthodox utilitarian.

questionable than thirty years ago that a major peculiarity of our environmental set-up in Sweden in the first decade after the First World War was the eminence of our teachers. David Davidson (1854–1942) was still active in the first post-war years as professor at Uppsala University and, when he became professor emeritus, as editor of *Ekonomisk Tidskrift*. Gustav Cassel (1866–1944), the somewhat younger Eli F. Heckscher (1879–1952) and Gösta Bagge (1882–1951), in Stockholm, were at the peak of their strength. Knut Wicksell (1851–1926) died before I had advanced in my graduate studies, but his influence remained strong and took in Sweden the form of a personal tradition. It was a hard crust of ability and authority to break through, tempting as well as deterring, to anybody trying to sprout into independent thinking.

Naturally, the main impact from our teachers was positive inspiration. In the analysis of dynamic economic processes, Wicksell's theory of the effects of disequilibrium in the money and capital markets, and of the cumulative development engendered when total demand and supply are not equal, gave us a start, considerably ahead of what was then thought and taught elsewhere. Wicksell had developed his ideas in a book in German before the turn of the century,[1] had presented them in simpler and more direct form in his published lectures,[2] and had refined and partly applied them in the protracted discourse he and Davidson kept up in *Ekonomisk Tidskrift*. This tradition, as it had developed over the years in teaching and oral discussion among us all, amounted to something considerably more diversified and accomplished than was ever put into print. Keynes's *Treatise*[3] and later his *General Theory*[4] appeared to us as brilliant and important writings on familiar lines and caused none of the shock and the sense of intellectual revolution which they did in his own country and elsewhere.[1] When the Great Depression descended upon the world, we were thus from the outset

[1] *Geldzins und Güterpreise*, Jena, 1898. English edition : *Interest and Prices*, London, 1936.
[2] *Vorlesungen über Nationalökonomie auf Grundlage des Marginalprinzipes* (2 vols.), Jena, 1913, 1922. English edition : *Lectures* (2 vols.) London, 1934, 1935.
[3] *A Treatise on Money* (2 vols.), London, 1930.
[4] *The General Theory of Employment, Interest and Money*, London, 1936.

Postscript

conditioned to turn to a realistic and practical discussion of anti-depression policy. About the so-called Stockholm School I shall make a few remarks later. My *Monetary Equilibrium*[2] is, of course, based on Wicksell.

Of greater immediate importance for the particular line of thinking pursued in the essays in this volume and the *Political Element* was, however, Cassel's influence. Cassel had come to economics from mathematics. Like Cournot three generations earlier, he attempted deliberately to avoid the value problem and to build his theory of price formation directly upon the functional relations between price, demand, and supply. His criticism of the value theories in *Theoretische Sozialökonomie*[3]—unfortunately in English available only in a translation which does not do justice to its content[4]—was weak. Cassel, with all his constructive intuition, had little gift for criticism, indeed little gift to understand clearly any thoughts other than his own. His philosophical foundations were superficial. While throwing away the subjective value theory as useless, he had not freed himself from uncritical utilitarianism. To thoughtful utilitarians like Edgeworth and Pigou, Cassel's thinking must have appeared as a retrogression to cruder natural law concepts, as they had been expressed before the elaboration of the subjective theory of value.

Of this I became aware as a result of my studies of the value

[1] It took Pigou twenty years to absorb the shock (*Keynes' General Theory*, 1950). Pigou was, of course, not typical. But it is strange to recall—and it was at that time difficult for us in Sweden to comprehend—that twenty or twenty-five years ago economists abroad actually believed in J. B. Say's law of equality between, or even identity of, total demand and supply. In justice, this environmental situation should be remembered for the explanation of the stress on his opposition to earlier writers and his insistence of being the great heretic, which marked Keynes's writings. Very differently from Keynes, Wicksell took pains to link his ideas with the monetary discussion after the Napoleonic wars and especially with Ricardo's theory of the relations between the amount of gold, the interest rate, and the price level. (Cf. Wicksell, *Interest and Prices* and Myrdal Vikt *Monetary Equilibrium*, p. 6, for references.)

[2] London, 1939. The original Swedish text, *Om Penningteoretisk jämvikt*, was published in *Ekonomisk Tidskrift*, 1931. A German version, entitled " Der Gleichgewichtsbegriff als Instrument der geldtheoretischen Analyse ", was included in *Beiträge zur Geldtheorie*, edited by F. A. Hayek, Vienna, 1933.

[3] Leipzig, 1918.

[4] *The Theory of Social Economy* (2 vols.), London, 1923. The English translations of Wicksell's books are not very good either.

241

problem. Nevertheless, there was, I felt, a healthy realism in his approach to economic problems, a desire to avoid metaphysical speculation and to get down to facts and figures.[1] There can be no doubt that familiarity with his approach, demonstrated so vividly in his tackling of topical practical problems in Sweden and the world, was exceedingly valuable to all of us and influenced us deeply. It helped to save us from getting entangled in the welfare scholasticism which was at that time, as it still is, fashionable at many centres of learning, and it made a preference for a direct and realistic analytical approach part of our habits of thought. My first major theoretical work on the integration of anticipations into the theory of price formation[2] owes much to Cassel, and more in regard to general approach than to details.

Heckscher, at that time, was finishing his classic book on *Mercantilism*[3] and was setting out on his great work on Sweden's economic history which occupied him until his death. Treating his subject from the broadest aspects, his ambition was to integrate the countless detailed historical facts into the framework of his economic theory.[4] He had a great and lasting influence on all of us, if comparatively less on myself, only because I took more interest in a sociological than a historical approach.

[1] Cassel's last attempt to formulate this approach is contained in a little book, *On Quantitative Thinking in Economics*, Oxford, 1935, which was an elaboration of his last lecture as Lars Hierta professor at the University of Stockholm, 1934. But much more than from his attempts at systematic methodology, which was not his strong side, his pupils learned from personal contact and from his way of handling various practical problems of the day in all sorts of reports and articles, among them those he regularly contributed to the main conservative daily newspaper in Stockholm, *Svenska Dagbladet*.

See further my obituary—the only one I have ever written— : " Gustav Cassel *In Memoriam* ", *Ekonomisk Revy*, February 1945. I tried there to write about Cassel's faults, which were so much on the surface, but in such a way as to explain why we, who knew him best, loved and revered him most.

[2] *Prisbildningsproblemet och föränderligheten*. (Price Formation and Changeability, still untranslated (Ed.)) Uppsala, 1927.

[3] *Merkantilismen*, Stockholm, 1931. English edition : *Mercantilism*, London, 1935.

[4] *Sveriges ekonomiska historia från Gustav Vasa*, (Sweden's Economic History from Gustav Vasa),. (4 vols., unfinished), Stockholm, 1935–1950. An earlier, short and synoptical treatment by Heckscher of Sweden's economic history is now available in English, *An Economic History of Sweden*, translated by Göran Ohlin, Cambridge, Mass., 1954 ; the volume contains an excellent introduction on Heckscher's place and role as an economic historian by Alexander Gerschenkron.

Bagge was mainly interested in social policy, viewed from a fundamentally conservative, even somewhat paternalistic, angle. While keeping to the classical line of equilibrium theory as represented by Cassel, his main work was directed towards analysing the institutional framework of society. He came therefore to take an intense interest in the new tendencies in contemporary economics in America, which he had visited already in 1904, and elsewhere outside the beaten track of economic theory as it had been carried on in Austria, England and at home by the rest of the older generation. In his lectures and seminars he opened to us a window to these new developments and exerted more influence on our orient ation than we were, at that time, fully aware of.

Davidson helped to keep the classics before our minds. He had studied Ricardo closely all his life, and we used to joke that as he became older he grew even physically more and more like the master.

The status of our teachers, their fame abroad and their professional relations with the leading economists elsewhere, opened doors for us in foreign countries to an extent that we did not deserve, and some of us grew accustomed to travel and work abroad early in our careers. I should add that the members of the younger generation of Swedish economists, whose intellectual milieu I am attempting to describe, also learned very much from each other. Our outstanding teachers were so utterly dissimilar that it never occurred to us that we formed a school. Fundamental differences of ideas were part of our heritage. But we continued discussions with each other and read each other's manuscripts, and we preserved close friendships between ourselves and with the members of the older generation. In this respect we were reacting consciously against the attitudes and behaviour of the older men, between whom, unfortunately, personal relations were extremely strained; many were not even on speaking terms with each other.

III

In the practical and political sphere, the teaching of economics by the older group was dominated by a rather uncompromising *laissez-faire* attitude. This became more pronounced in the second half of the 'twenties, after the death of Wicksell. Overcoming the powerful predilections in favour of *laissez-faire*, inherent in the utilitarian philosophy[1] of which he was a persistent adherent, Wicksell, as a radical in his political attitudes, was in principle an interventionist, however narrowly he drew in practice the limit for interventions.[2] When he had left the arena, *laissez-faire* had a much freer hand.

Cassel, it is true, to the great dismay of his colleagues and, in particular, to Heckscher's, made somewhat irregular excursions into protectionism.[3] More generally, Cassel's

[1] Cf. my *Economic Theory and Under-developed Regions*, London, 1957, Chapter 10,

[2] Wicksell early criticised on logical grounds the notion of interest harmony and the predilection for *laissez-faire*, particularly as they permeated Walras's and Pareto's equilibrium systems. In his political allegiance Wicksell was not a socialist, still less a Marxist, but a liberal, though in many questions he was more radical than the socialists. He never joined the Labour Party. See the excellent biography of Wicksell by Torsten Gårdlund (*Knut Wicksell. Rebelli det nya riket.* Stockholm, 1956), which I hope will soon be available in English.

Wicksell had the integrity of a saint : few persons have gone through life so untouched by moral compromise as he. I have often wondered whether, and how, his exceptional personality was conducive to the great originality he demonstrated when, rather late in life, he came to work seriously in economic theory.

Personally, Wicksell was unpretentious and deeply human in all his contacts. At the same time he was unbendingly inhuman in adhering to, and following *ad absurdum*, his own moral convictions as those became crystallized in his strangely puritan and mathematical mind. Social conventions, national pride and undisturbed relations to individuals or the general public were of no concern to him, when such considerations conflicted with his convictions, and he was then always prepared to sacrifice his own material interests and those of his beloved family.

Just as Sweden's greatest author August Strindberg was not considered fit to become a member of the Swedish Academy, so Wicksell was never co-opted into the Academy of Science, while there was in both places, then as later, besides the real authors and scientists, room for dilettantes and plodders who belonged to the right society and held inoffensive views. Evidence of the integrity of the strict Swedish procedure for university promotions was, however, the fact that Wicksell did become ordinary professor in Lund in 1904—though he had preached Neo-Malthusianism, expressed opinions towards Russia which were considered treacherous in Sweden at that time, lived with his wife (the young Norwegian-born Anna Bugge, later lawyer and Sweden's representative to the League of Nations for a number of years) without their being formally married, and in spite of the fact that he did not even find it possible to compromise his conscience by applying for the chair to the King in the appropriate and customary form.

[3] It became known that Cassel, though not a member himself like Heckscher had aided the protectionist members of a Royal Commission on commercial policy to draft their Minority Report (*Tull- och traktatkommitténs Betänkande angående tullsystemets verkningar i Sverige före varldskriget*, del I, Statens offentliga utredningar 1924/37, Stockholm, 1924).

intense interest in practical issues and his realism led him time and time again to take up positions that deviated from liberal orthodoxy. Heckscher once remarked in a conversation about Cassel that, however he jumped, he always came down on his feet, like a cat. Though this observation was not meant to be entirely kind, it revealed Hecksher's grudging admiration.

Heckscher himself would have strongly objected to the characterization of his own views as in line with *laissez-faire*. Indeed, with the intellectual enthusiasm of having gained a very important insight, he presented in a popular book on Old and New Economic Liberalism[1] the usual theoretical qualifications to the *laissez-faire* doctrine and foremost among them John Stuart Mill's important reservation (widely accepted since the middle of the nineteenth century) that, strictly speaking, the economic rule of non-interference applied only to the sphere of production and exchange but not to distribution where, on the contrary, interferences in the interests of justice and welfare were legitimate. It was difficult, however, to find in Heckscher's treatment of practical problems much consideration for this large qualification. On the contrary, as a general judgment I think it can be said, without doing him an injustice, that he, as well as other economists of the older generation, shared a tendency to come out on the conservative do-nothing side in most of those questions of income distribution which became important in the 'twenties : wage policy, compulsory regulation of the working week, measures to mitigate unemployment and to compensate the unemployed, housing policy, and the pending big social security reforms.[2]

Bagge, as a true conservative, had, of course, fewer doctrinal inhibitions. Long before, in the 'thirties, it had become a commonly discussed, though not generally accepted view, Bagge had, for instance, drawn the conclusion from Wicksell's theories that the volume of public investment should fluctuate

---

[1] *Gammal och ny ekonomisk liberalism*, Stockholm, 1921.

[2] If Heckscher succeeded in remaining a practical conservative in questions of distribution, in spite of his adherence in principle to Mill's big qualification, his personal honesty was never in doubt. He was a Puritan in the Victorian style and he harboured much of the inconsiderate moralistic rectitude of Wicksell which in his case, too, was primarily directed upon himself.

counter—cyclically in order to stabilise general business conditions. He enjoyed playing with this idea and many other equally unorthodox ones, but they never became part of what he then thought practical. In most of the issues of the day his conservatism kept him well in line with his liberal colleagues.

The economists of this generation abstained as a matter of principle from entering politics or even from formally belonging to a political party.[1] But they were definitely active politicians in another sense, *viz.* as political economists.[2] And as economists they spoke with real conviction. The liberal views were asserted as clear and almost self-evident truths. Cassel later gave his autobiography the title : *In the Service of Reason.*[3] Even if the other economists of the older generation were conditioned by education to be personally more

---

[1] Again Bagge was atypical. He had already in his youth been the leader of the Conservatives in the Stockholm City Council. After a period of retreat to scientific pursuits in the late 'twenties and early 'thirties—which is however, the period I am now trying to characterize—he became a member of Parliament and soon the leader of the Conservative Party.

[2] In this respect the following generation, to which I belong, broke with that tradition. Through the circumstances of the time and our own ambitions, several of us were brought into political life or became lost in administration. The older generation generally took a charitable view of our political adventures. I recall an episode at a dinner party which Cassel gave when he passed his seventieth birthday, in 1936. In a little speech he referred to the fact that, while he himself had remained " unpolitical ", his pupils were all becoming members of Parliament: Bagge representing the Conservative Party, Wohlin the Farmers' Party, Ohlin the Liberal Party and I the Labour Party. As we, in spite of our dispersion over different parties, remained faithful economists, he suggested that, perhaps, this would contribute to more sense in Sweden's political life, though he still felt that we would have been more influential outside than inside the party councils.

Looking back on our experiences, I believe we must now concede that it is highly questionable whether this departure from the tradition has brought advantages large enough to compensate for the disadvantages. We learned a lot, it is true, but we also lost much valuable time and became less effective as researchers and teachers, at least for the periods when we were more fully occupied in practical and political tasks. It may be held, perhaps, that it ought to have been an advantage for the nation to have economists engaged in politics. But the question is whether Cassel was not right in thinking that we would have had an even greater influence on the political affairs of our country, if we had, like our elders, exerted it from outside. Undoubtedly, also, some of us had occasionally to compromise our thinking, and all of us were suspected of doing it when we were classified as party politicians.

On this point Heckscher very strongly shared Cassel's views. Even Bagge once remarked that one should not " harness Apollo to drag the plough " ; he added that he did not mean himself.

[3] *I förnuftets tjänst* (2 vols.), Stockholm, 1940 and 1941.

unassuming in their expressions than Cassel, there is no doubt
that in all sincerity they really believed that the policies they
were propounding were the inferences from principles which
were true in the sense that they were undeniably promoting
the public welfare.   Cassel, Heckscher and some others who
were less well known abroad, e.g. Sven Brisman and Gunnar
Silverstolpe, were prolific writers of popular books besides
learned treatises, and all were regular contributors to the
daily press.   They exerted an enormous influence over public
opinion, Cassel, indeed, far beyond Sweden. With adult education on the upsurge, even many labour politicians became
converted to the liberal church.

It is not easy to grasp clearly the historical circumstances
—the interplay between events and people's reaction to them—
which make it understandable that Swedish economists in this
period early after the end of the First World War held these
views and played this role in rationalizing and moulding public
opinion in the liberal direction.   The spirit and the general
outlook in the years preceding the crash on the New York
Stock Exchange seem so far off that it is difficult to recall them
now.   After thirty years we find ourselves in a continual
sequence of international and national crises, each new one
mounting on the reverberations of earlier ones.   We fix the
origin or, at least, the beginning of this era of sustained
abnormality at the First World War and we are apt to forget
that there was a short *lucidum intervallum* when that war—then
called the Great War or, in America, the European War—
was believed to be a one-time and never-recurring aberration
from the normal course of evolution.   The world was then
expected to return to normalcy.   And, as a matter of fact,
for a few years it did go a long way in this direction.

It would be interesting to review the main features of
the political and economic development in this short period,
its mental climate, and the way in which it affected the
economic discussions that then took place.   Here I will have
to restrict myself to emphasize that the 'twenties were an era of
gradually increasing confidence in restored stability and progress.
Conditioned by later events, we sometimes forget that people
then trusted in the future and used as criteria for policy pre-war

concepts and values. This mood was even stronger in Sweden, which had stayed out of the war and which, after the war, was favoured by a number of accidental historical developments.

To the older generation of economists this mental climate of the time itself implied a return to normalcy. Their main ideas, their system of theories, their research interests, and their accustomed ways of pursuing them, in short, their scientific personality had been moulded in the progressive and innocently secure decades towards the end of the long era of peace. During the war the regimentation of the economy, allocations, rationing, price-fixing, and all the paraphernalia of economic controls had been to them an ordeal and anathema even intellectually.

They must have felt also professionally frustrated. For in the First World War the controls were managed almost entirely by officials and practical men from law, business and politics. The professional economists remained largely outsiders. They were rarely consulted ; whenever they were, their advice was not heeded and, in most cases, could not have been followed. They could criticize and did criticize : but as their basic conception was that all these policies violated nature and the well-established laws of sound economics, their criticism was apt to be exasperating to those carrying political responsibility. And, still more importantly, even if they had tried, as some of them did, to take a more positive approach, they would have been unable to follow it up, as they lacked the theoretical tools for accomplishing it. This contrasts sharply with the role economists were to play in the Second World War, when all countries drew upon the services of a whole cadre of economists ; they had already been trained in the depression years in collaborating with the politicians and the administrators on planning and even executing control schemes.

The younger generation had from the beginning a different background. They had no deep personal roots in the pre-war period, least of all as economists. Stability and normalcy they had only read about. They had thus not the same personal motives to trust the illusion of normalcy, which was the mark of the 'twenties, and to feel it as a fulfilment of deep longings. Controls never appeared to them so objectionable on grounds of principle.

Perhaps it is also natural for young people turning to

Postscript

economic studies to want to be in on action aimed at improving the world. In any case, when they faced undesirable situations, such as unemployment, they had fewer inhibitions than the older generation to think constructively about measures which would mitigate them. But, more generally, they were inclined to approve of interventions when these were likely to lead to desirable results. The very facts that the older generation was so far out on the liberal wing, that they were intellectually so strong and had such a powerful influence over public opinion were also undoubtedly extra spurs to opposition on the part of the younger generation who did not want to stand in the shadow. And, in addition, the tradition of Wicksell's political radicalism played its role, at least with some of us.

To this group of economists who grew up in Sweden after the war belonged Erik Lindahl and Bertil Ohlin, who were out a little earlier than the rest of us, and the late Fabian von Kock. For the type of critical approach to the value problem, represented by the views expressed in this volume and the *Political Element*, Alf Johansson was a main inspiration.[1] To the group belonged, furthermore, Karin Kock, Dag Hammarskjöld, Tord Palander and, as they emerged from their studies, Erik Lundberg, Ingvar Svennilson, Richard Sterner and, still later, Torsten Gårdlund. In spite of individual differences, our generation of Swedish economists had much in common, particularly in contrast to the older men. Politically, we were, in varying degrees, less conservative.[2]

[1] Alf Johansson played for all of us the role of the ideal Oxford and Cambridge don : learned and circumspect, never hurried, always prepared to let his fountain of wisdom sprinkle to the delight and edification of those who were around. I mention this here, because his influence cannot be known to foreign economists and hardly to the younger generation of economists growing up in Sweden a quarter of a century later. For, in this respect also resembling many of the most influential English dons, he did not write much himself ; from early in the 'thirties he was drawn into Swedish housing policy, for which he since then has been the main source of inspiration and, later, the chief administrator as Director-General of the Housing Board.

[2] The late Nils Wohlin, of the same generation as Heckscher and Bagge, was an economic historian, demographer, politician and administrator, and did not pretend to be an economist. Arthur Montgomery was more exclusively an economic historian ; he also identified himself with a liberal view in line with the attitudes of the older generation, as did Gustav Åkerman. Johan Åkerman was already then so exclusively himself that it is difficult to allocate him to either of the two age groups I have here distinguished. Per Jacobsson, David Davidson's only lamb, disappeared to the new League of Nations before finishing his doctorate studies.

Value in Social Theory

The less conservative political outlook would not, however, necessarily have led any of us of the younger generation to the type of criticism against the basic philosophy of the old school which is carried out in *The Political Element*. As I mentioned, Wicksell had been a political radical all his life but he, more than anybody else, remained faithful to utilitarianism and hedonism which he explicitly placed at the foundation of his economic thinking. The same was true of his pupil Lindahl who shared the political views of the younger generation but remained classical in philosophy and methodology.

But two or three amongst us felt not only the negative inspiration of the older generation, but also a strong positive stimulus from the remarkable Uppsala philosopher, Professor Axel Hägerström (1868–1939) who, unfortunately, has remained almost unknown abroad. His major works were devoted to a critique of the notions, concepts and methods of reasoning in jurisprudence, which he showed to be self-contradictory, false or meaningless. With the aid of much learning he traced their origin to primitive magic in pre-historic times, from which stems also our prevailing tendency to conceptualize. These works are rather forbidding and were not studied thoroughly by any of us. But in some more general writings and in his personal teaching, which in the 'twenties reverberated among the young intellectuals in Sweden far beyond Uppsala, he clearly and strikingly expressed the importance of drawing a line between beliefs about reality and valuations of it. The two are not on the same logical level, for beliefs can, valuations cannot, be judged by the criteria of true and false.

Hägerström had a considerable influence on the post-war generation of jurists and social scientists in Sweden. In a general and sometimes vague way many of us were made familiar with the thought that there were no objective values to be established and known, scientifically, only subjective valuations which, of course, could be observed—and made the object of new subjective valuations—but whose significance for social theory had no claim to any other validity than that they were actually held by certain individuals and groups. By his thorough going scepticism about all kinds of metaphysics

250

and his insistence on critical clarity of the concepts used in social analysis, he also helped to save the whole post-war generation of Swedish intellectuals from becoming Marxists. The remote and rather indirect influence of Max Weber worked in the same direction.

Since it was against the *laissez-faire* teaching of our elders that we were—in varying degrees of intensity—reacting, it is understandable that those of us who, like myself, were inclined to hold radical views, were the more susceptible to Hägerström's criticism of value metaphysics. I have already accounted for the radical tradition from Wicksell as a positive inspiration for our critical attitude. On the personal plane of political valuations, I always felt myself in line with Wicksell. Deprived of Wicksell's utilitarian foundations, but subject to the stimulus of his political radicalism, I was receptive to Hägerström's philosophical scepticism. And Cassel, although the main proponent of the superficial *laissez-faire* doctrine, against which we reacted, played an important role in preparing the way for a deeper and systematic criticism of the value and welfare approach with his rationalistic urge to throw away empty speculations of the type represented by the marginal utility theory, his constant insistence on the necessity to quantify all our notions, and his masterly manner to get down to a realistic treatment of facts and figures, all of which broke through his *laissez-faire* prejudices. In this complicated way positive impulses weaved themselves into the negative inspiration that we received from our teachers.

I have already said that the personal relations between our teachers were not very harmonious. But it would be a mistake to ascribe their differences to their ideals or opinions. They all were sharply cut individuals of rather unbending character. But as economic thinkers they were clearly members of the same generation, conditioned by their time to a very similar general approach to problems. They were alike also in their unquestioning appreciation of independence and originality in scientific work and their unhesitating acceptance of criticism. They were convinced that progress in science emerges from free discussion and controversy.

This was indeed a vital element in the intellectual atmosphere in which we, the younger generation, grew up. Absolute academic freedom went much beyond inability to fire men for their views. Looking back over my youth, I cannot remember that the thought ever entered my mind that the political or scientific views which I held and expressed could ever have the slightest influence on my future academic career. This, I knew, would solely depend on the quality of my work. In that respect also we were singularly fortunate. Conditions were not the same in some other countries at that time, and, I am afraid, in this respect the standards of the academic world have since tended to deteriorate.

IV

It came to some heated controversies in the Economists' Club which had been gathering round Wicksell when, as emeritus, he had moved to Stockholm from Lund and which still flourished in the latter part of the 'twenties after his death. It is interesting to remember that Bagge, who was older than we but who, as I mentioned, unlike Cassel and Heckscher, was a true conservative and not a *laissez-faire* liberal, sided with the young Turks. But the fight was not to have been carried on only *intra muros*. I think it was Alf Johansson, with whom I had most in common in my philosophical interests, who once suggested that a carefully documented criticism of the dominant *laissez-faire* school should be worked out and presented in the form of a popular pamphlet, and steal the public support from the elders. This I set out to do in the autumn of 1927.

So much for the background and for the motives for my early studies in the value problem. Books have, however, their peculiar fate even while they are being written. In the course of my work, I gradually lost interest in what I had set out to criticize, *viz.* the popular teaching of my older colleagues and, indeed, the controversies of the day in my home country. I became more and more deeply involved in the history of economic theory. In particular, I became increasingly fascinated by the basic philosophies of natural law and utilitarianism, and their preservation in economic theory.

Instead of the two months I had intended to give to it, I spent two years. The book was, of course, a complete failure from the publisher's point of view and had little influence outside academic circles. When it finally appeared in 1930 the world had moved into the Great Depression, and even in Sweden the inescapable need for large-scale state intervention had changed the focus of public interest from the issues of the 'twenties. *Laissez-faire* had lost because of events, not intellectual criticism.

The study was almost entirely devoted to criticism. The positive suggestions in the last chapter for a solution of the problem of how to introduce valuations into economic analysis and thus to draw political conclusions on a scientific basis are very sketchy. This was pointed out by the critics and I was deeply conscious of the defect myself.[1] It is easy to tear down but difficult to build up. I could, of course, have answered with the young August Strindberg that reason enough for demolishing old dilapidated buildings and clearing the slums is to provide space and let air through. But even before the book was published, I had become aware of a basic superficiality in my whole approach to the value problem.

I still considered the critical analysis of the inherited body of economic theory correct and worth doing. But I had begun to doubt the correctness of a fundamental thought underlying the critical argument in the book, *viz.* that, once the metaphysical elements were radically cut away, there would remain a positive theory which would be independent of all subjective valuations; that it should then be possible to reach solutions of practical and political problems simply by adding to the theoretical knowledge of facts and relations a set of premises from the sphere of valuations and by drawing the conclusions. But was this thought not just naïve empiricism, at heart not dissimilar to the crude belief in " facts " established without

---

[1] I was also made conscious of another systematic defect of the book, namely its one-sidedness. Heckscher once remarked to me that we seem always to write about what we are against : Marx wrote the history of Capitalism, he himself of Mercantilism, and I analysed and criticized Liberalism (*sans comparaison*, he added). If I wanted to be an impartial scientist I should now make the same autopsy of theoretical Marxism. I accepted the challenge and started on a manuscript which, however, was never finished. I found the work too tedious, I did not feel enough personal urge. In our *milieu*, Marxism was never the pressing problem which Liberalism had been. We did not have to " work it off ".

theory, of which I saw so distressingly much in America where I then spent a year ?

In America this was the time of the institutionalist revolt against classical economic theory. Under Wesley C. Mitchell's leadership the young American economists criticised everything —except the basic value and welfare notions.[1] Their own approach remained, as a matter of fact, considerably more naïve in this particular respect than that of the economists in the classical tradition against whom they were revolting with so much vehemence. Typical and revealing of this approach was the title of a book published in these years by Frederick C. Mills, *The Behaviour of Prices*.[2]

But social facts or the behaviour of their quantitative characteristics do not organize themselves into a scientifically analysable system merely by being observed and recorded. A viewpoint, indeed a correlated complex of concepts, is needed, which constitutes a theory. Prior to answers there must be questions, and the questions we raise stem from our interest in the matter, from our valuations. Indeed, our theories and all our scientific knowledge are necessarily pervaded by valuations. It is therefore not enough to demolish, as I had attempted to do, the traditional clumsy methods of fettering human valuations by pressing them into a grid of stale and abstract metaphysical notions, or to demonstrate how the institutionalists deceived themselves when they denounced theory and only succeeded in suppressing explicit valuations which remained as implicit biases. The question was legitimate : By what did I replace the old value notions?

Again I have to confess that besides all the positive things I learned from my new American friends of the institutional school, I also received a strong negative inspiration from them. By their naïve empiricism, which was flagrant, they forced me to become aware of the need for a rational method of introducing value premises into economic research. Value premises are required not only in order to enable us to draw practical and

[1] I remember an abortive discussion with Mitchell on this question. However I tried and tried, I never got Mitchell to see the point—and this in spite of Mitchell's considerable learnedness in the history of economic doctrine : he gave for many years a course on the history of economic theory at Columbia University.

[2] New York, 1927.

political inferences from observations and economic analyses, but already in order to formulate a theory, to direct our observations, and to carry out our analysis.

I pondered over this problem during my American year 1929–30 and afterwards, but all my brooding yielded no more than the article on " Ends and Means " which is included in the present volume.[1] The attempt must be deemed largely abortive. The article elaborates the logical difficulty, not to say impossibility, of inserting value premises into economic analysis. I could understand Joseph Schumpeter, at that time professor in Bonn and co-editor with Emil Lederer of *Archiv für Sozialwissenschaft und Sozialpolitik*, when he did not accept the article for publication, as in his view it was too negative in its findings. To me the problem was very serious and personal. Because of my inability to find the way out of the maze, I felt a deep frustration in my scientific work and did not write much more for two years.

V

MEANWHILE, the happy 'twenties had ended. The gathering Great Depression and the practical economic problems raised in its wake rescued me from my critical philosophy and restored my scientific productivity.[2] My outer life had already placed forcefully before me that important phenomenon : Social Crisis! and I have remained, with the rest of the world, under that sign ever since. I arrived in New York for a year's Rockefeller Fellowship in America only two days before the crash on the Stock Exchange in the Fall of 1929. When, during the academic year 1930–31, I led a seminar at the Post-Graduate Institute of International Studies in Geneva on world economic problems, we inevitably turned our attention increasingly to an analysis of the financial crisis. I was in Germany when, in the Summer of 1931, the banks stumbled. I returned home to Sweden just in time for the crisis which developed when, in

[1] Chapter X.
[2] This statement should not be read as a careless cynicism but as an ascertainment of a fact. The Great Depression, like wars and other deeply tragic events, did stimulate economic thinking and did put speculative economists to useful practical work.

September of the same year, England and, forced to accompany her, Sweden and a group of other countries, were violently and unpreparedly thrown off the gold standard and for a time sailed a monetary course without compass and direction. Under the premises of crisis and depression the methodological problem of practical economic research was put into a new light.

The crux of the matter is, of course, that when the old liberal postulate of a harmony of interest is renounced, political conclusions—and ultimately theoretical research—must be founded on explicit value premises which must be concrete and take into account the actual conflicts of interests between different social groups. However, in a situation experienced as a crisis, it is a matter of empirical fact that interests converge and that conflicts of valuations disappear. Political conclusions can then be drawn from value premises which are homogeneous and defined in concrete terms, not as a result of metaphysical speculation but established by empirical observation of actual interests.[1]

During the next years I was happily busy on all sorts of theoretical and practical problems. The Labour Government which came into power after the election in the Autumn of 1932—and which, incidentally, is essentially the same now after twenty-five years—decided to introduce an under-balanced budget and I presented in an appendix to the Bill

[1] In a book for the general public on Sweden's way through the Monetary Crisis, propounding a certain monetary policy after the collapse of the gold standard in September 1931 (*Sveriges väg genom penningkrisen*, Stockholm, 1931) this thought was expressed as follows :

" This book outlines a programme for monetary policy. Such a programme can, of course, not be determined except from the viewpoint of the interests and ideals of the several different groups in society. This field of interests will be studied. The book should not have been written—at least not in its present form —were it not possible to ascertain that in the present crisis the interests of most social groups actually converge in such a way that it affords a basis for a considerable agreement on policy once the facts have been established." The analysis was thereafter focused on the situation in the labour market in various sectors, profitability in various industries, relation between the several types of price indices, employment rates, et cetera. On the basis of this analysis, taking into account also the institutional framework which in the short run can be assumed to be a constant, the conclusion was reached that there was, as a matter of fact, a common interest in a rise of the price level of industrial products. Upon this value premise a monetary programme could be formulated after a further analysis of international relations in the particular situation and available means to regulate the money market. This monetary programme had only validity for the given situation and did not provide a principle for monetary policy in general.

the theoretical motivation.[1] It was also the time when, among other things, our generation of Swedish economists were engaged on writing learned treatises on various aspects of anti-depression policy for the Unemployment Commission, on which Bagge was the economist member[2] and of which Hammarskjöld the secretary. Our writings during these years in the early 'thirties, and before we were engulfed in practical and political tasks, are the foundation for what doubtful claim we may have to the esteem in which the so called Stockholm school has occasionally been held abroad. If it ever existed, now at any rate it is dispersed.

Like the others, I was also drawn into work on all sorts of Royal Commissions and Committees and was a member of Parliament from 1935. From my philosophical period I had kept as a hobby the ambition to attempt always a clarification of the chosen value premises for practical proposals. A specimen of this type of philosophical meticulousness was an appendix to the principal report of the Population Commission.[2]

[1] " Konjunktur och offentlig hushållning " (The Public Finances and the Business Cycle), Bihang till riksdagens protokoll, 1933, 1 saml., Bilaga III.

[2] Ernst Wigforss—who was to become Minister of Finance from 1932 until 1949 when he retreated to writing his memoirs—was a member of the Commission for the Labour Party. Wigforss had his earlier scientific training in Scandinavian languages but was from the late 'twenties for all practical purposes an economist and an adopted member of the Club. Though older than the rest of the generation I have above characterized as the younger one, he should rightly be counted into our group. He never gave himself time to venture into original economic analysis—or, perhaps, did not think he had the ability for it—but he read the literature more copiously than any of us, he was thoroughly familiar, and in complete sympathy, with all the new ideas of the time and took a lively part in the discussions between us which run parallel to our various writings.

[2] " Några metodiska anmärkningar rörande befolkningsfrågans innebord och vetenskapliga behandling " (Some Methodological Notes on the Population Problem and its Scientific Treatment). Bilaga I, *Betankande i sexualfrågan*, avgivet av Befolkningskommissionen, Statens offentliga utredningar 1936/59, Stockholm, 1936. The Commission had been set up in 1935 as a consequence of a book in the writing of which I had collaborated and which bore the title *The Crisis in the Population Problem* (*Kris i befolkningsfrågan*, Alva and Gunnar Myrdal, Stockholm, 1934). The operative word is again " Crisis ". Cf. Alva Myrdal, *Nation and Family, The Swedish experiment in democratic family and population policy*, New York and London, 1945.

Notes on the methodological problems involved are contained in several writings on practical and political issues of this period, as, for instance, in regard to fiscal policy : *Finanspolitikens ekonomiska verkningar* : (The Economic Effects of Fiscal Policy). Statens offentliga utredningar 1934/1, Stockholm, 1934, Introduction, especially pp. 9 ff. ; in relation to agricultural policy : *Jordbrukspolitiken under omläggning*) (The Evolution of Agricultural Policy). Stockholm, 1938, First Part.

I should add that from the short-term point of view of reaching agreement on a policy among a group of practical-minded people such an insistence on logical clarity and explicitness with respect to value premises is not always conducive to success. Usually it is easier to reach agreement on practical matters if the premises are kept under the table. But there are certain long-term pedagogical advantages in the more pedantic procedure. And it expresses a *reservatio mentalis* that definitely helps to save the conscience of a collaborating scientist, at least to his own satisfaction, and does make a return to science subjectively more feasible.

In 1938 I divested myself of all the practical and political responsibilities that I had accumulated. I now faced the task of directing a comprehensive study of the American Negro problem ; I was accompanied and aided by Richard Sterner. The problem is immense in scope and importance, it is as complicated as life itself, it is permeated by the most intense valuations and these valuations clash violently. I was asked to look at things as an outsider. Indeed, I was to be both the subject and the object of a cultural experiment in the social sciences. And it was expected that the result would be an objective study. It was to " be undertaken in a wholly objective and dispassionate way ". Here, if ever, was there need for methodological clarity. We attempted to work with explicit value premises, to base them as far as possible on observation, to stress them throughout the study, and to define the concepts used in terms of the chosen value premises. Excerpts from, or condensations of, some of the chapters of *An American Dilemma* which touch upon these methodological problems and the methodological appendices are contained in this volume.[1]

In the Autumn of 1942 I returned to Sweden and had again for almost five years new experiences of the political process which is part of the social reality that we are studying: as member of the Swedish Parliament, as member of the Board of Directors of the Swedish Bank, as Chairman of the post-war Economic Planning Commission in Sweden and, later, as member of the Swedish Government. As far as scholarly writings

[1] Part II.

are concerned, this period is barren. Since 1947 I have as Executive Secretary directed the Secretariat of the Economic Commission for Europe. My main contribution to the comprehensive research work, which over the years has been carried out under the sponsorship of ECE, has mostly been the merely auxiliary one of building up, defending and preserving the Secretariat as a free and independent scientific agent: guided in its research by the established standards of our profession, without sideward glances at what would be politically opportune, and recruited solely on the criterion of professional competence.[1]

I also managed to do some writing of my own. The article on " The Relation between Social Theory and Social Policy ", which is included in this volume,[2] is an excursion into the methodological field from this period. In more recent years my scientific interests have increasingly been absorbed by the problems of under-developed regions. Again, as always when entering a new field, the methodological questions have come to the fore. The first and the last essays in this volume are excerpts from two recent books on the problems of under-development and development. In particular the last of these publications, *Economic Theory and Under-developed Regions*, is almost entirely devoted to questions of methodology.

VI

IT is in the nature of a collection of contributions, ranging over such different periods during which I have been engaged in practical and theoretical work on such diverse problems, that terms are not used consistently, and that the views expressed are not always the same. I have already mentioned the development of my thoughts from my original attempt to tackle the value problem in *The Political Element* almost thirty years ago.

I do not feel that I have arrived at any final conclusions in this development. The note on which I should want this

---

[1] Cf. my article " The Research Work of the Secretariat of the Economic Commission for Europe", *25 Economic Essays in Honour of Erik Lindahl*, Stockholm, 1956.
[2] Chapter II.

volume to end is that I do not pretend to have solved the value problem in the social sciences. The task is bigger and more exacting than merely to criticize the old system of political economy which we inherited. This system is undoubtedly based on metaphysical notions and can therefore be demolished under logical scrutiny, as I think I demonstrated already in *The Political Element* : I am not prepared to withdraw my complete negation of value and welfare theories. But it is equally certain that valuations are necessary in all scientific work, from the beginning to the end. The final solution of the value problem in economics and in the social sciences generally must therefore be to set up a method by which human valuations are rationally and openly introduced into theoretical and practical research to give it direction and purpose, to make it both unbiased and relevant to life. These valuations must themselves be ascertained as social facts ; and the value premises by which they are represented in our scientific work must be tested as to relevance and significance in our society.

I do not believe that the experiment in *An American Dilemma* to apply systematically explicit value premises to the analysis of a social problem, even if deemed successful in this particular case, is a convincing proof of the general practicability of the method. In spite of its enormous complexity, the American Negro problem is in one respect relatively simple. As the discussion in the book shows, in America there is a set of rather homogeneous valuations, ready-made for the use of the social scientist, in the form of the American Creed, which is particularly explicit about the Negro problem. This set of valuations is so widely accepted, has such authority and is so important as a real social trend, that it is admissible to use it—with many qualifications—as an "instrumental norm" for research. This is, however, largely a historical accident. It is not to the same extent true of other problems in America or elsewhere. The possibility of working with a single uniform set of value premises renders the Negro problem in one respect similar to the analysis of an economic depression where interests converge. Since 1931 all—or most of—my writings have belonged to one or other of these two categories.

The real difficulty, however, arises when analysis has to be based upon a number of different sets of conflicting value premises. The complexities of an analysis attempting to do this are enormous and, perhaps, not soluble, as the basis concepts themselves are determined by the value premises. I am not unaware that to work with an 'instrumental norm' can then be looked upon as a trick and may turn out to be the means of forcing a particular system of ideals upon a study. In my recent publications on the problems of under-development and development I have used as value premises the desirability of equality of opportunity and of political democracy, and I am now setting out to use these value premises for a more intensive study of the problems of development and integration in South-East Asia. I fully understand the criticism that I am giving one particular set of value premises a strategic advantage, while these problems could also be treated from other points of view.

In defending the method, I would base myself on the fundamental thesis that value premises are necessary in research and that no study and no book can be *wertfrei*, free from valuations. To make them an explicit part of the argument is already a logical advance, because this displays them for criticism. I would continue my defence by pointing out that keeping to a single set of value premises is motivated only by the practical consideration of the unmanageable complexity in which one would be bogged down if one were to use several and conflicting sets of value premises. Being clear about the methodological desirability, in principle, of using more than one set of value premises also implies that one pays, constantly, attention to the sphere of valuations, and that one uses every possibility of viewing the problems also from other angles.

Nevertheless, as I pointed out, by relying mainly on one set of value premises, we give this set a strategic advantage. Unquestionably, from a strictly scientific point of view, this is a weakness—indeed a weakness which our method shares with the traditional value approach. The difference is, however, not only that with our method the set of value premises is kept explicit at all stages of the argument, and that the logical relativism of all valuations is recognized as well as the desirability, in principle, of applying other sets of value premises

whenever practically possible.   An even more important difference is that, by not objectifying the value premises and not
pressing them into the stale grid of a doctrine, they can be more
closely modelled on concrete human valuations actually held
by people.   Indeed, both the choice of the set of value premises
which is given the advantage of being used as the " instrumental
norm", and their more specific definition ideally can, and
should, be made on the basis of a realistic study of people's
actual valuations. They can then by empirical research be
tested for relevance and significance.

That we never reach more than a makeshift is true.   Indeed,
clarity about the imperfection of all our scientific endeavours
in the social field and about its deeper reason is, in itself, an
important and healthy result of methodological study.   It
gives a broader perspective to the fact of which every writer—
who is not a fool—is well aware, *viz*. that no scientific work
can be anything other than a contribution to an ever-continuing
process of growing knowledge through discussion and controversy.   Naturally, we should be as clear as we can about
what we are undertaking, present relevant material as fully
and analyse it as well as our resources allow.   But it will never
be anything other than, at best, a step forward in a development.   No book is definitive; nobody ever says the last word
on anything that really matters.

This is also true of methodological study itself.

INDEX

Index

Negroes: amalgamation, 166–7; *see also* race

noninterference, where applicable, 4–5

norm, instrumental, 161–2

North, of U.S., Negroes in, 114–16; *see also* America

nutrition policy, 30

OBERLIN College, 185

objectivity: complete, unattainable, 119; scientific, 129; and specification of valuations, 155

occupied countries, social scientists in, 28

Ogburn, William F., 144–6

Ohlin, Bertil, 246n, 249

opinion(s): American, disparities in, 69; beliefs and valuations in, 83–4; as cause of social change, 80; dynamics of, 80; elements in average, 83; illogicality of, 72; meaning of, 71; need of empirical study, 2; personal and political, 86 ff; political, often conditional, 88; *see also* public opinion

opinion research, results of, 83

optimism-pessimism bias scale, and Negro problem, 124–5

PALANDER, Tord, 249

panaceas, for Negro problem, 190

Pareto, V., 244n

Park, Robert E., 141–3, 146

parties, political, 21

'passing', 182

paternalism, 186

Patten, Simon, 153

perfectionism, 129n

physiocrats, 207

Pigou, A. C., 241

planning, 14, 29; and democracy, 43–4

policy and theory, distinction, 9

political economy, *see* economics

politicians, limited freedom of, 20–1

poor, condition of, studies on, 18

population theory, and social policy, 16

Positivism, 129n

Powdermaker, Hortense, 183

power, as aim of politicians, 20

'practical', *see* 'theoretical'

practical problems, approach to, 40

prejudices, 77

prices, levelling of, 4

problem, choice of, and valuations, 155

production, maximization of, 4

professional ethics, 36–8

prognoses, and programmes: correlation, 53; interdependence, 159

programmes, *see* prognoses

progress, economic, and equality of opportunity, 5

Prohibition, 67

'projects', State-sponsored, in universities, 45–6

propaganda, 28, 29; *see also* warfare, psychological

psychiatry, 11

psychologists, and group differences, 12

psychology, industrial, 28

public opinion: changes in, 80; research, 28, 39

public relations, 28, 29

publicity, for Negro problem, need of, 118

Puritanism, 67

QUESTIONS, in opinion studies, 84–6

RACE, 11; as overtone in social relations, 91; use of term, 181; *see also* Negroes

race prejudice, 192 ff; in liberals, 59; Park on, 142–3

race purity, 167–8

race relations, in America, changing, 17

racial identification, of Negroes in America, 92–3

radical-conservative scale, and biases, 123–4

radical and conservative attitudes, difference, 10

radical premises, in social sciences, 10 ff

radicalism, *see* liberalism

rationalism: and moralism, in America, 56–7; secularist, 11; of Western culture, 135–6

rationality: in politics, 21–2; social scientists and, 24–5, 35

rationalization(s), 72; mechanism of, 71 ff; scientist and need for, 120

'realism', of conservative sociologists, 12

reality, of situations, 61

'reasons', desire for, 71

reconciliation, of conflicting valuations, 74–5

Index